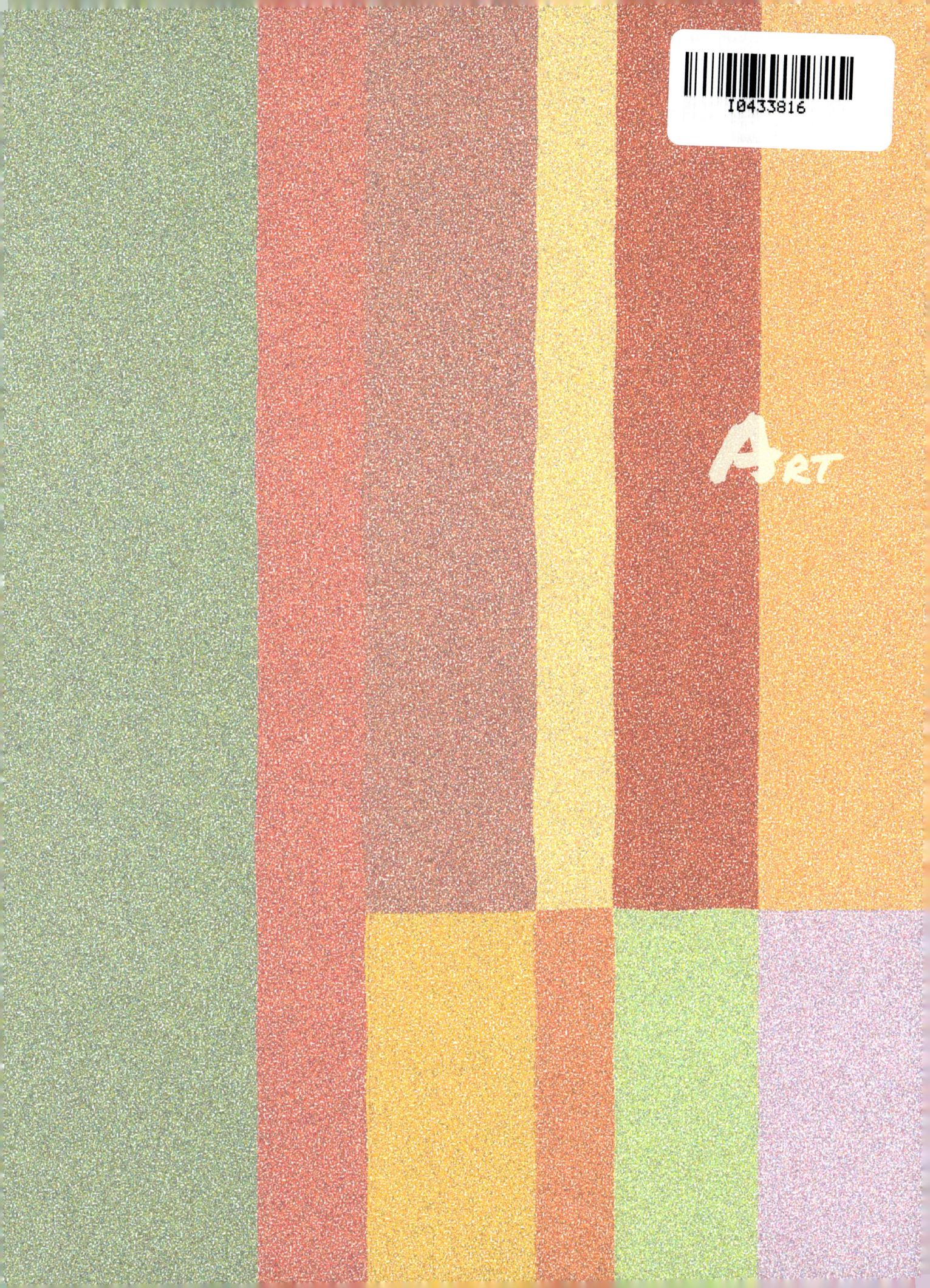

YOUth

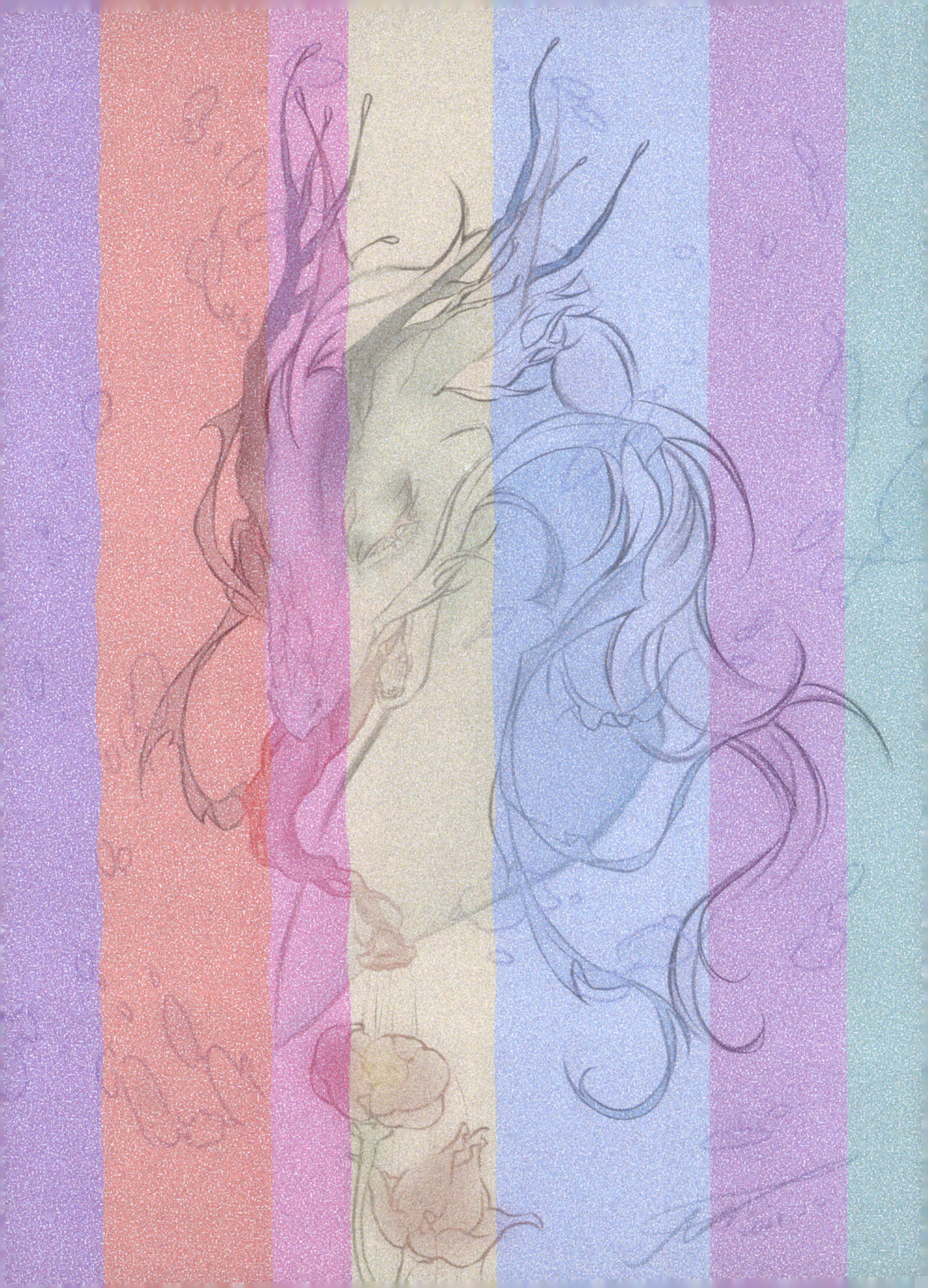

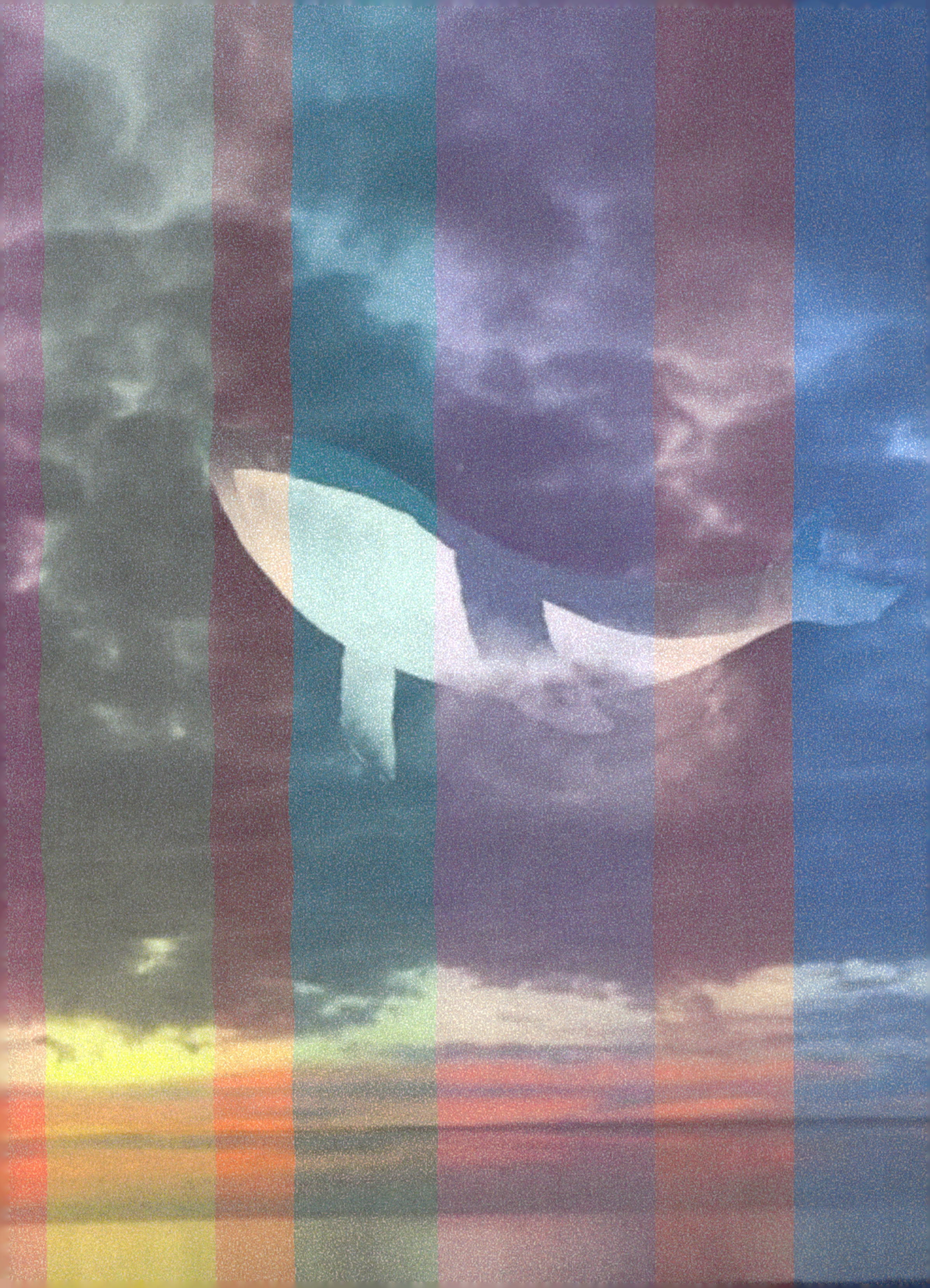

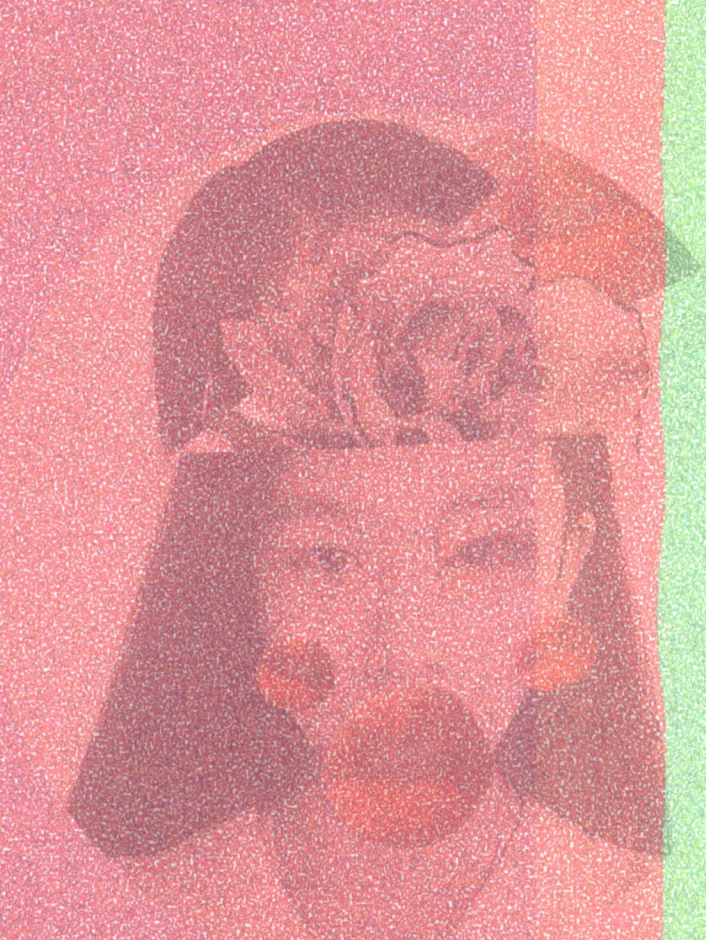

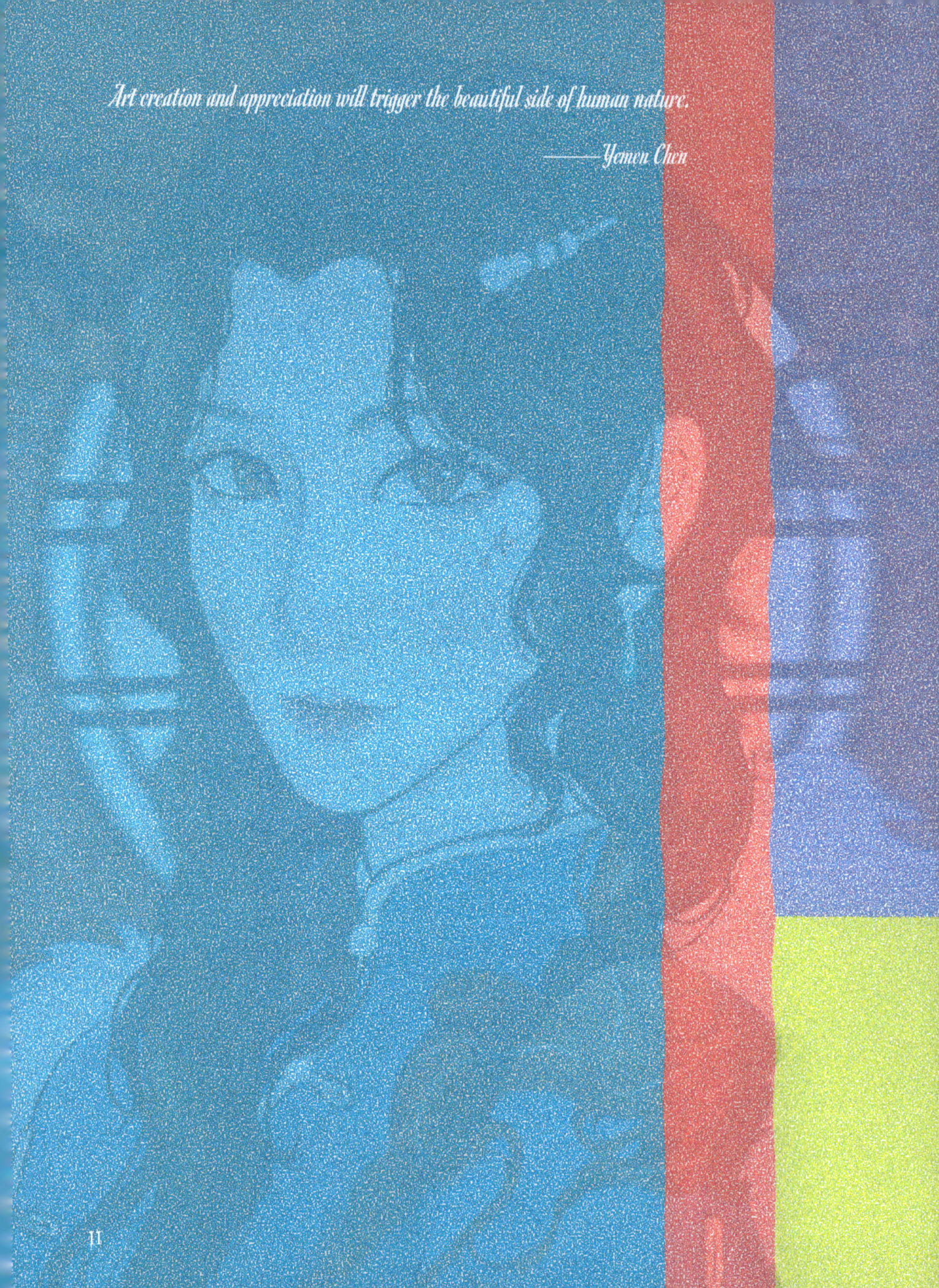

Art creation and appreciation will trigger the beautiful side of human nature.

―― *Yemen Chen*

"The Vibrant Future" International Education Project for Young Artists

Beaming Youth
International Youth Artist Artwork Series-2

EDITOR-IN-CHIEF Yemen Chen
ASSISTANT EDITOR-IN-CHIEF Jiajun Deng
EDITORS Jia Zhong, Yue Liu, Xunyan Kuang
COVER DESIGN BY Yue Liu
BOOK DESIGN BY Jia Zhong
ARTISTS Boyang Jiao, Caleb R. Wu, Changlu Xu, Fangyu Ren, Jiajun Chen, Jiajun Deng, Jiaxin Leng, Jia Zhong, Jinchang Zhang, Jinghan Xu, Jinglin Guo, Jingyi Yang, Junkai Gong, Kun Wang, Leyi Yang, Liyu Zhang, Peiyu Wu, Qingxia Song, Rong Hong, Rui Li, Shuo Pang, Timothy X. Wu, Wanchen Zhang, Xikai Xu, Xin Wen, Xunyan Kuang, Yifei Wang, Yihan Zhang, Yu Jiang, Yue Liu, Yue Wang, Yuning Yang, Yuting He, Ziqi Meng, Ziyan Chen

Losget Press
2021

The publication of this book is part of a benevolent program – "The Vibrant Future" International Education Project for Young Artists, sponsored by the International Society of Young Artists. All of the earnings from the publication of this book will be donated to improve education for young artists.

EDITOR-IN-CHIEF Yemen Chen
ASSISTANT EDITOR-IN-CHIEF Jiajun Deng
EDITORS Jia Zhong, Yue Liu, Xunyan Kuang
COVER DESIGN BY Yue Liu
BOOK DESIGN BY Jia Zhong
ARTISTS Boyang Jiao, Caleb R. Wu, Changlu Xu, Fangyu Ren, Jiajun Chen, Jiajun Deng, Jiaxin Leng, Jia Zhong, Jinchang Zhang, Jinghan Xu, Jinglin Guo, Jingyi Yang, Junkai Gong, Kun Wang, Leyi Yang, Liyu Zhang, Peiyu Wu, Qingxia Song, Rong Hong, Rui Li, Shuo Pang, Timothy X. Wu, Wanchen Zhang, Xikai Xu, Xin Wen, Xunyan Kuang, Yifei Wang, Yihan Zhang, Yu Jiang, Yue Liu, Yue Wang, Yuning Yang, Yuting He, Ziqi Meng, Ziyan Chen

Copyright © 2021 by International Society of Young Artists
All rights reserved.
Published in the United States by Losget Press, Los Angeles
Originally published in Paperback in the United States by Losget Press, in 2021
Title: Beaming Youth: International Youth Artist Artwork Series-2
Description: First Edition. | Los Angeles: Losget Press, 2021.
Identifiers: LCCN: 2021900120 | ISBN-13: 978-1-951364-07-6 | ISBN-10: 1-951364-07-4
www.losget.com
E-mail: contact@losget.com
First Printing. 2021.

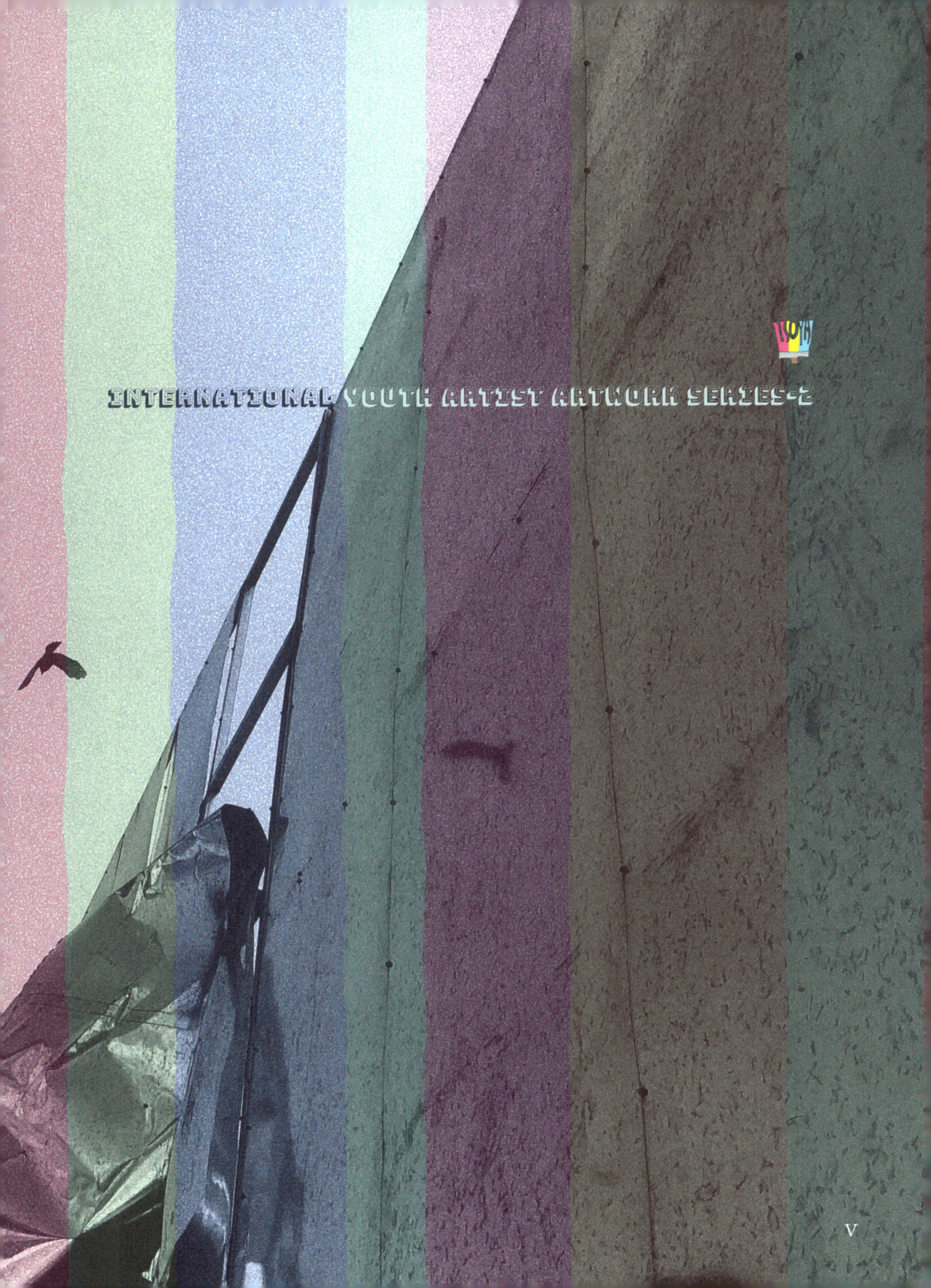

CHILDREN WHO LOVE ART WILL BECOME PEACE-LOVERS IN THE FUTURE

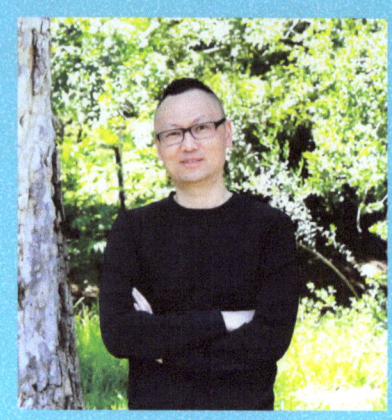

YEMEN CHEN
PRESIDENT OF THE INTERNATIONAL SOCIETY OF YOUNG ARTISTS

FOREWORD

The International Society of Young Artists, established on August 18, 2018, headquartered in Los Angeles, is a non-profit organization aiming to provide a platform for young artists to develop their creative talents.

For a long time, the public believed that art was only related to artists engaged in art work. The fact is, art is closely related to everyone's life. The rapid development of technology has changed the world. Today's young generation faces unprecedented opportunities and challenges. The power of art education not only makes people elegant but also improves people's competitiveness. Art is an important part of competitiveness in today's business world: the design hidden in the product attracts the audience; creating an idol star requires dozens of art industries; Steve Jobs has achieved significant commercial success because he knows people Fascinated by the art hidden in the product. The fundamental purpose of learning art is to enhance people's sensitivity to things and cultivate people's concentration, insight, and creativity. The acquisition of these abilities is essential for engaging in any industry.

"Love" is an essential creative theme of art. The process of artistic creation will provide a positive effect on people's psychology. Art creation and appreciation will trigger the beautiful side of human nature. Children who love art will become peace lovers in the future.

The International Society of Young Artists welcomes everyone from 8 to 28 years old. Whether you intend to pursue an artistic career, we hope to sow the seeds of art in the rich soil deep in your heart.

The International Society of Young Artists is willing to gather young people from all over the world who love art and provide them with opportunities to learn and communicate. We welcome volunteers and donors from all over the world to contribute to this cause. We hope to make the world a better place by cultivating young people's love for art.

Yemen Chen
January 2019

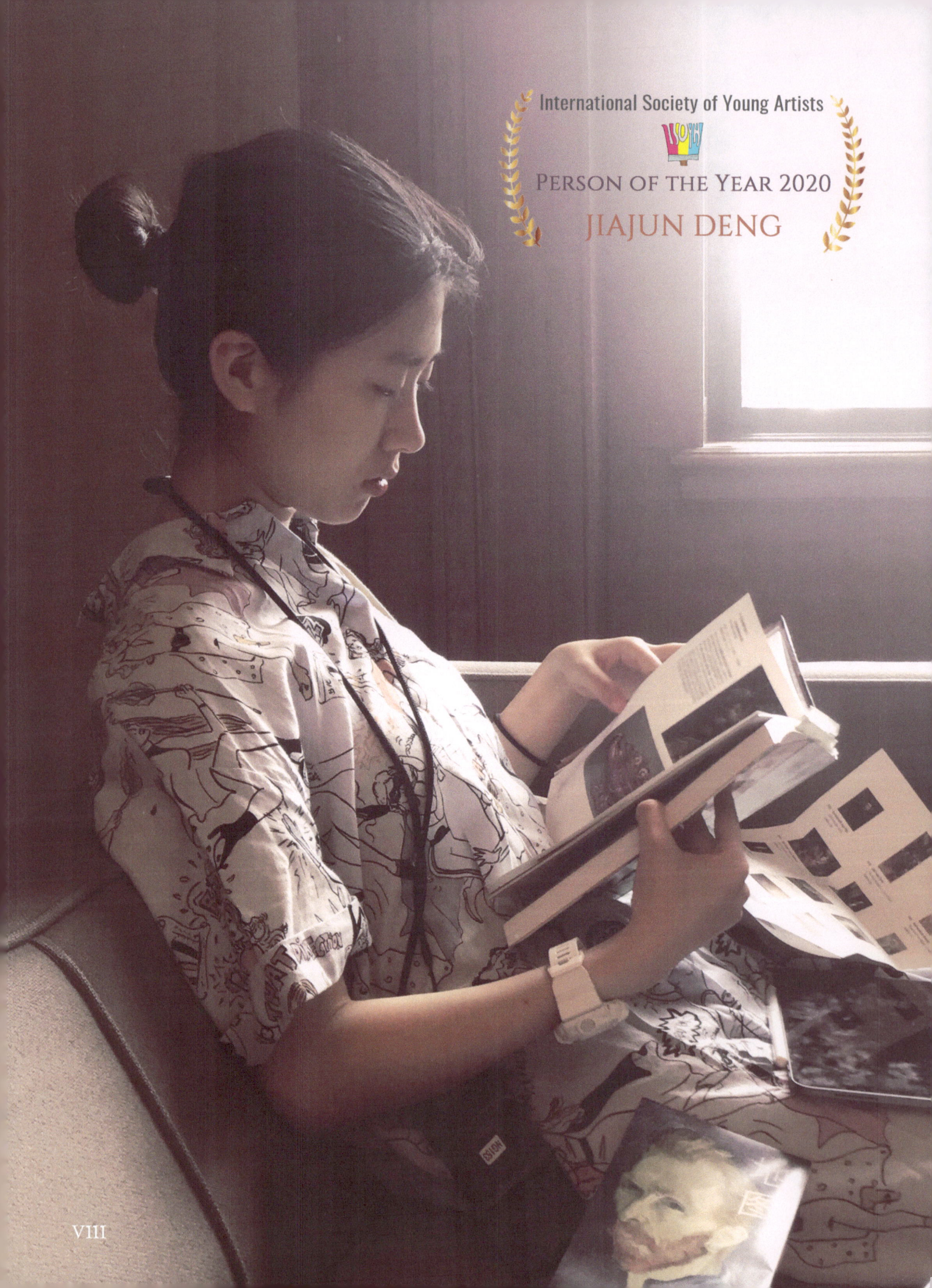

Hello everyone!

I am Jiajun Deng, 16 years old this year, and I am currently studying in the 2019 entry art class of the No 17 High School in Qingdao City, Shandong Province. This time, as a member of the International Society of Young Artists (ISOYA), I used my spare time to follow the chairman of the association, Mr. Chen, to coordinate the publication of the ISOYA's artwork album. Although my daily study is very stressful, the coordination work is very meaningful to me. It has taught me how to communicate effectively and how to accomplish something efficiently.

I have been studying art with Mr. Chen since I was very young, and nowadays I have been communicating with Mr. Chen remotely. I remember when I was a little girl, Mr. Chen took me and other students to read the English magical literature Harry Potter as well as the famous Chinese ancient literature Dream of the Red Chamber, and played beautiful music for us while we were painting, let us experience the similarities of different types of creative forms. This all-around teaching method has broadened my understanding of arts and helped me understand that arts are interlinked. This has benefited me a lot. Now, I will appreciate a literary work as a work of art and experience the conflict and harmony, color and sound hidden. Maybe it's because Mr. Chen has seen me growing up and knows me well, whenever I have an art problem that I can't solve, he can answer me in a way that I can easily understand. I also know that some of the difficulties we encountered in our studies were mostly caused by psychological factors. Mr. Chen has a magical power that other teachers rarely have. He can accurately judge whether the student is experiencing a professional problem or a psychological problem and provide practical help.

Painting has also improved my imagination, allowing me to perceive things around me so as to simulate the imagination. The soul of art lives in my body, like a fantasy dream, taking me to tour various magical worlds. Painting is full of magic, and it is like a living medicine, bringing peace to my mind. Painting makes me happy and makes me curious about everything. The soul of art lingers between my wrists and gives me precious intuition so that my inspiration can flow continuously on the drawing paper.

Jiajun Deng-

JIAJUN DENG
Person of the Year 2020
January 16, 2021, Qingdao

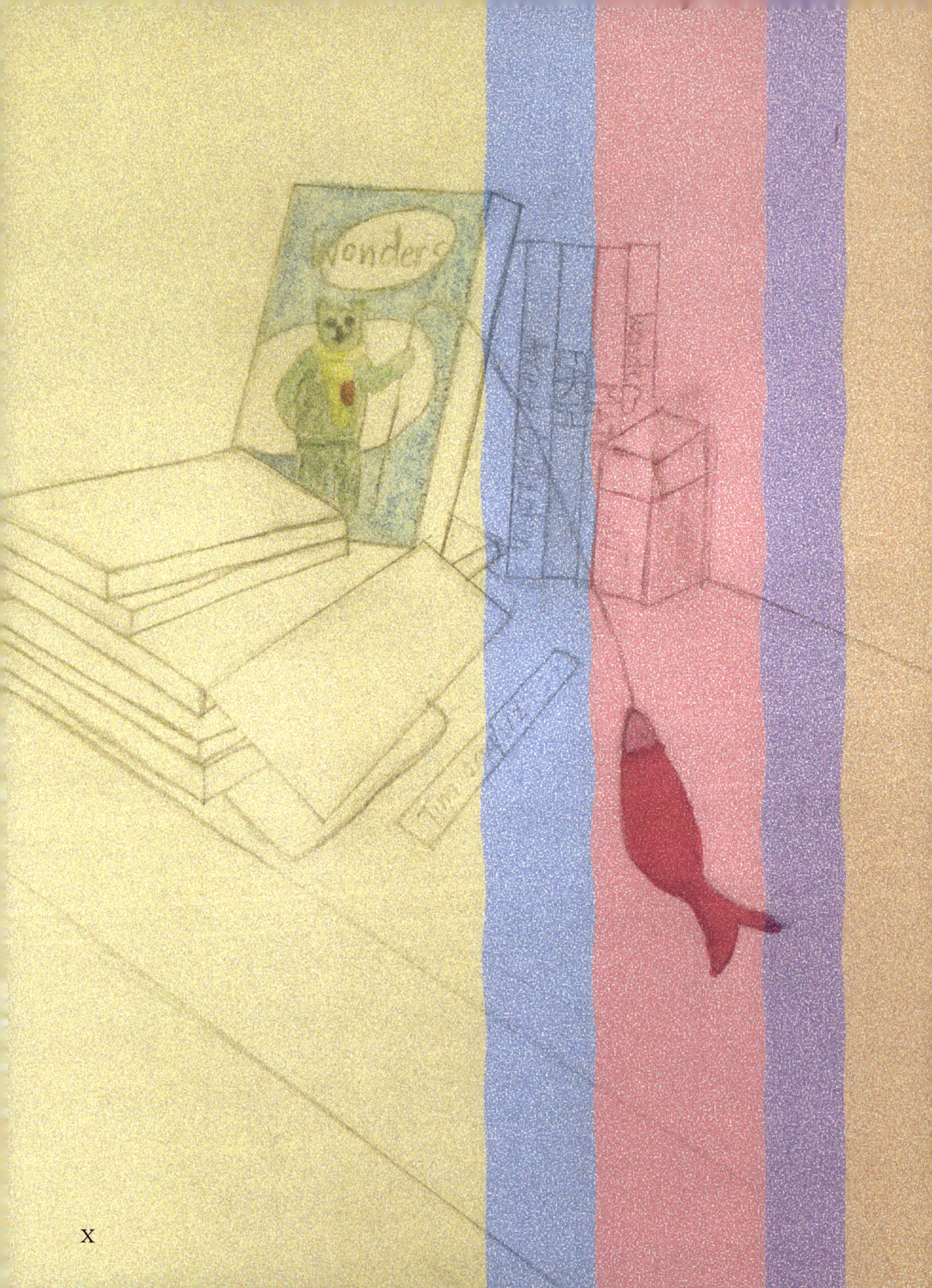
x

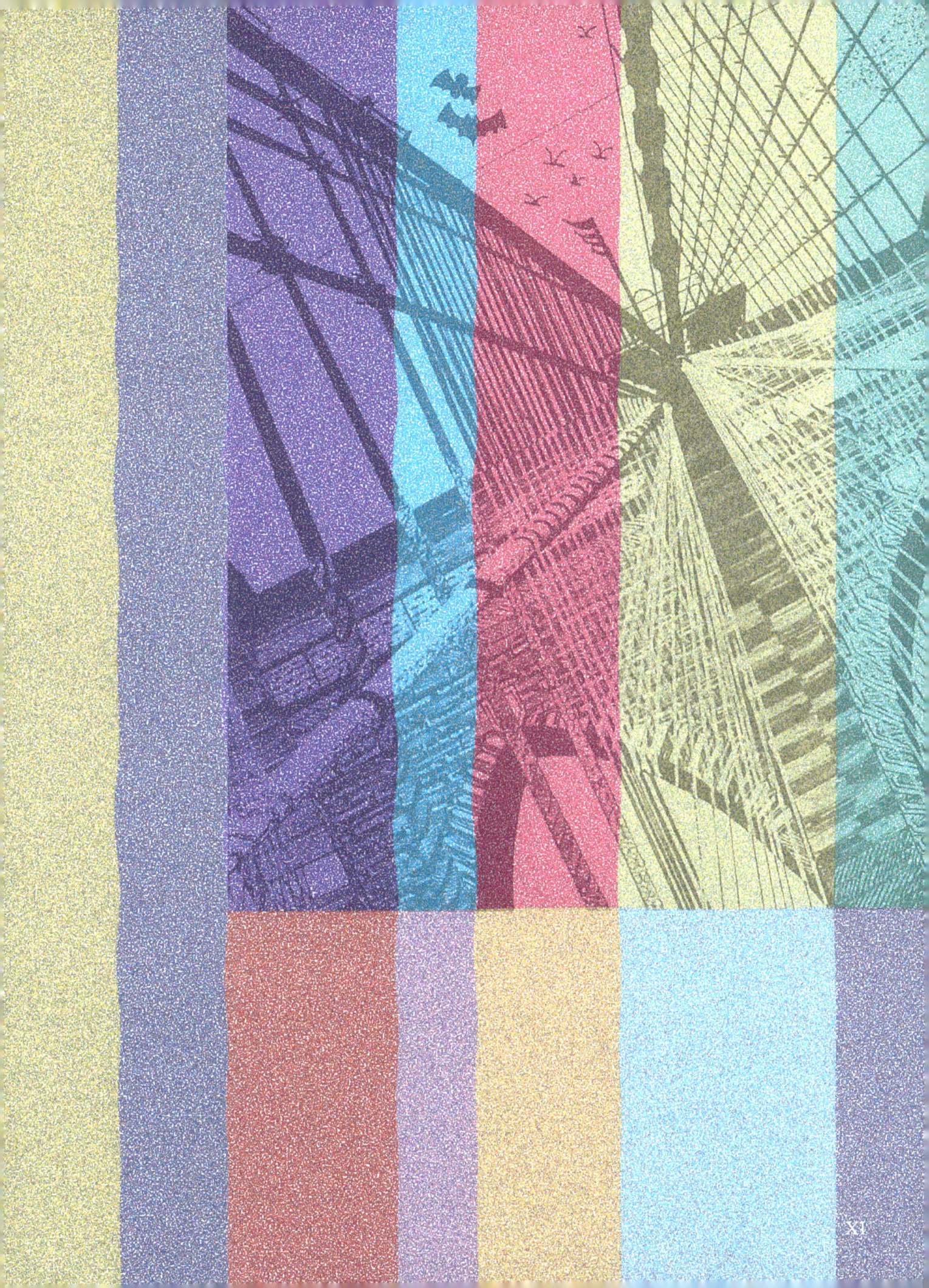

Contents

Boyang Jiao 1
Caleb R. Wu 3
Changlu Xu 7
Fangyu Ren 11
Jiajun Chen 15
Jiajun Deng 19
Jiaxin Leng 23
Jia Zhong 25
Jinchang Zhang 31
Jinghan Xu 35
Jinglin Guo 41
Jingyi Yang 45
Junkai Gong 49
Kun Wang 51
Leyi Yang 53
Liyu Zhang 57
Peiyu Wu 59
Qingxia Song 61
Rong Hong 65
Rui Li 69
Shuo Pang 73
Timothy X. Wu 77
Wanchen Zhang 81
Xikai Xu 83
Xin Wen 83
Xunyan Kuang 87
Yifei Wang 93
Yihan Zhang 97
Yu Jiang 99
Yue Liu 101
Yue Wang 107
Yuning Yang 109
Yuting He 111
Ziqi Meng 115
Ziyan Chen 117

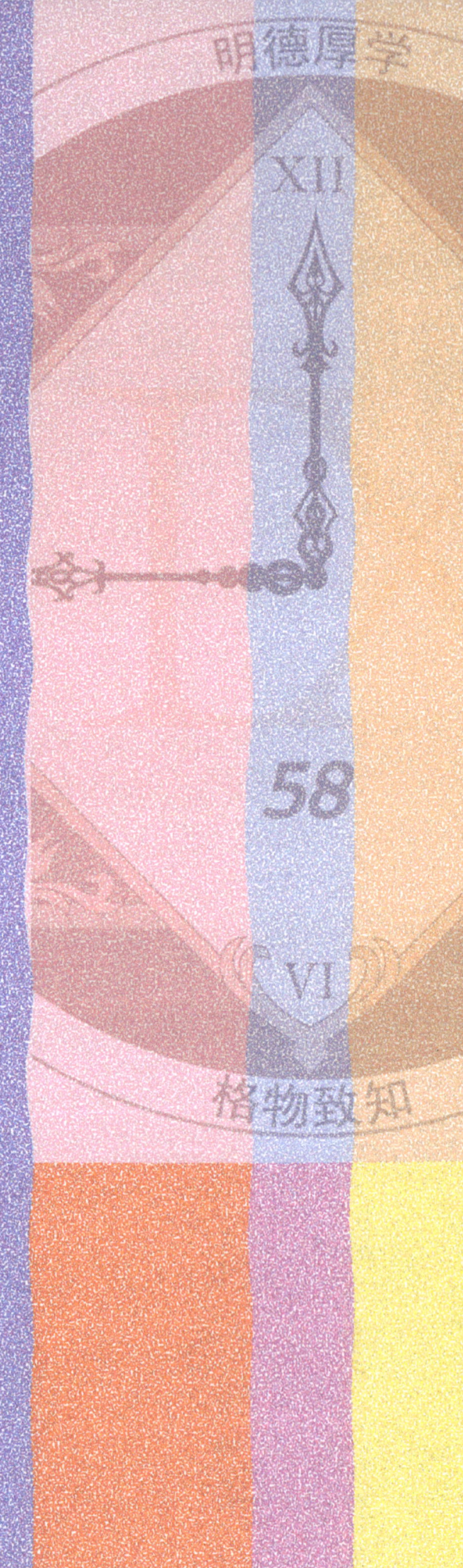

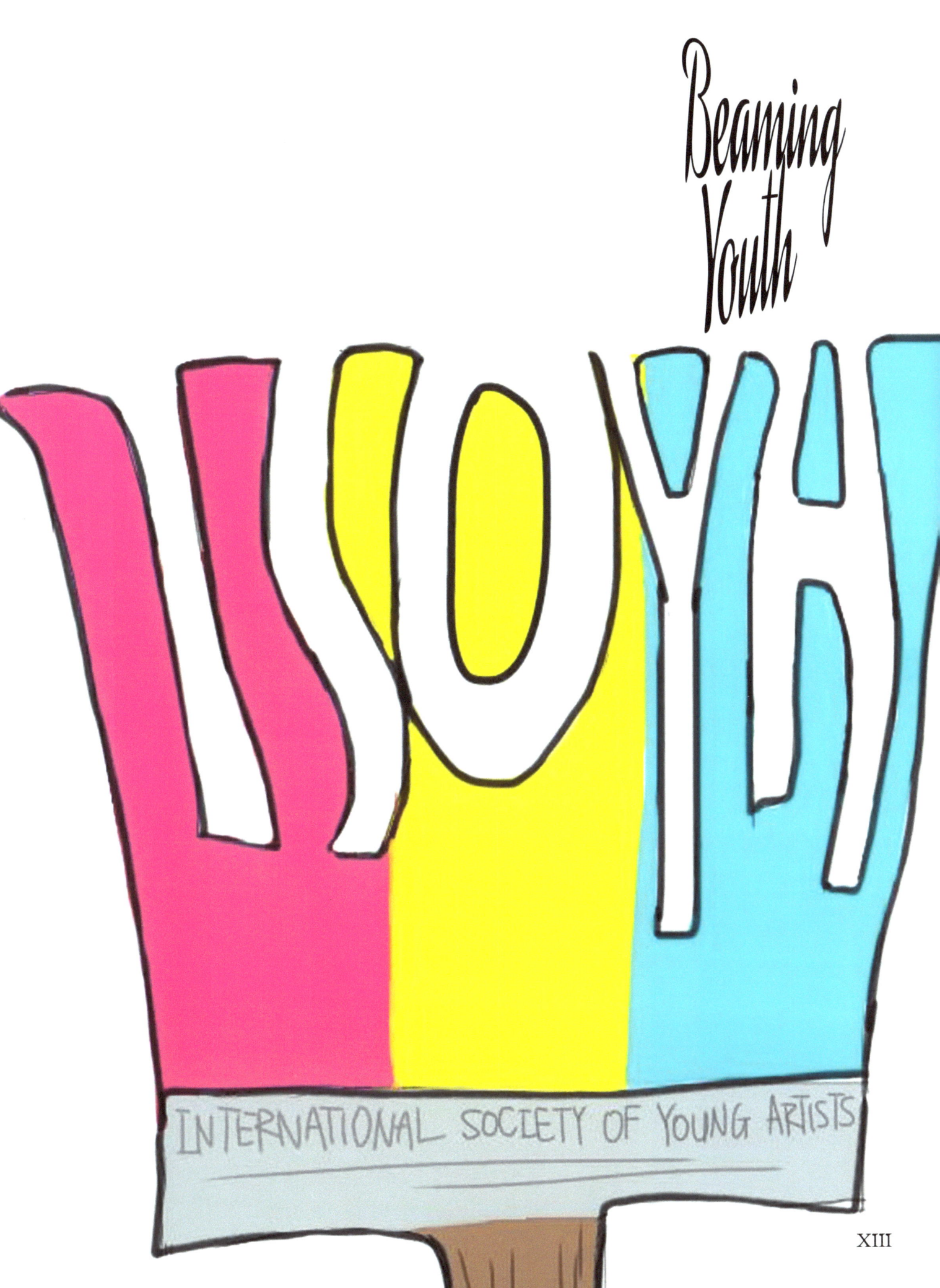

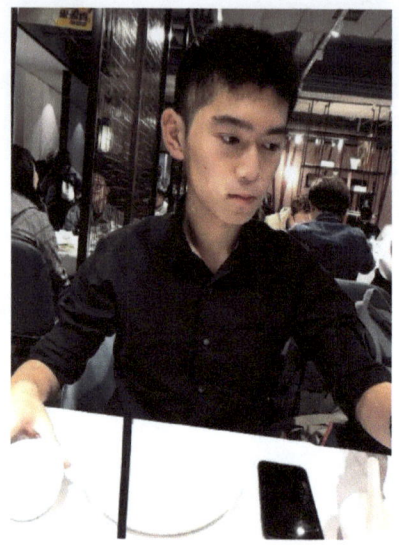

BOYANG JIAO

Beijing University of Chinese Medicine, China

Silver Award for Art, 2nd Liberty Awards, International Society of Young Artists, USA, 2019
Silver Award for Art, 1st Liberty Awards, International Society of Young Artists, USA, 2018

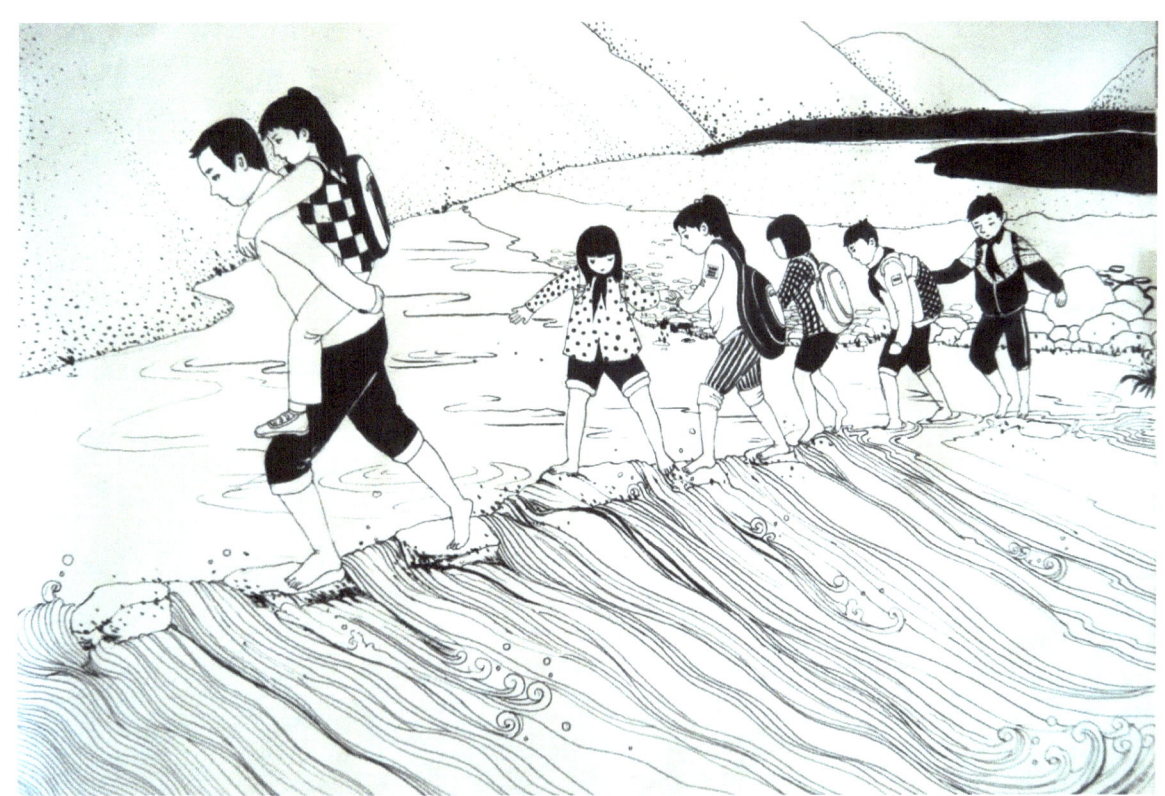

Teacher and Students, ink on paper, 2012

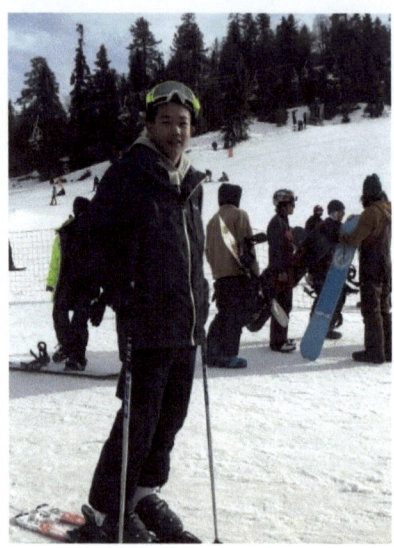

CALEB R. WU

Chino Hills High School, USA

Silver Award for Art, 3rd Liberty Awards, International Society of Young Artists, USA, 2020-21
Gold Award for Art, 2nd Liberty Awards, International Society of Young Artists, USA, 2019
Bronze Award for Art, 1st Liberty Awards, International Society of Young Artists, USA, 2018

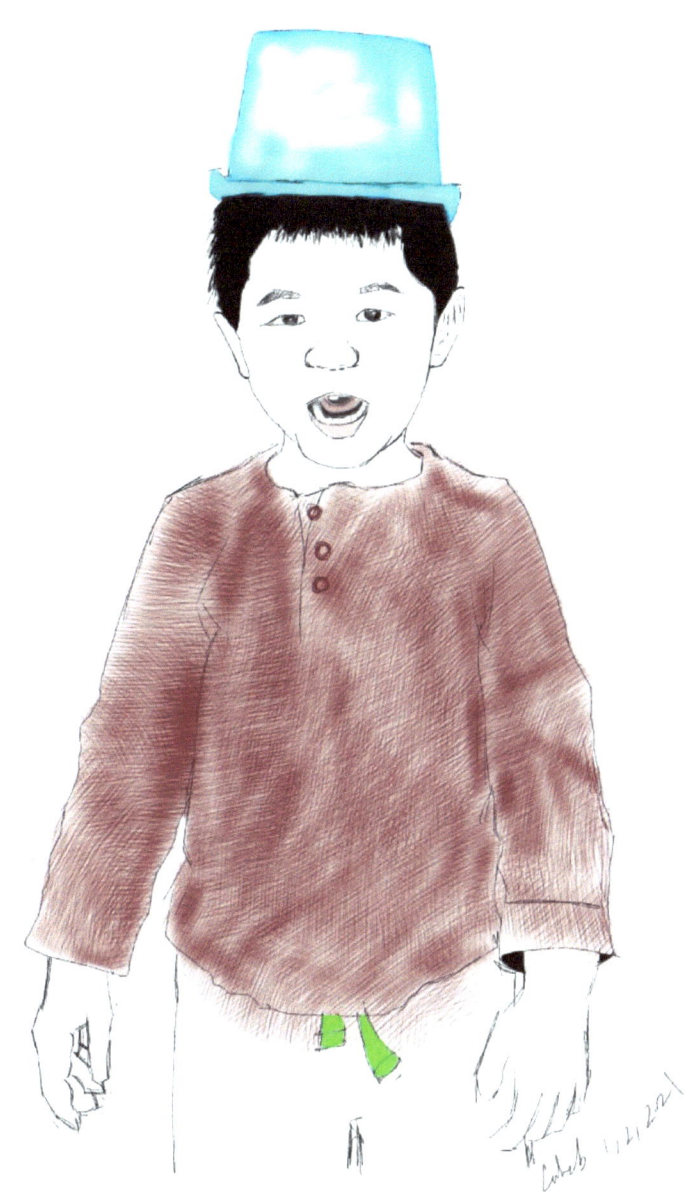

Lucas, digital, 2021

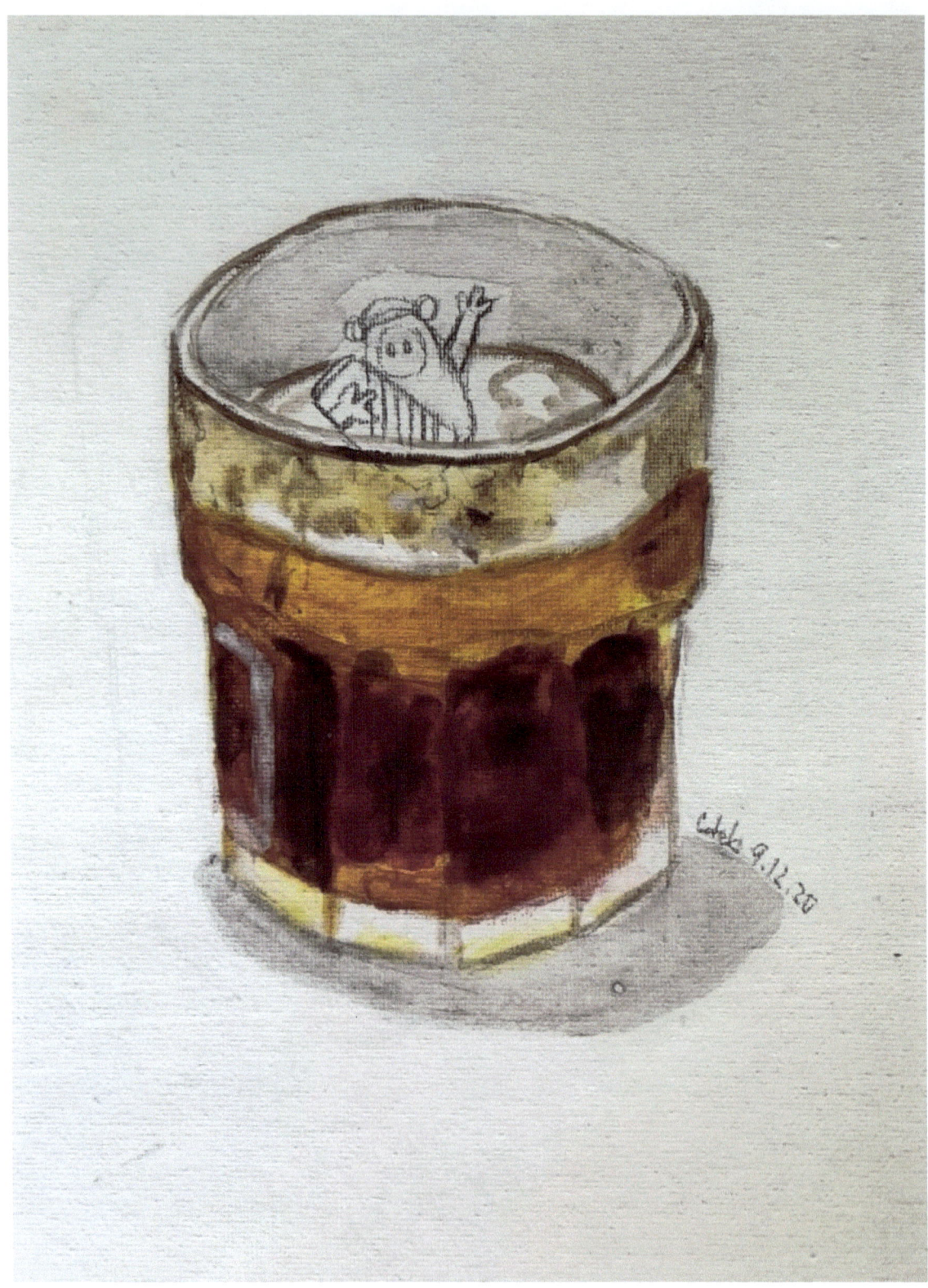

Elf in the Glass, acrylic on paper, 2020

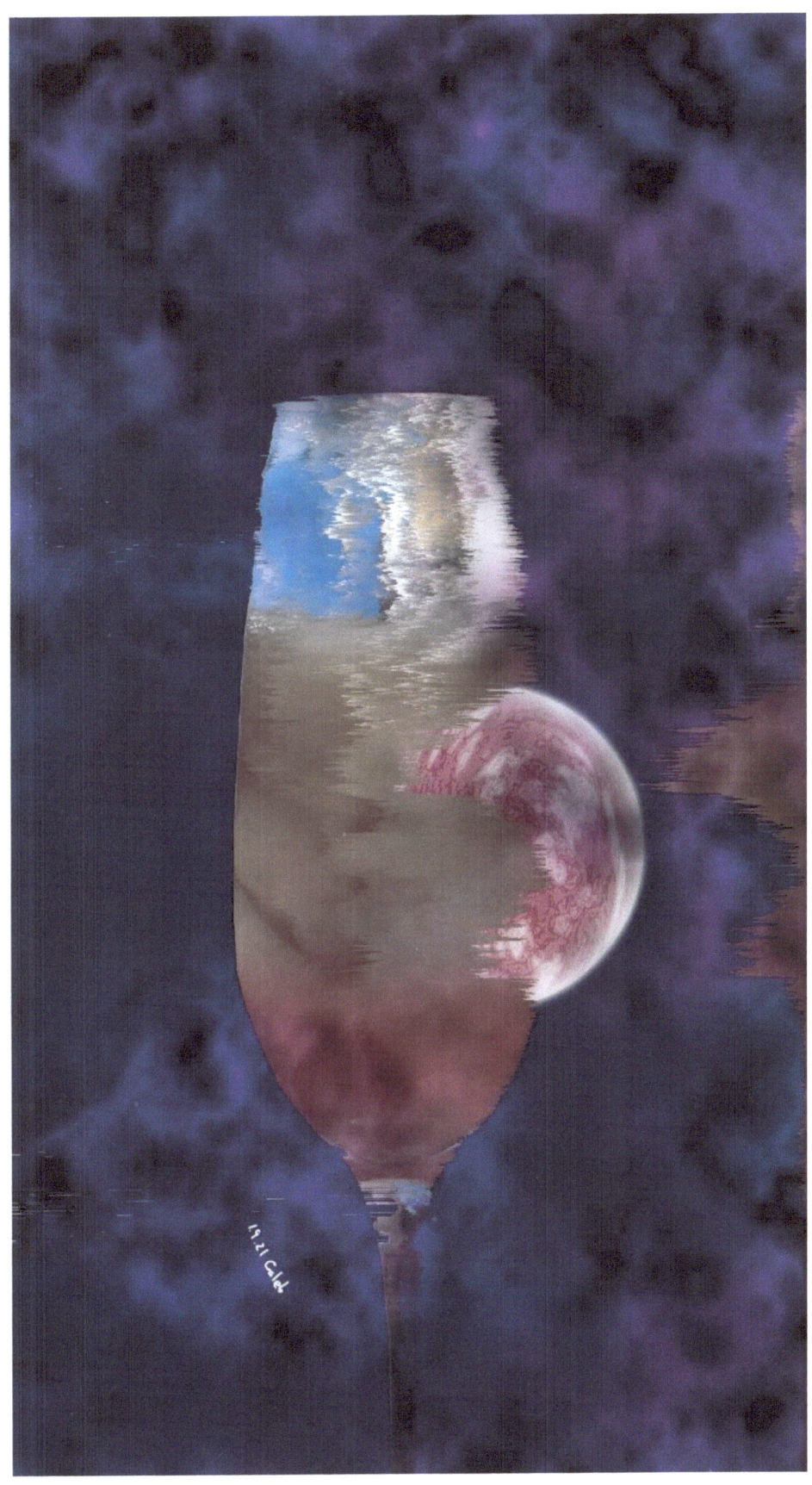

Moon Cocktail, digital, 2021

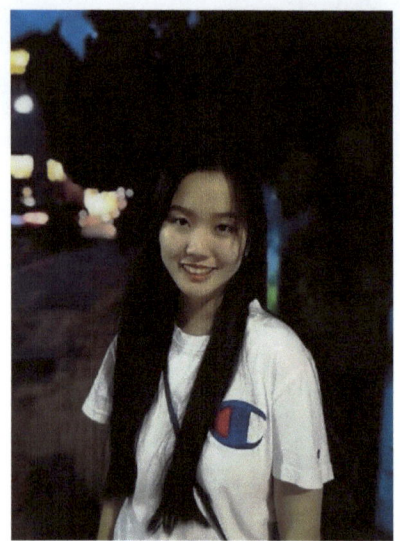

CHANGLU XU

Qingdao Haishan School, China

Silver Award for Art, 3rd Liberty Awards, International Society of Young Artists, USA, 2020-21
Rising Star Award, 2nd Liberty Awards, International Society of Young Artists, USA, 2019
Rising Star Award, 1st Liberty Awards, International Society of Young Artists, USA, 2018

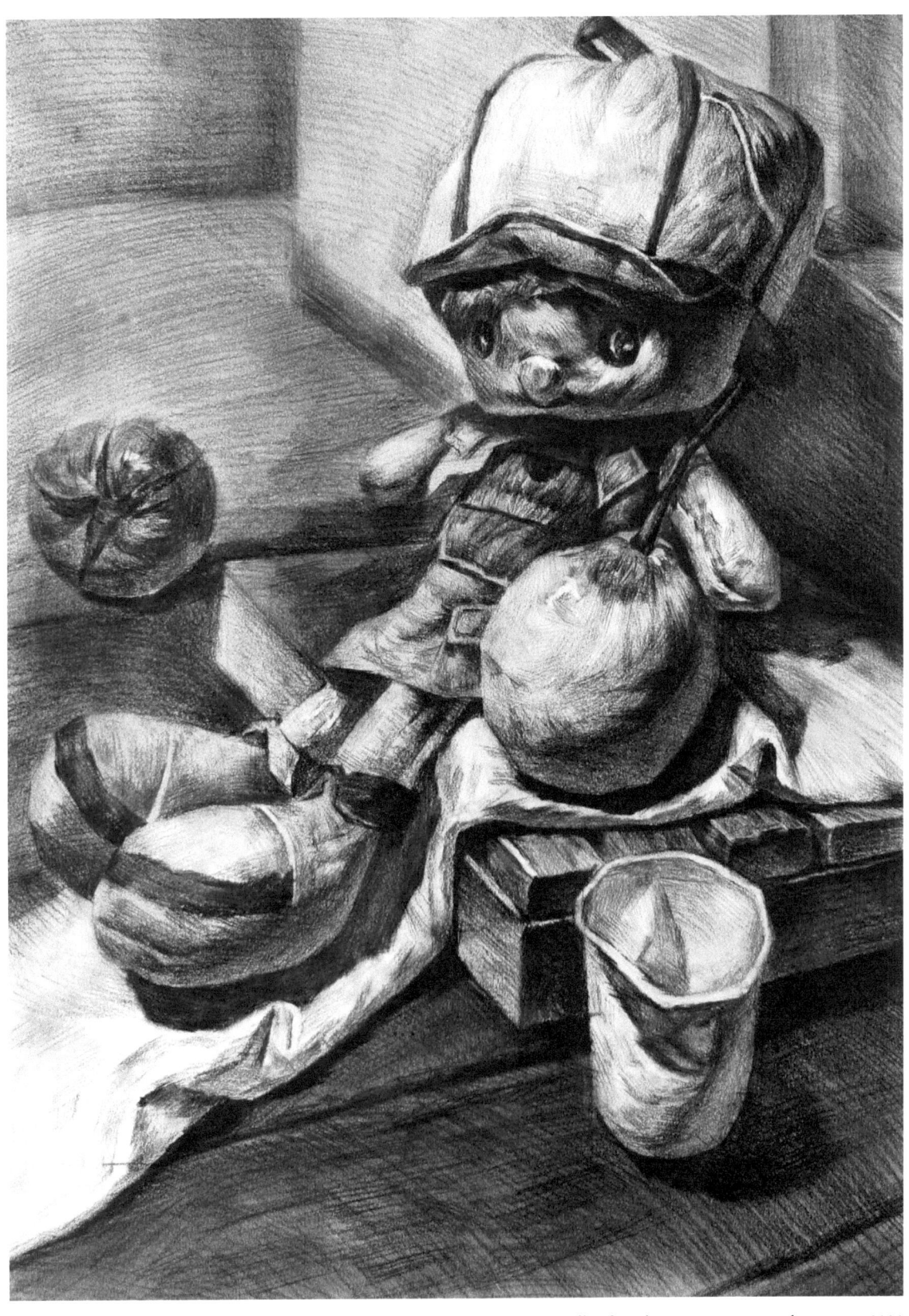

Still Life with a Boy Puppet, pencil on paper, 2020

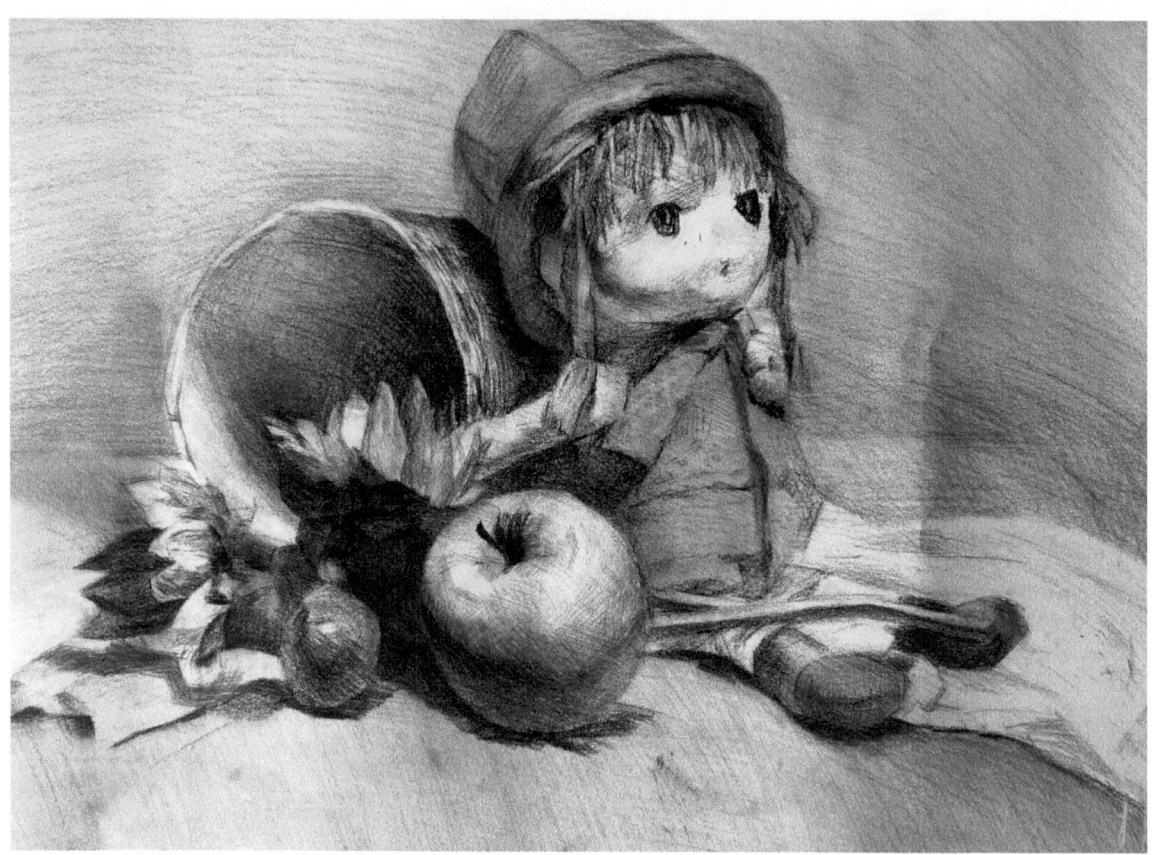

Still Life with a Girl Puppet, pencil on paper, 2020

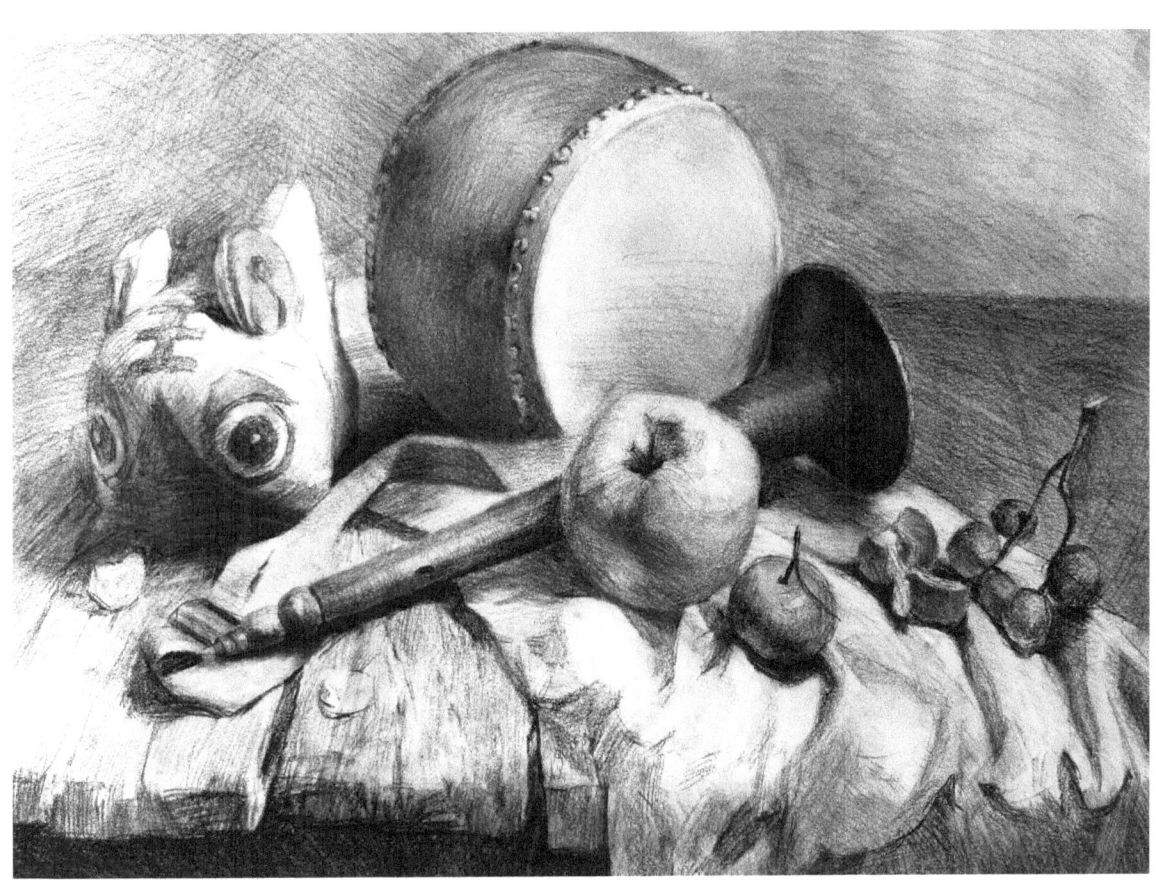

Still Life with a Cloth Tiger, pencil on paper, 2020

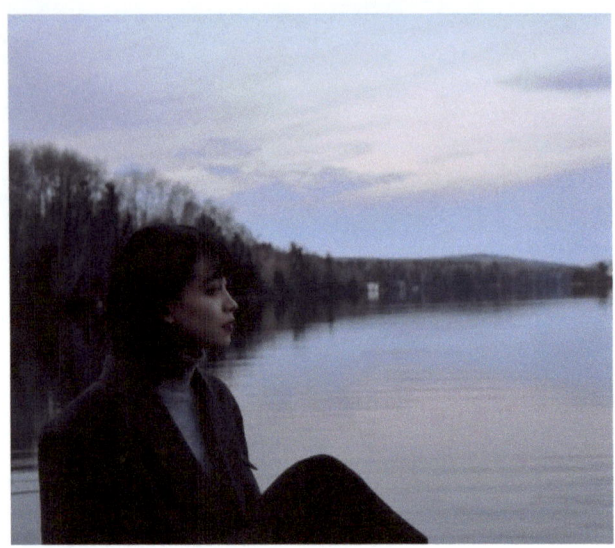

FANGYU REN

University of Toronto, Master of Science in Biomedical Communication, Canada

Gold Award for Art, 3rd Liberty Awards, International Society of Young Artists, USA, 2020-21
Gold Award for Art, 2nd Liberty Awards, International Society of Young Artists, USA, 2019
Gold Award for Art, 1st Liberty Awards, International Society of Young Artists, USA, 2018
Excellence in Teaching Award, Losget Academy, USA, 2018
Excellence Press Award, Losget Press, USA, 2018
Excellence in Mentoring, "The Colorful Peace" Art Project Honoring the 100th Anniversary of the WWI Armistice, International Society of Young Artists, USA, 2018

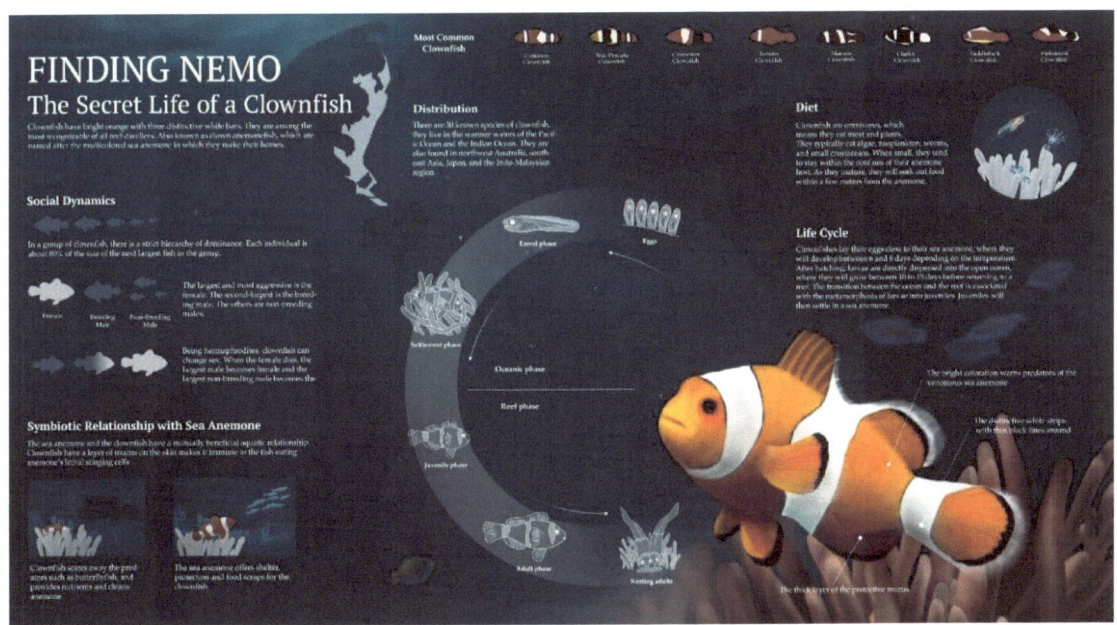

Infographic Design: *Finding Nemo*, digital, 2020

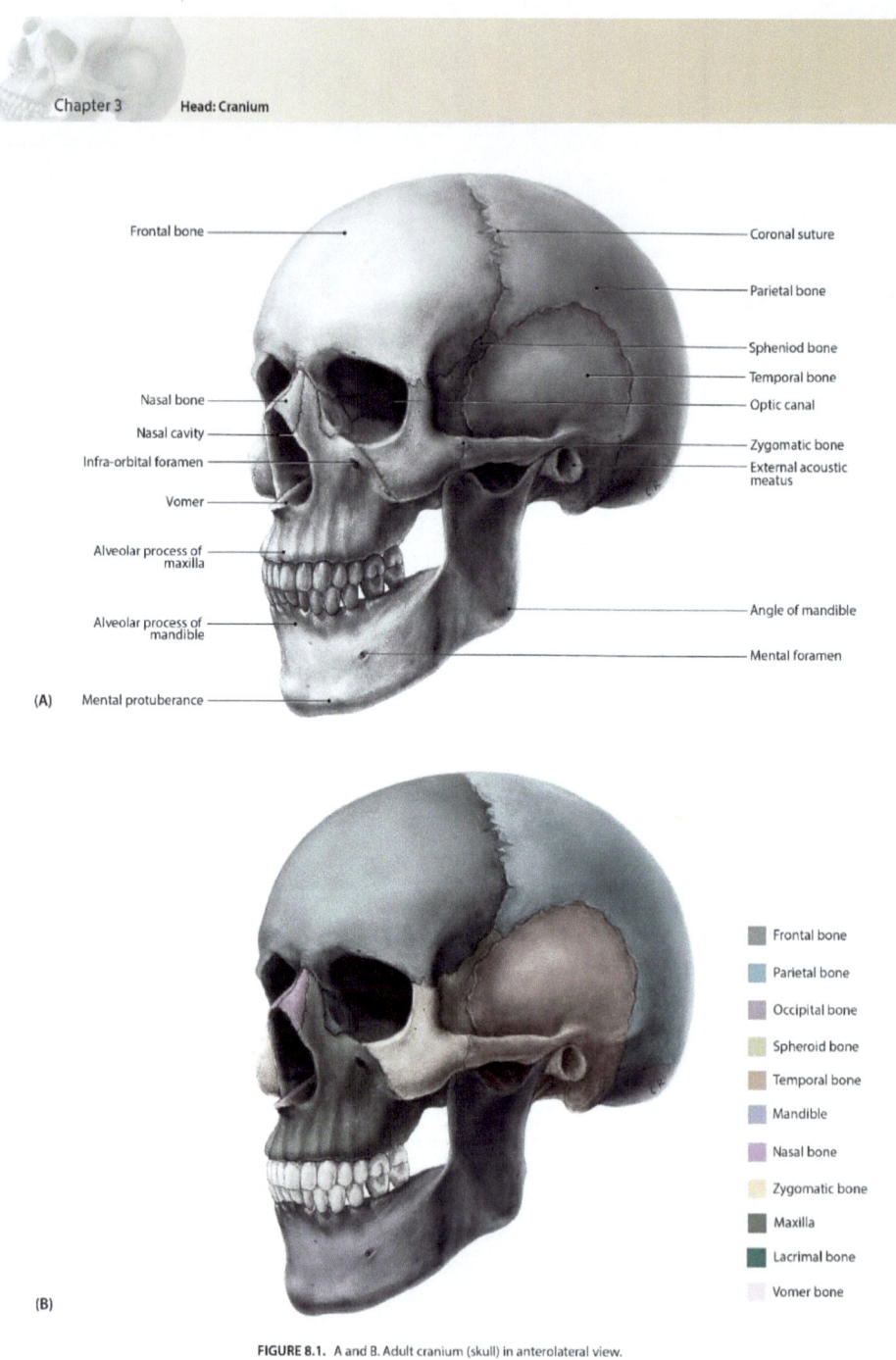

Medical Illustration: *Human Skull Anterolateral View*, carbon dust and digital, 2020

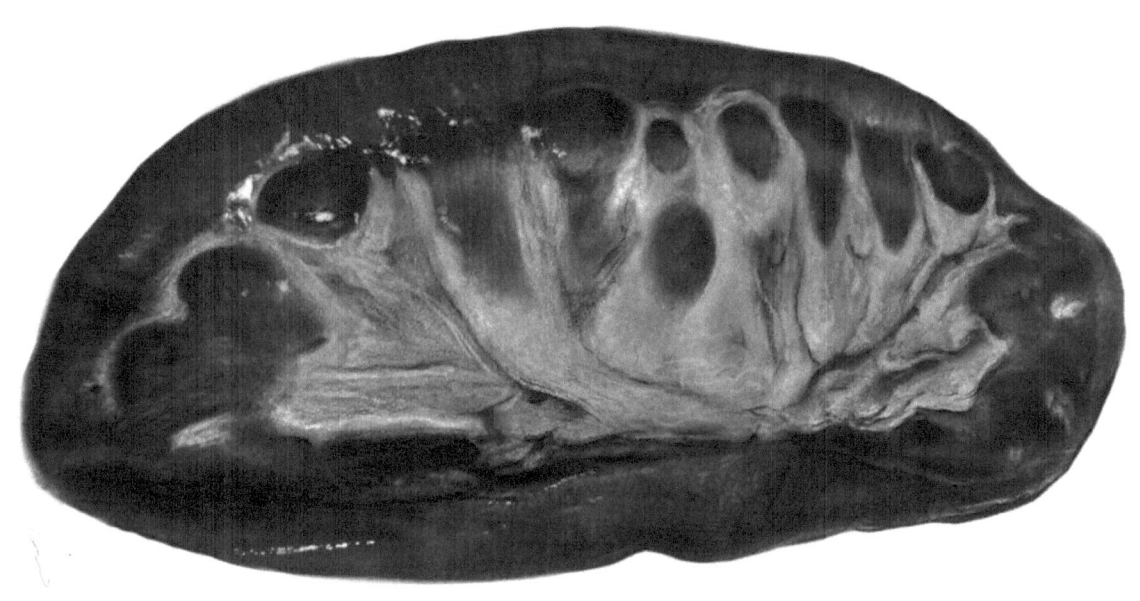

Medical Illustration: *Human Kidney Cross Section*, carbon dust and digital, 2020

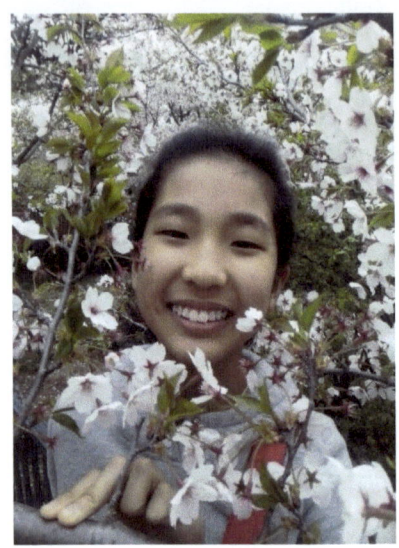

JIAJUN CHEN

Qingdao No.17 High School, China

Silver Award for Art, 3rd Liberty Awards, International Society of Young Artists, USA, 2020-21
Bronze Award for Art, 2nd Liberty Awards, International Society of Young Artists, USA, 2019
Rising Star Award, 1st Liberty Awards, International Society of Young Artists, USA, 2018

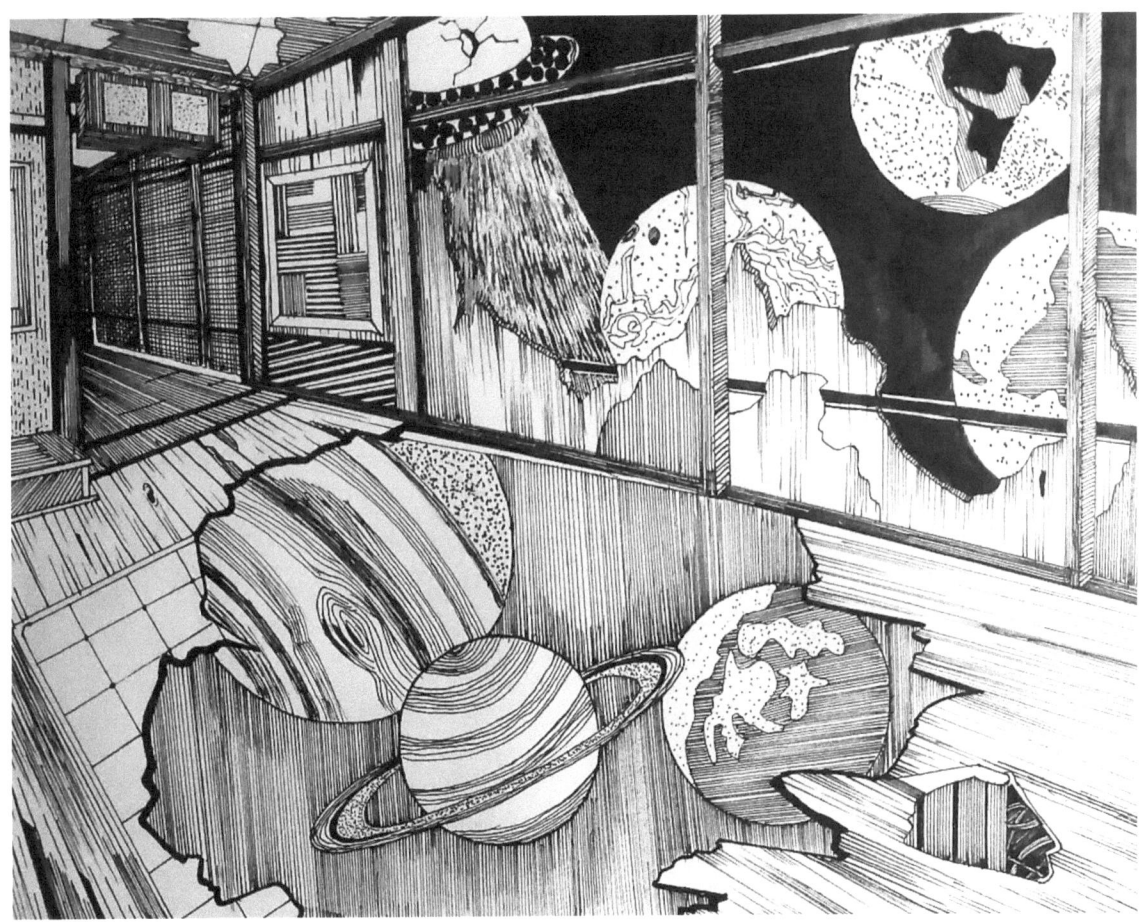

Planet House, ink on paper, 2020

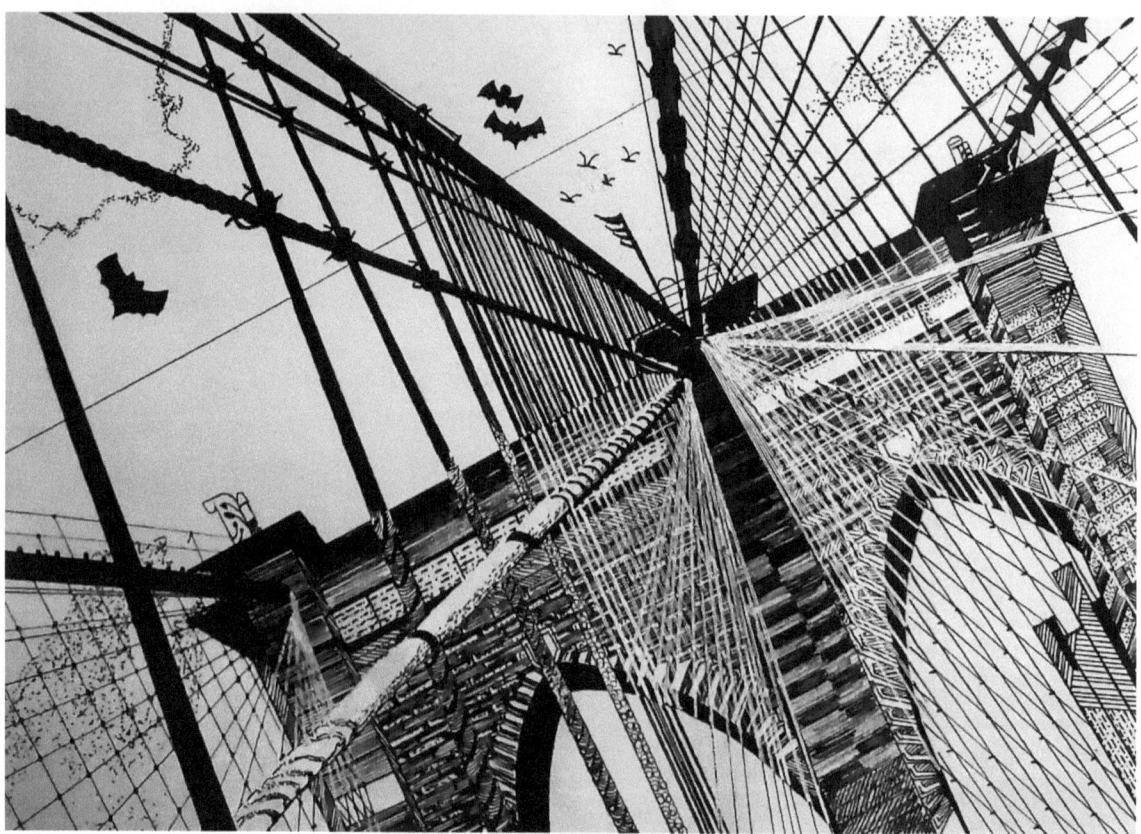
Bridge, ink on paper, 2020

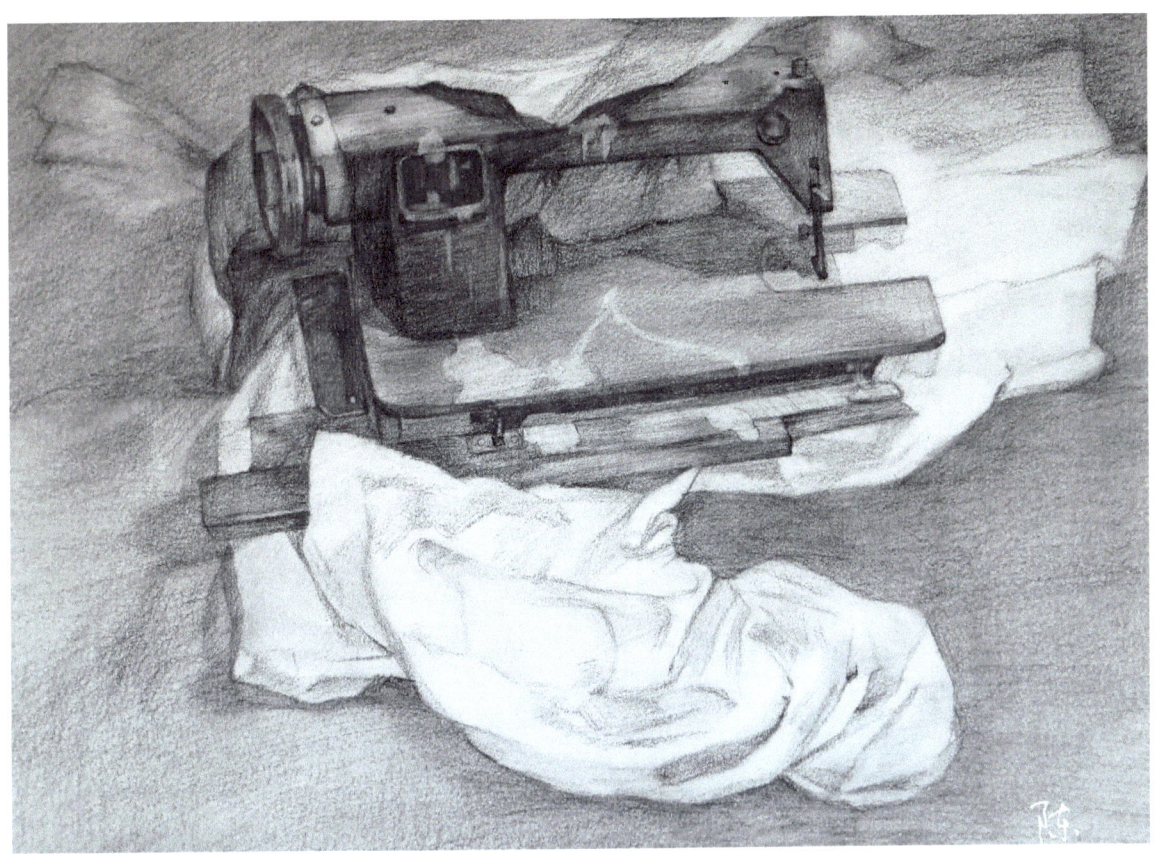

Sewing Machine, pencil on paper, 2020

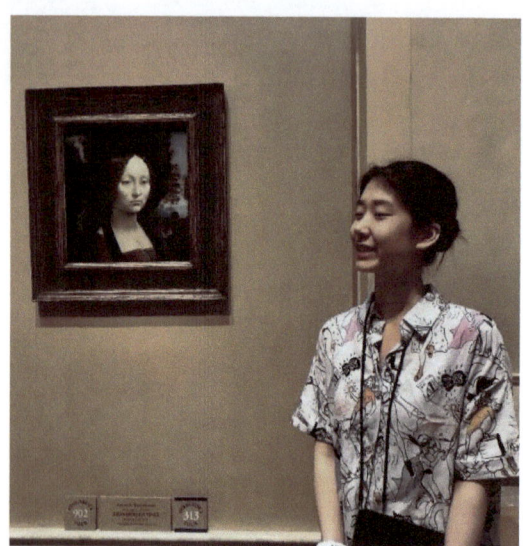

JIAJUN DENG

Qingdao No.17 High School, China

Person of the Year 2020, International Society of Young Artists, USA, 2020

Gold Award for Art, 3rd Liberty Awards, International Society of Young Artists, USA, 2020-21

Silver Award for Art, 2nd Liberty Awards, International Society of Young Artists, USA, 2019

Gold Award for Art, 1st Liberty Awards, International Society of Young Artists, USA, 2018

Gold Award, "The Colorful Peace" Art Project Honoring the 100th Anniversary of the WWI Armistice, International Society of Young Artists, USA, 2018

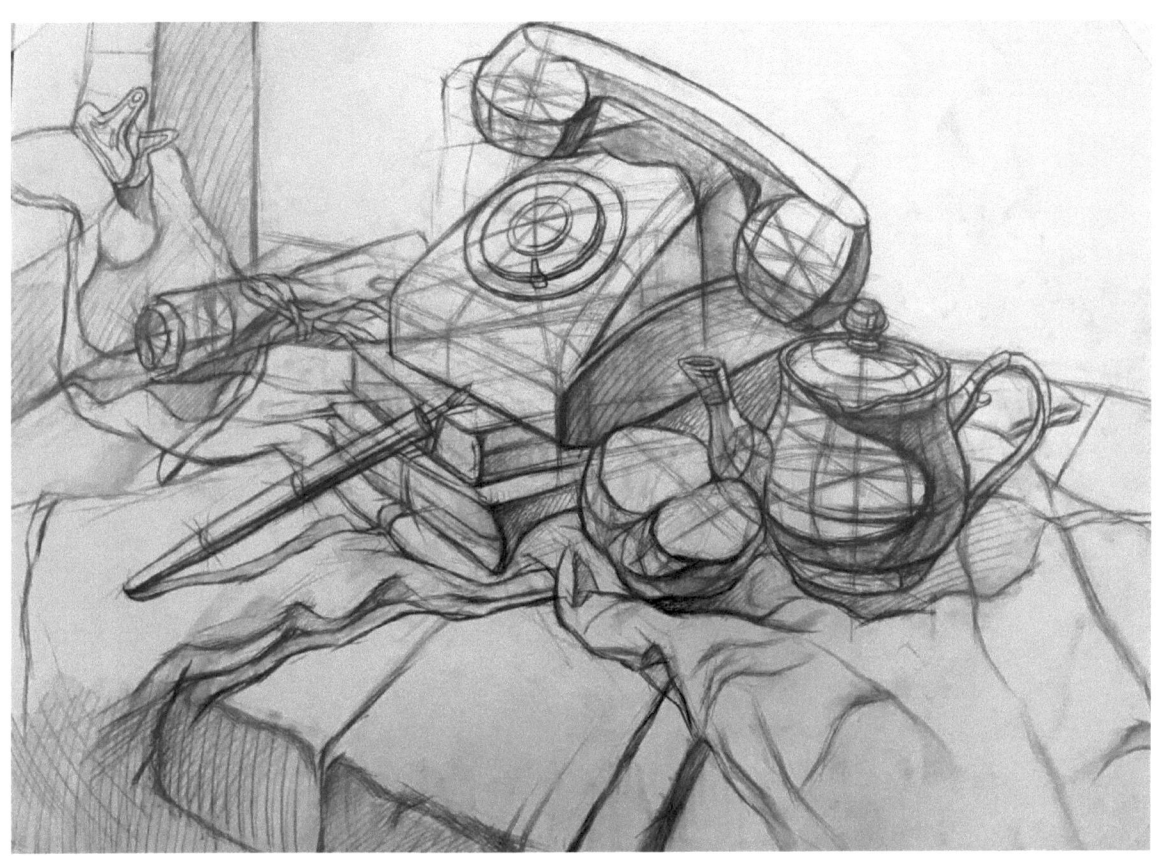

Still Life with a Telephone, pencil on paper, 2020

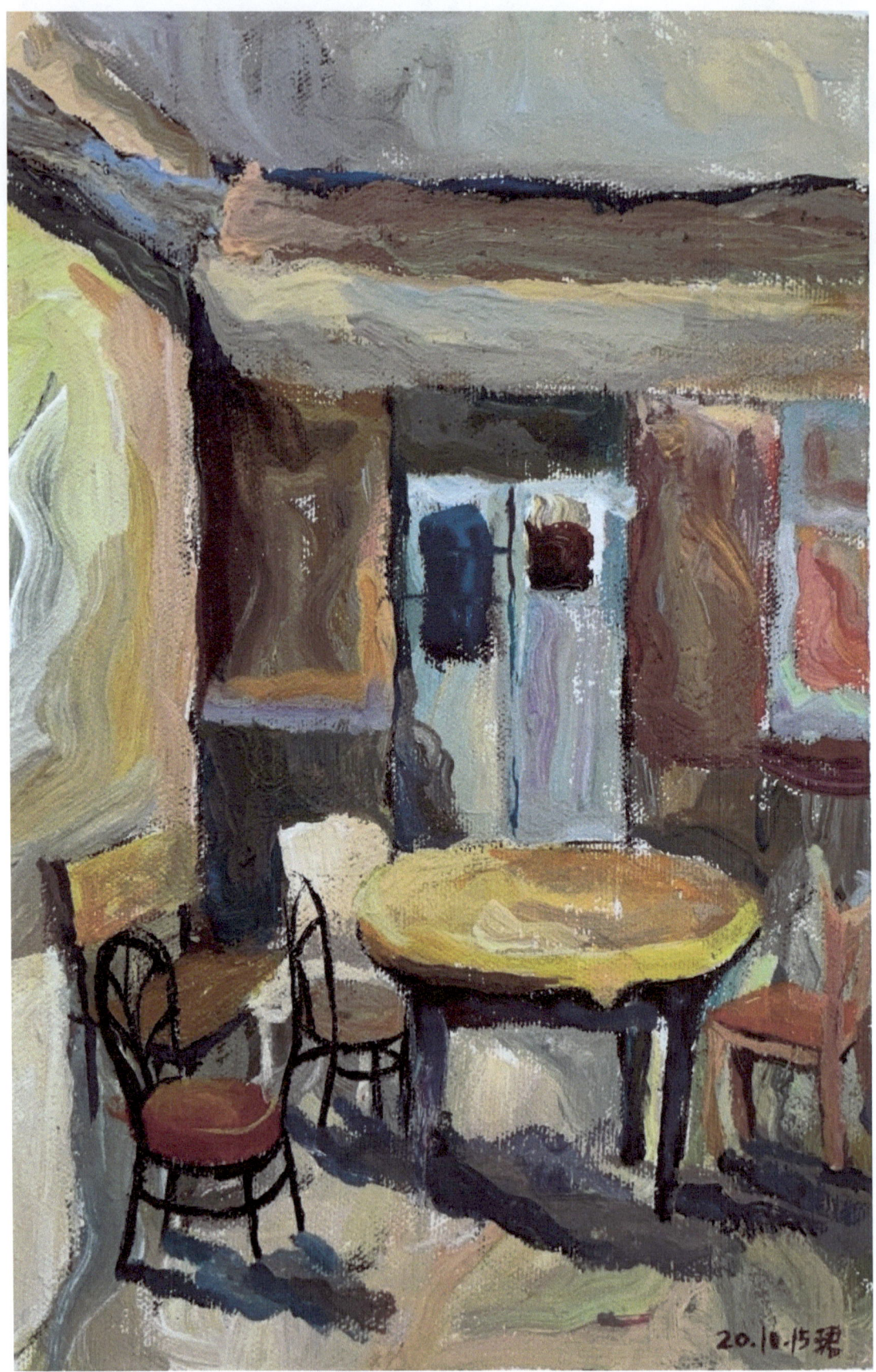

A Corner of the Courtyard, gouache on paper, 2020

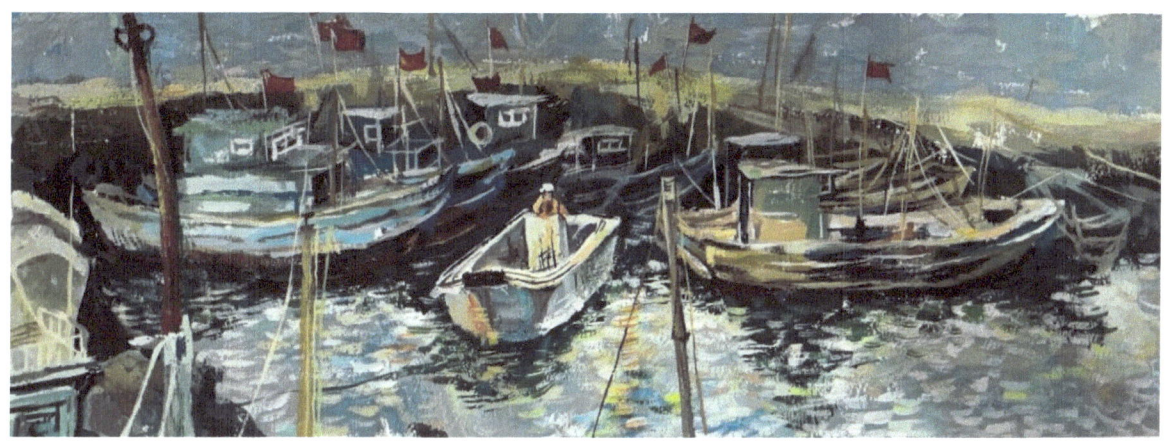

Old Fishing Harbor, gouache on paper, 2020

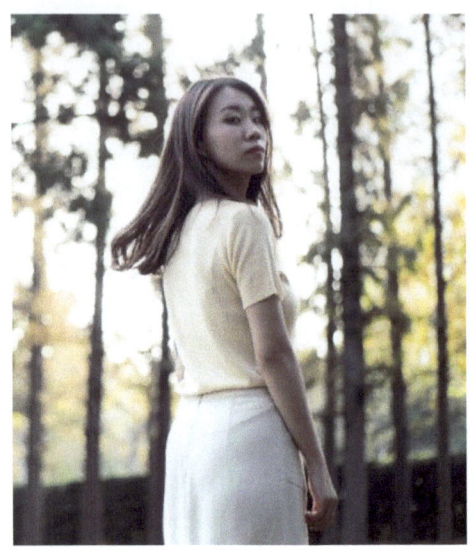

JIAXIN LENG

Zimo Clothing Co., Ltd, China

Gold Award for Art, 2nd Liberty Awards, International Society of Young Artists, USA, 2019
Gold Award for Art, 1st Liberty Awards, International Society of Young Artists, USA, 2018

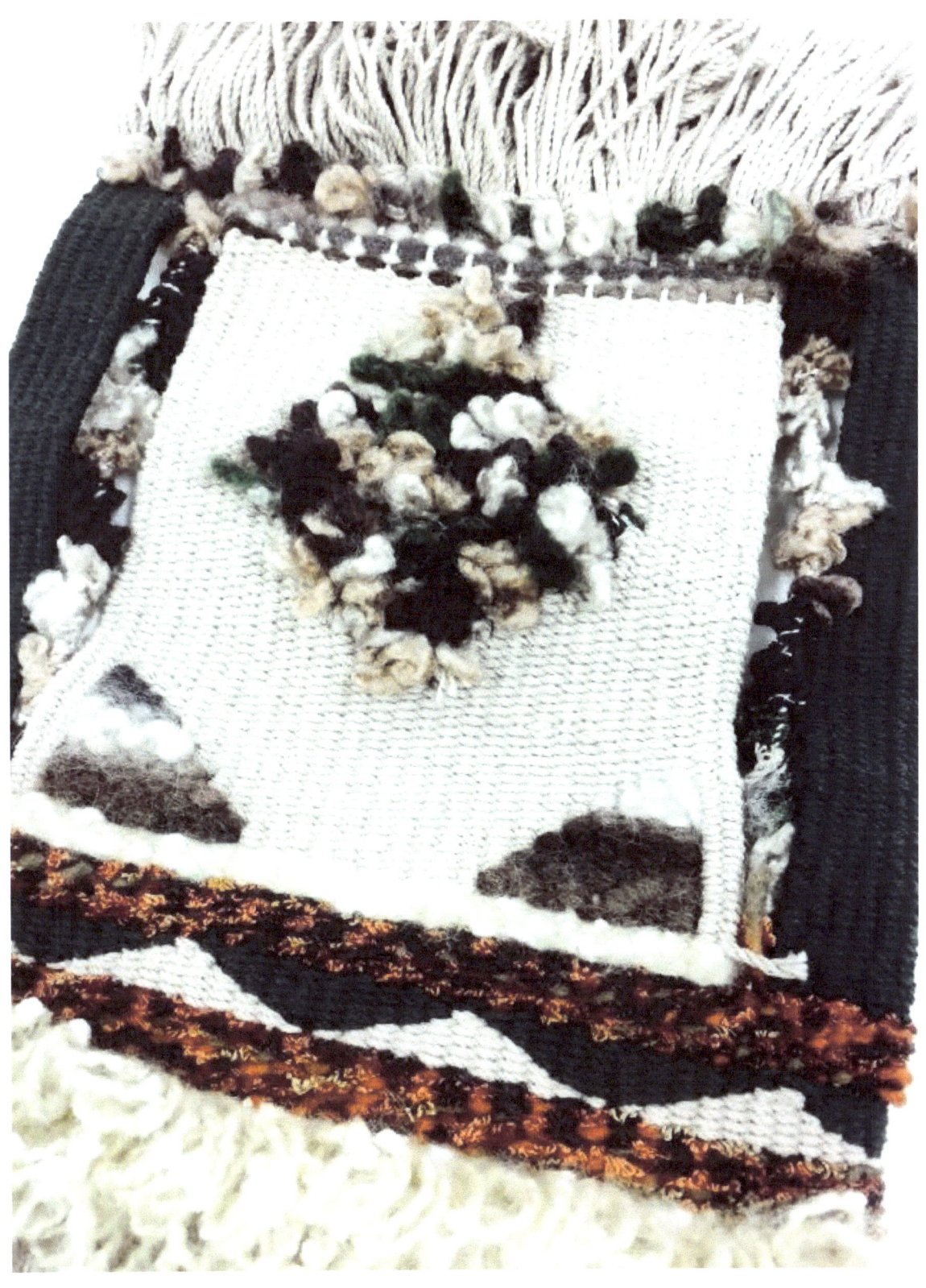

Wall-hanging Woven Piece, braiding rope and woolen thread, 2018

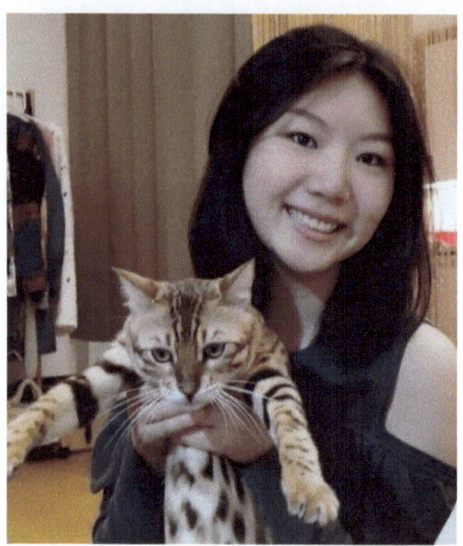

JIA ZHONG

School of Visual Arts, USA

Gold Award for Art, 3rd Liberty Awards, International Society of Young Artists, USA, 2020-21
Gold Award for Art, 2nd Liberty Awards, International Society of Young Artists, USA, 2019
Gold Award for Art, 1st Liberty Awards, International Society of Young Artists, USA, 2018
3rd Prize, 10th "Earth Doctor" National Geographic Science and Technology Competition, the Geographical Society of China, 2016

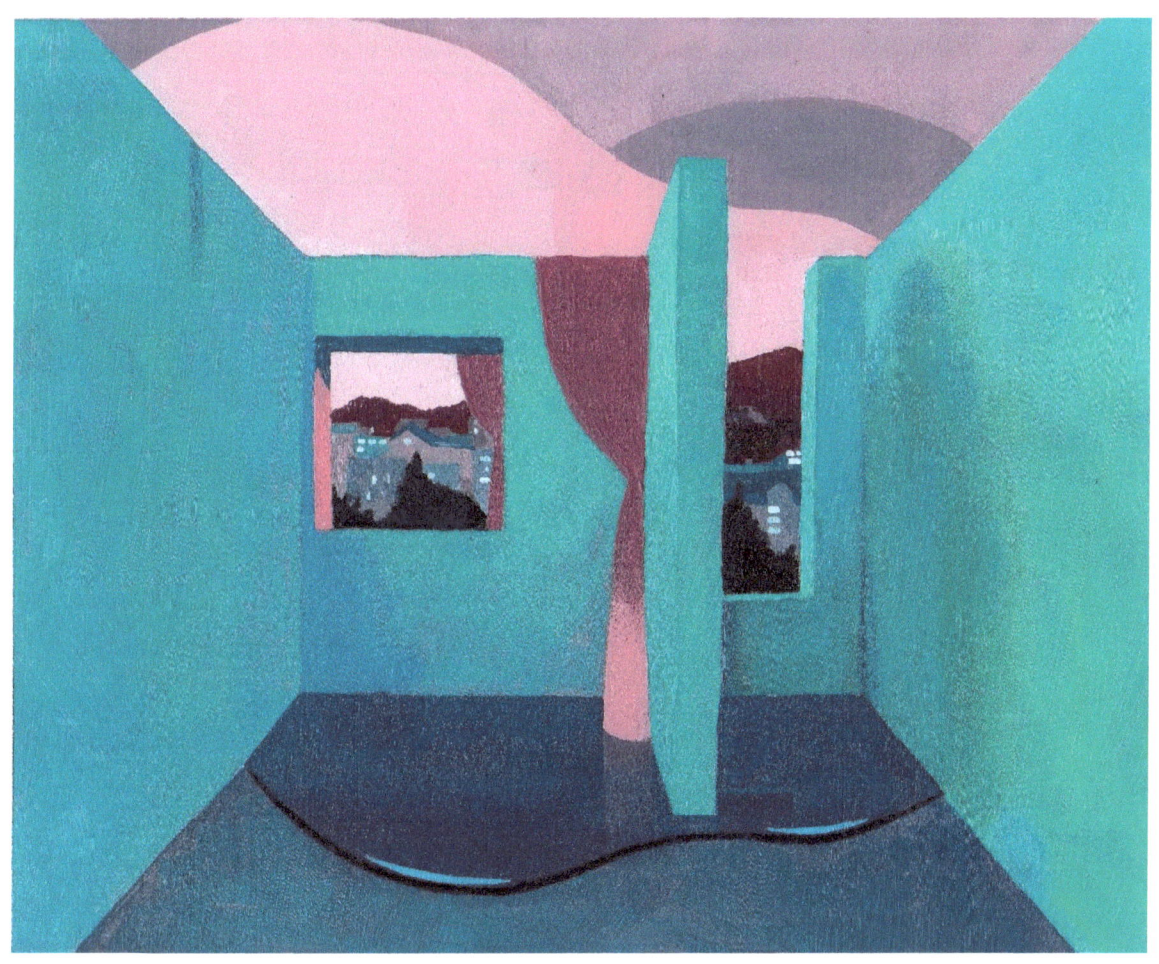

36°04′13.8″N 120°25′37.8″E, acrylic on paper, 2020

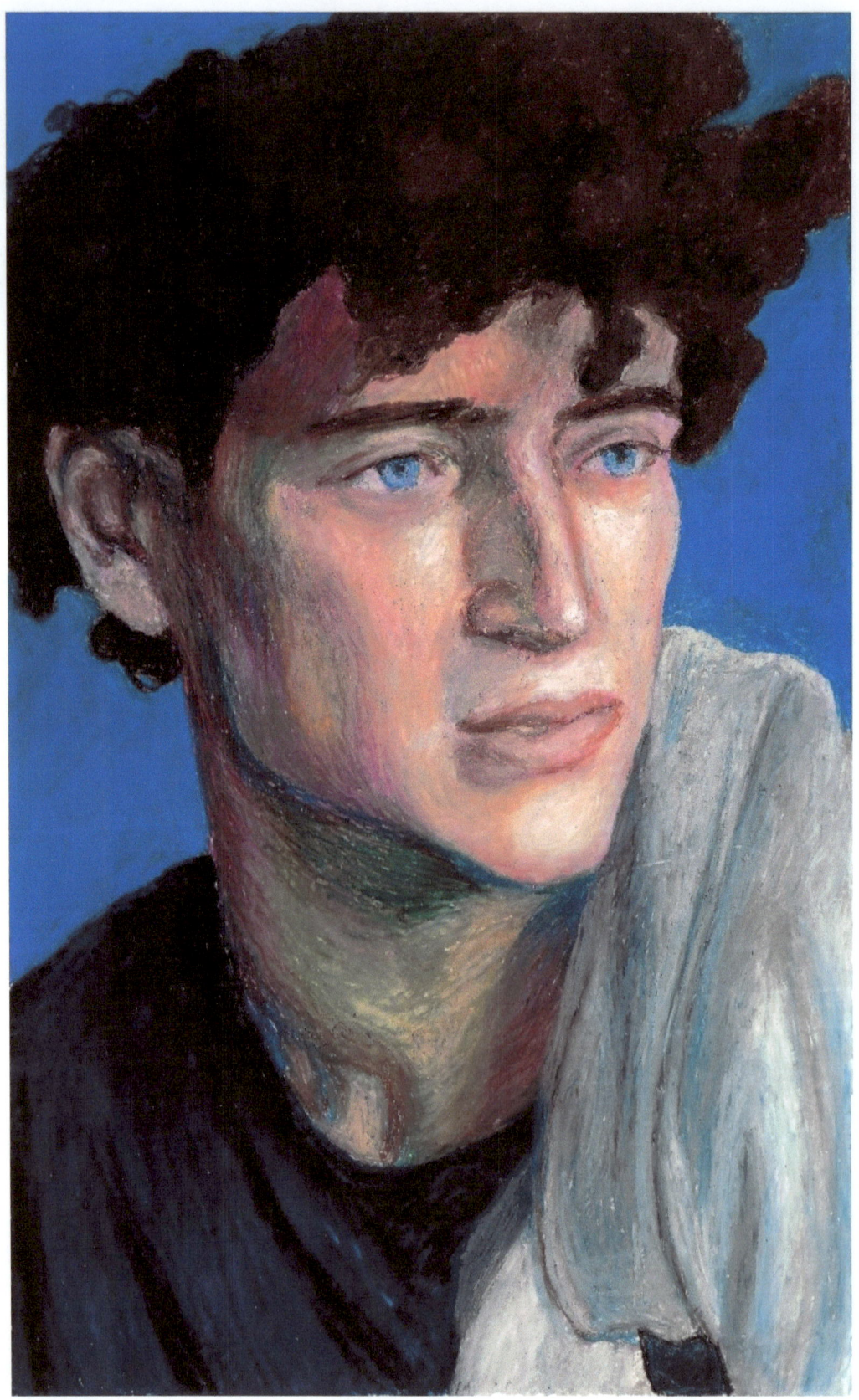

5:27 P.M., oil pastel on paper, 2020

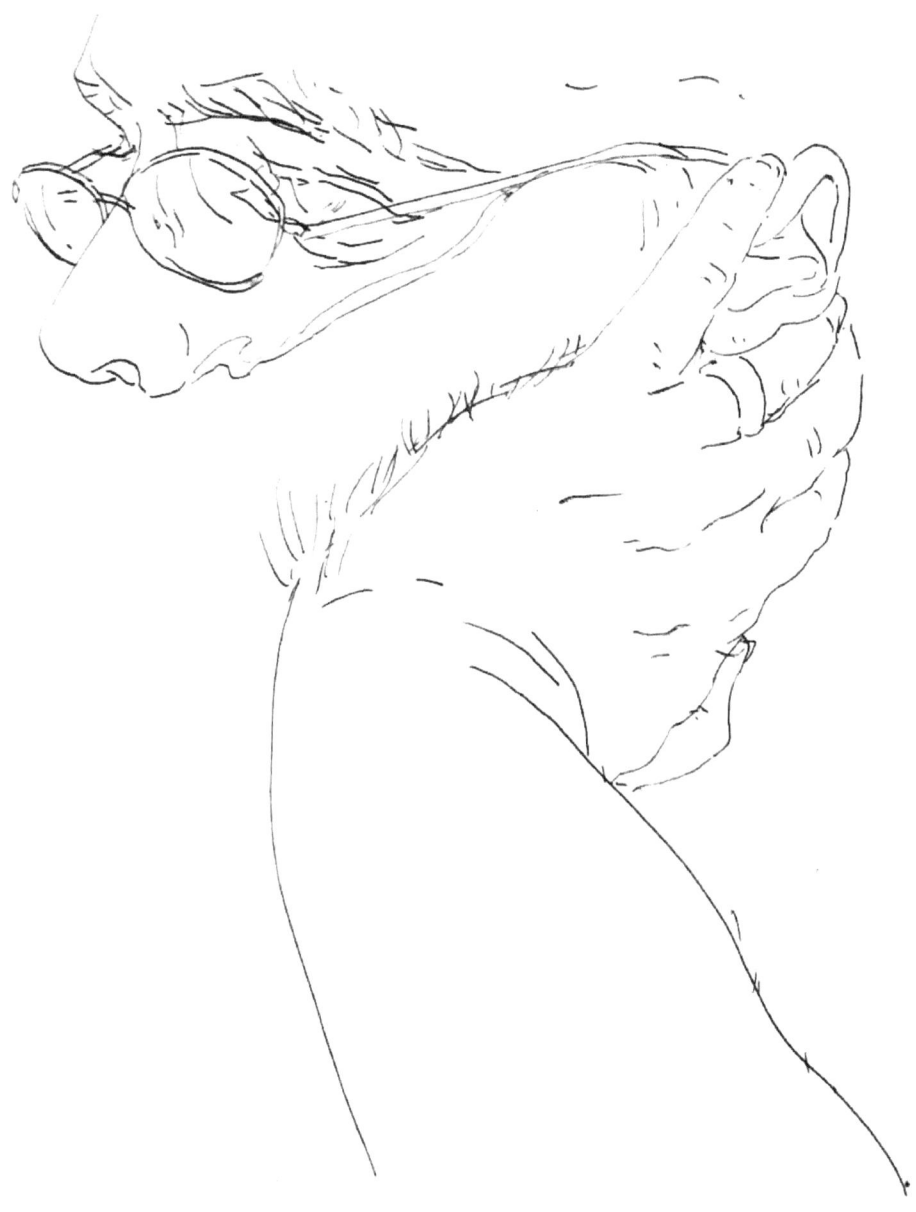

Midlife Blessing, ink on paper, 2020

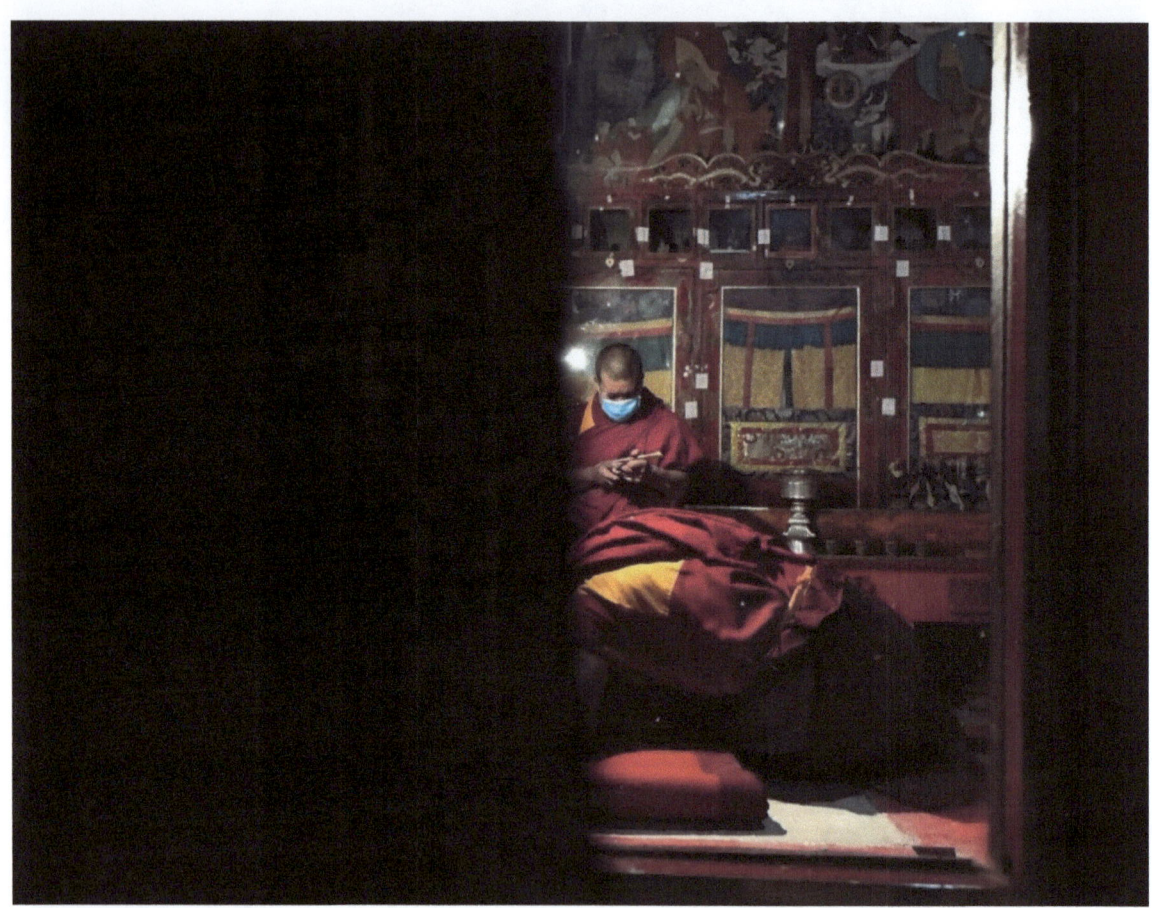

The Halves, photo, 2018

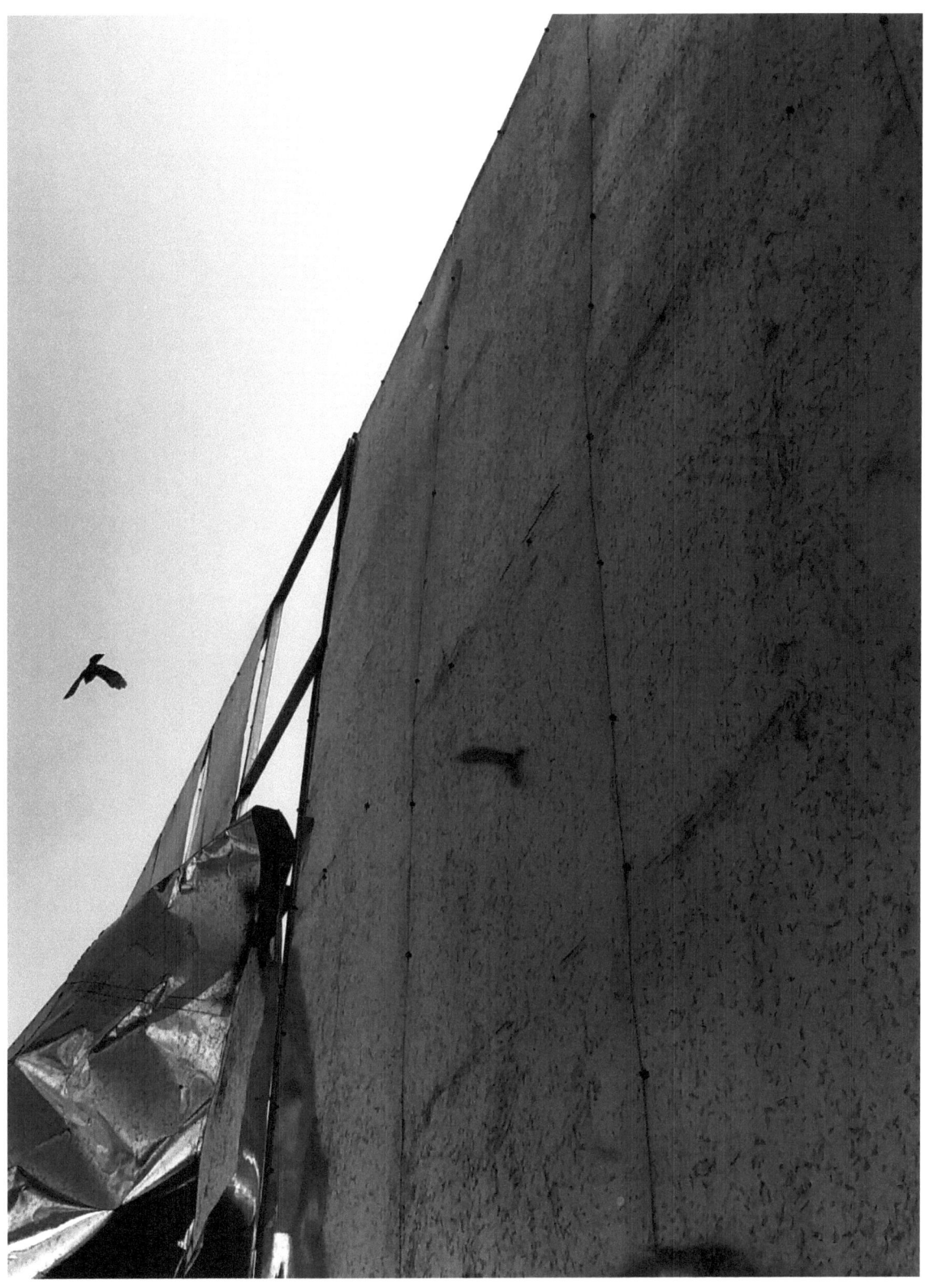

Upon the Barrier, photo, 2018

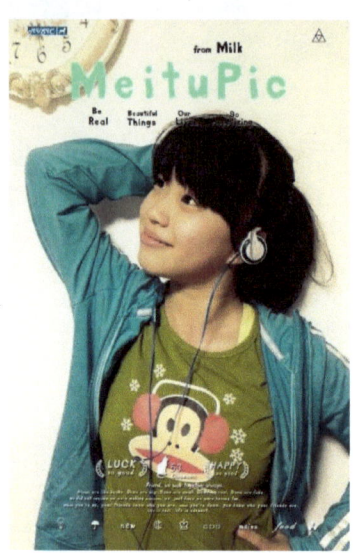

JINCHANG ZHANG

Qingdao Haishan School, China

Bronze Award for Art, 3rd Liberty Awards, International Society of Young Artists, USA, 2020-21
Silver Award for Art, 2nd Liberty Awards, International Society of Young Artists, USA, 2019
Silver Award for Art, 1st Liberty Awards, International Society of Young Artists, USA, 2018

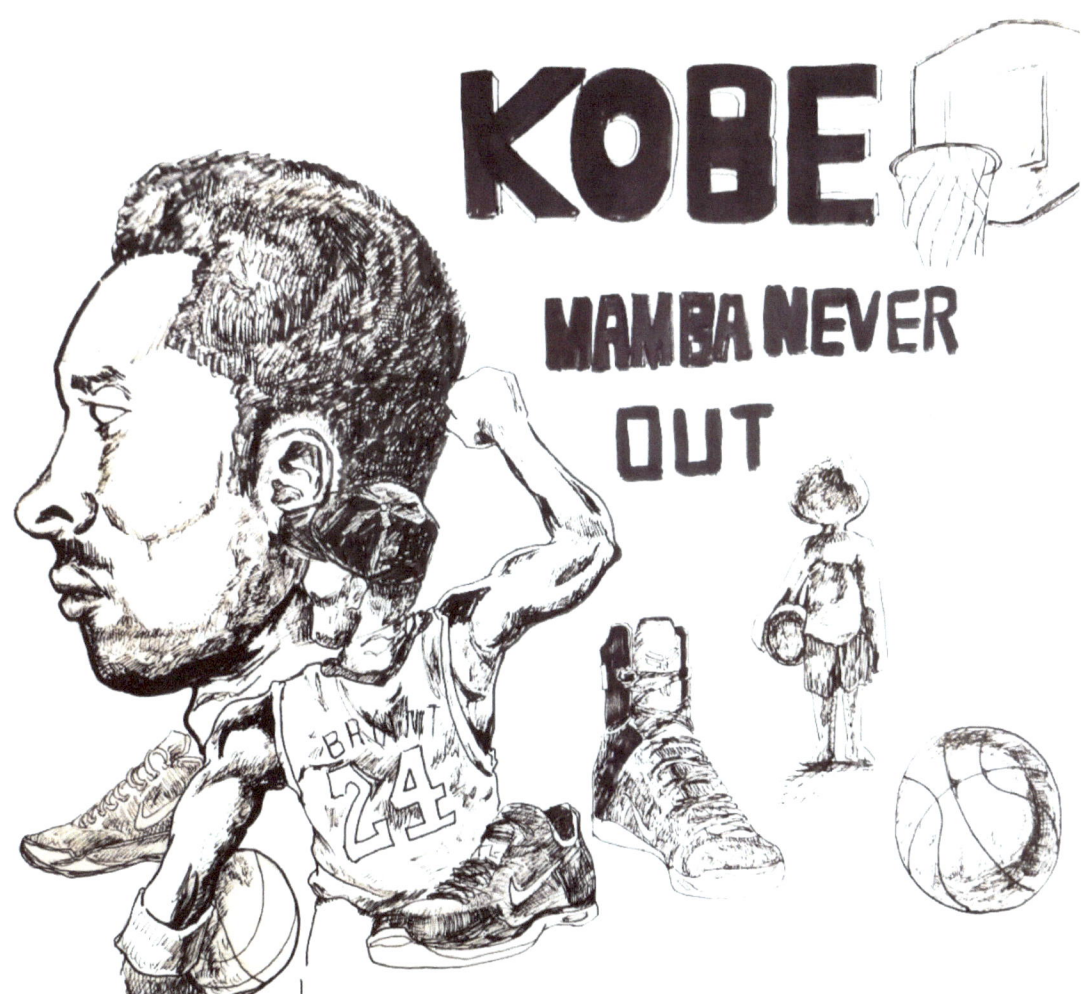

Kobe, ink on paper, 2020

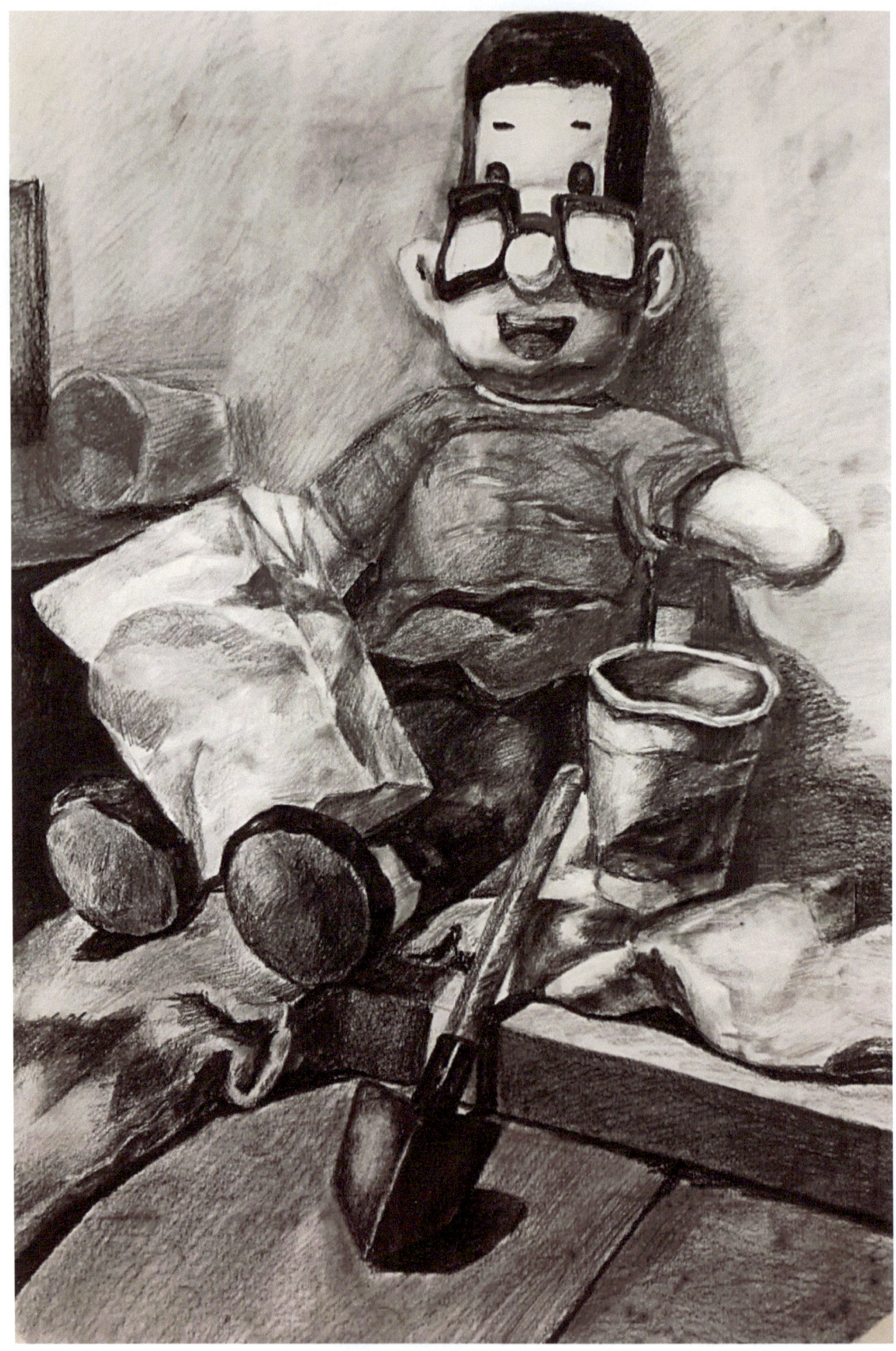

Still Life with a Man Puppet, pencil on paper, 2020

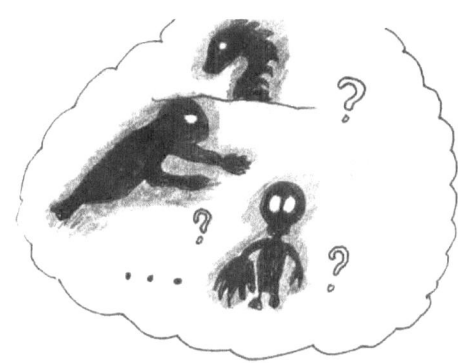

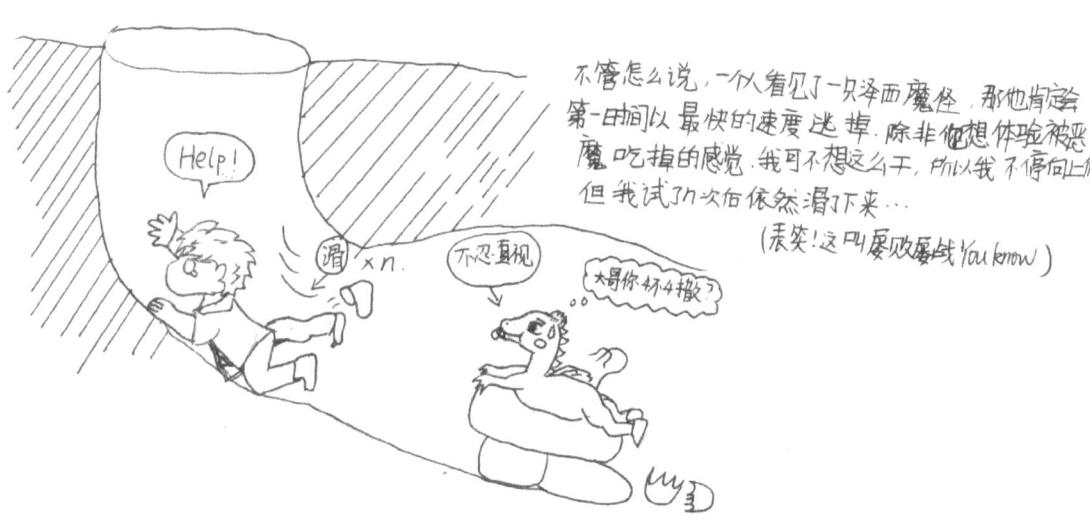

Comics Anthology *New Jersey Family* Page 2, ink on paper, 2017

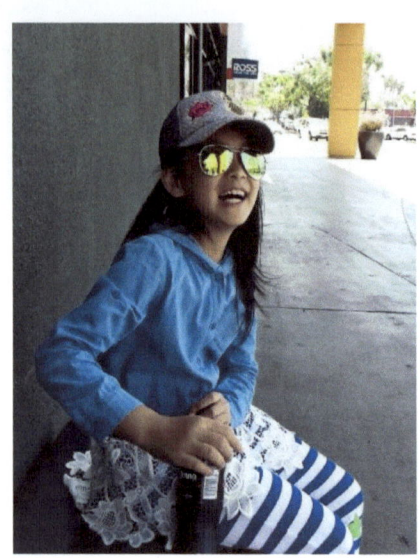

JINGHAN XU

Chino Hills High School, USA

Gold Award for Art, 3rd Liberty Awards, International Society of Young Artists, USA, 2020-21
Silver Award for Art, 2nd Liberty Awards, International Society of Young Artists, USA, 2019
Rising Star Award, 1st Liberty Awards, International Society of Young Artists, USA, 2018

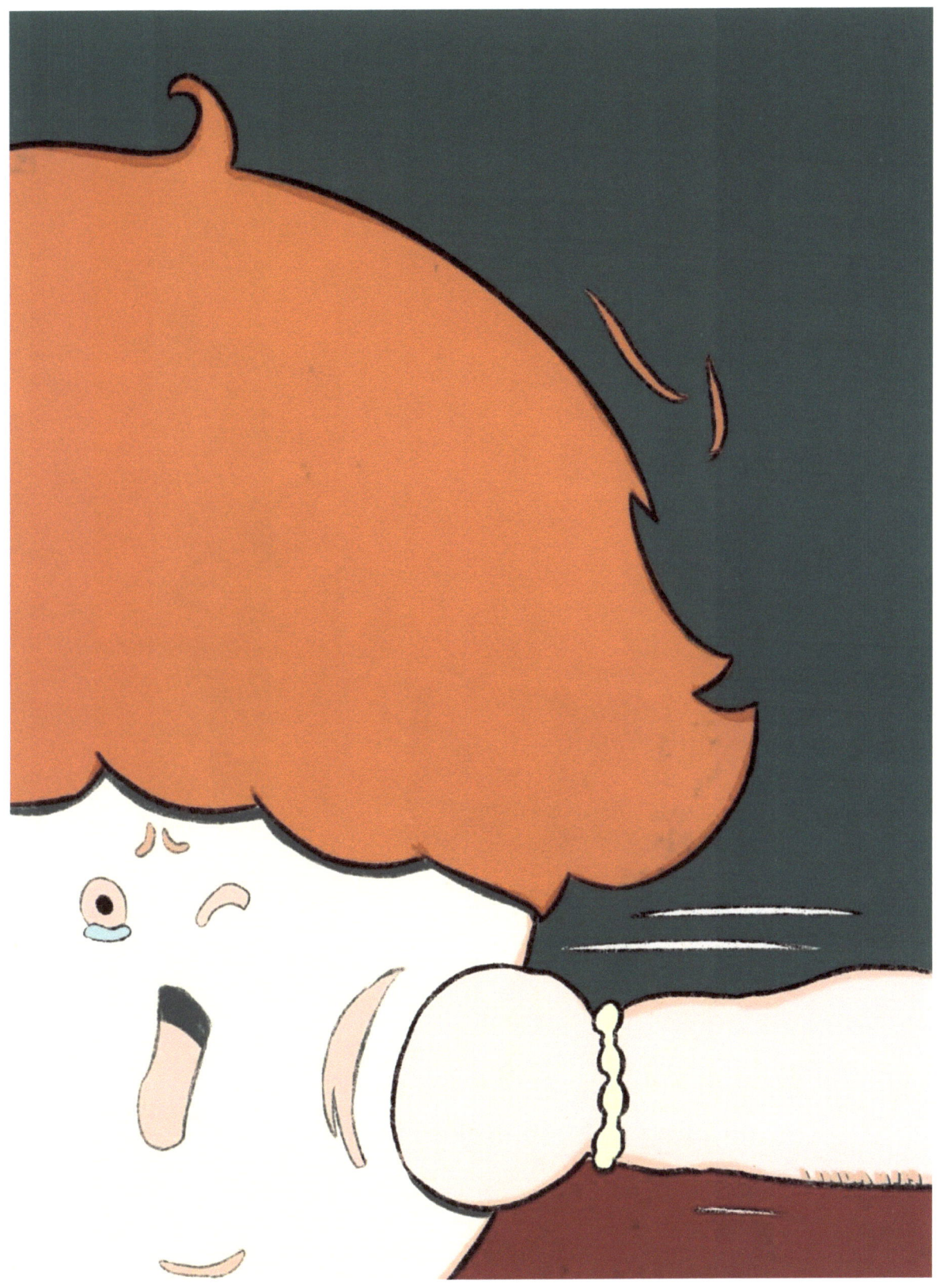

Sorr…, digital, 2020

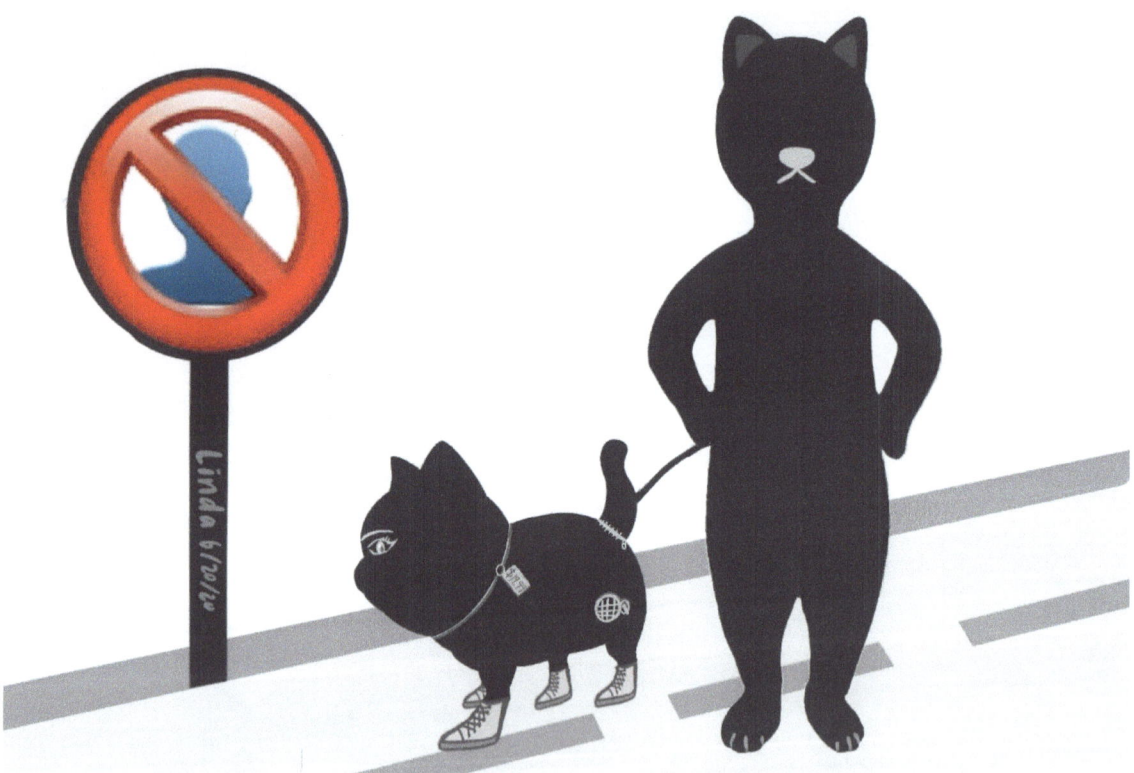

$19.99, digital, 2020

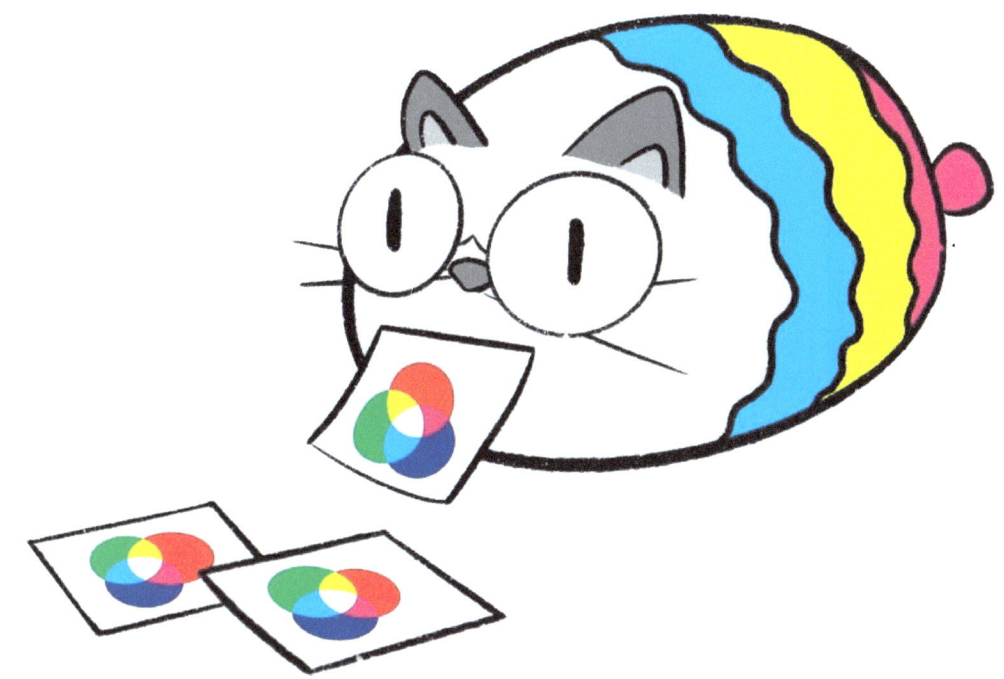

Pet Printer, digital, 2021

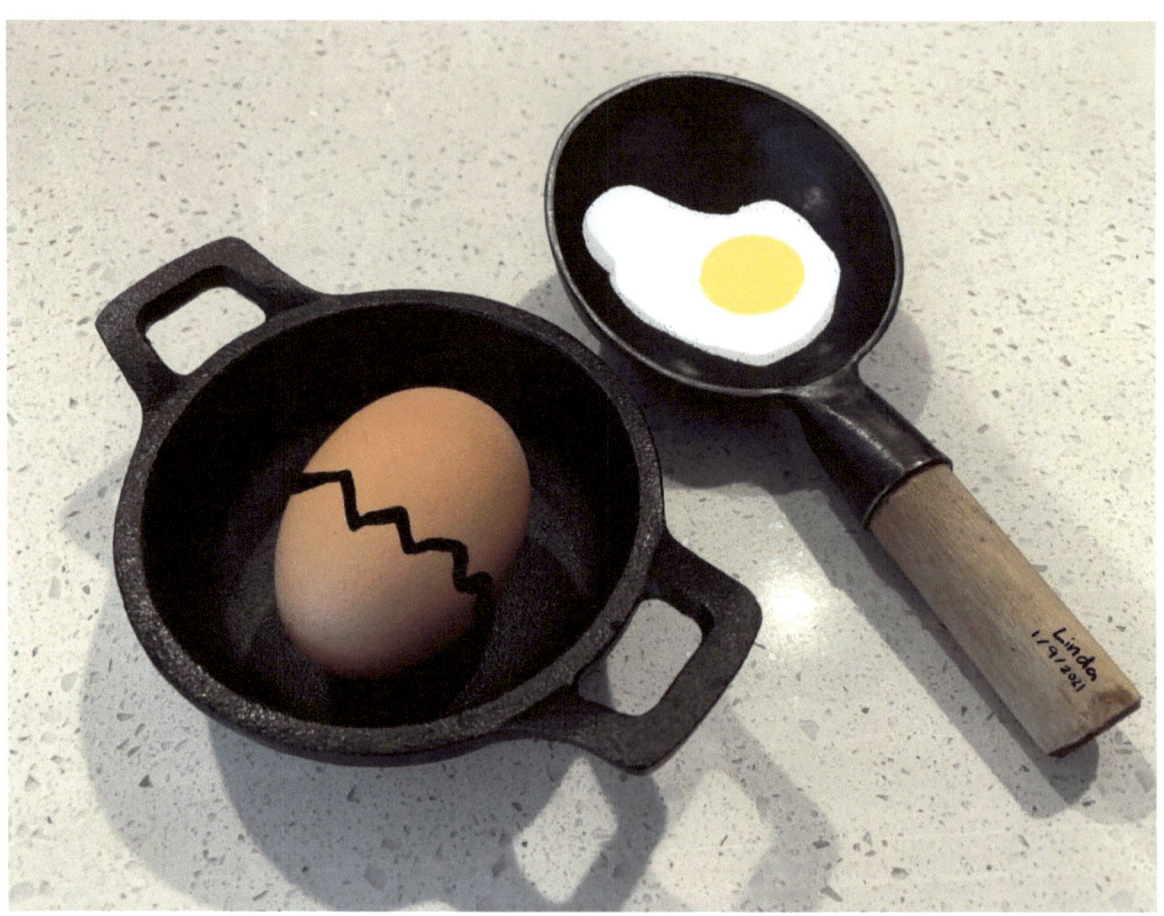

A Naked Egg, photo and digital, 2021

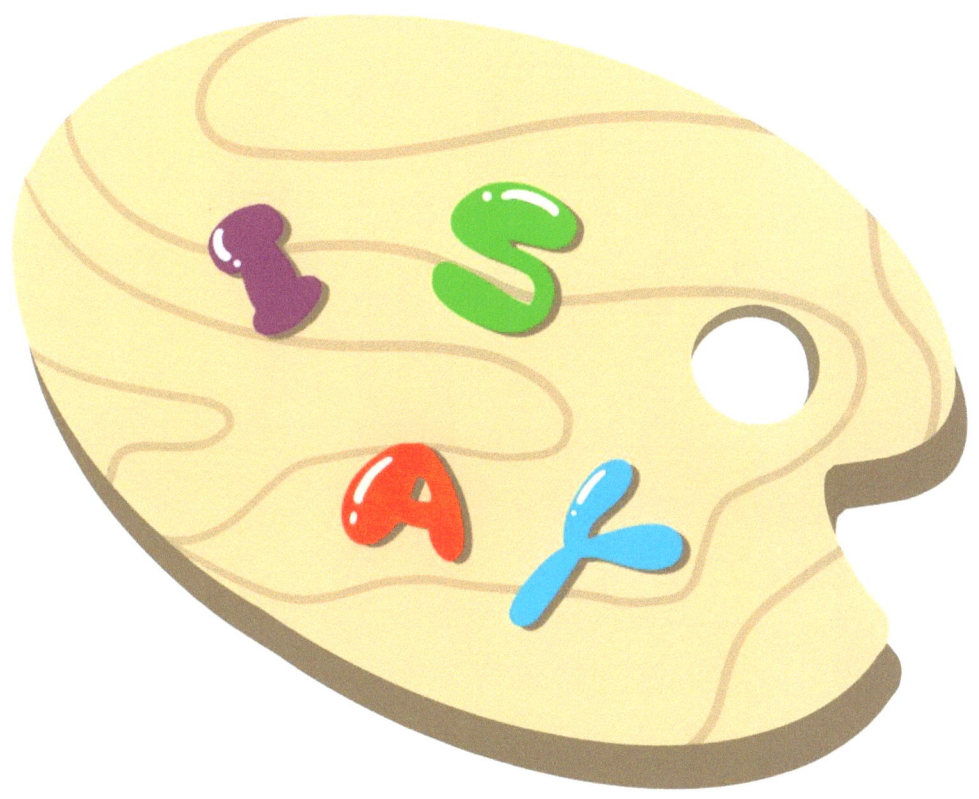

The Logo of International Society of Young Artist, digital, 2021

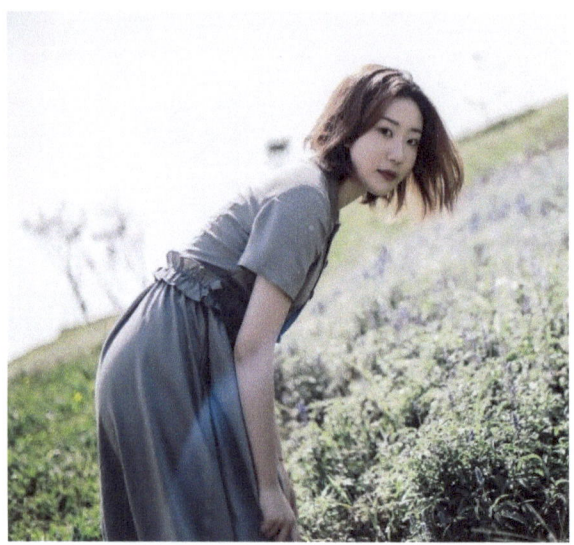

JINGLIN GUO

Maryland Institute College of Art, USA

Gold Award for Art, 2nd Liberty Awards, International Society of Young Artists, USA, 2019
Silver Award for Art, 1st Liberty Awards, International Society of Young Artists, USA, 2018

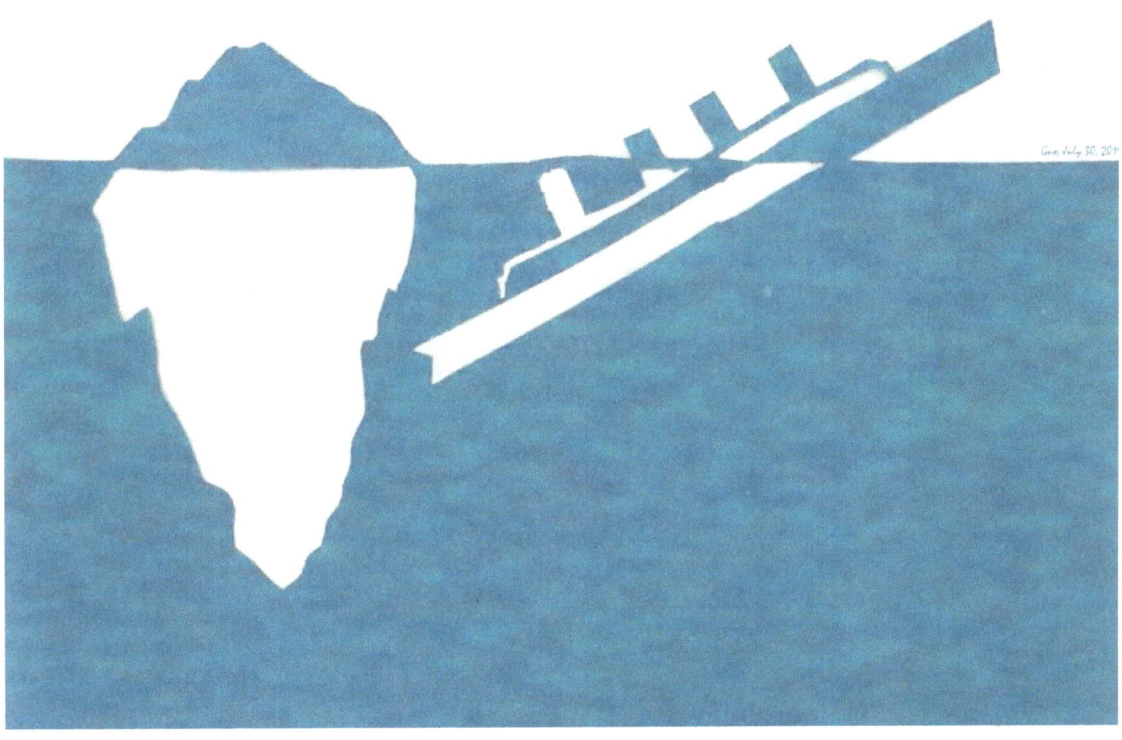

Illustration about the Report of RMS Titanic Incident in The New York Times, papercutting, 2019

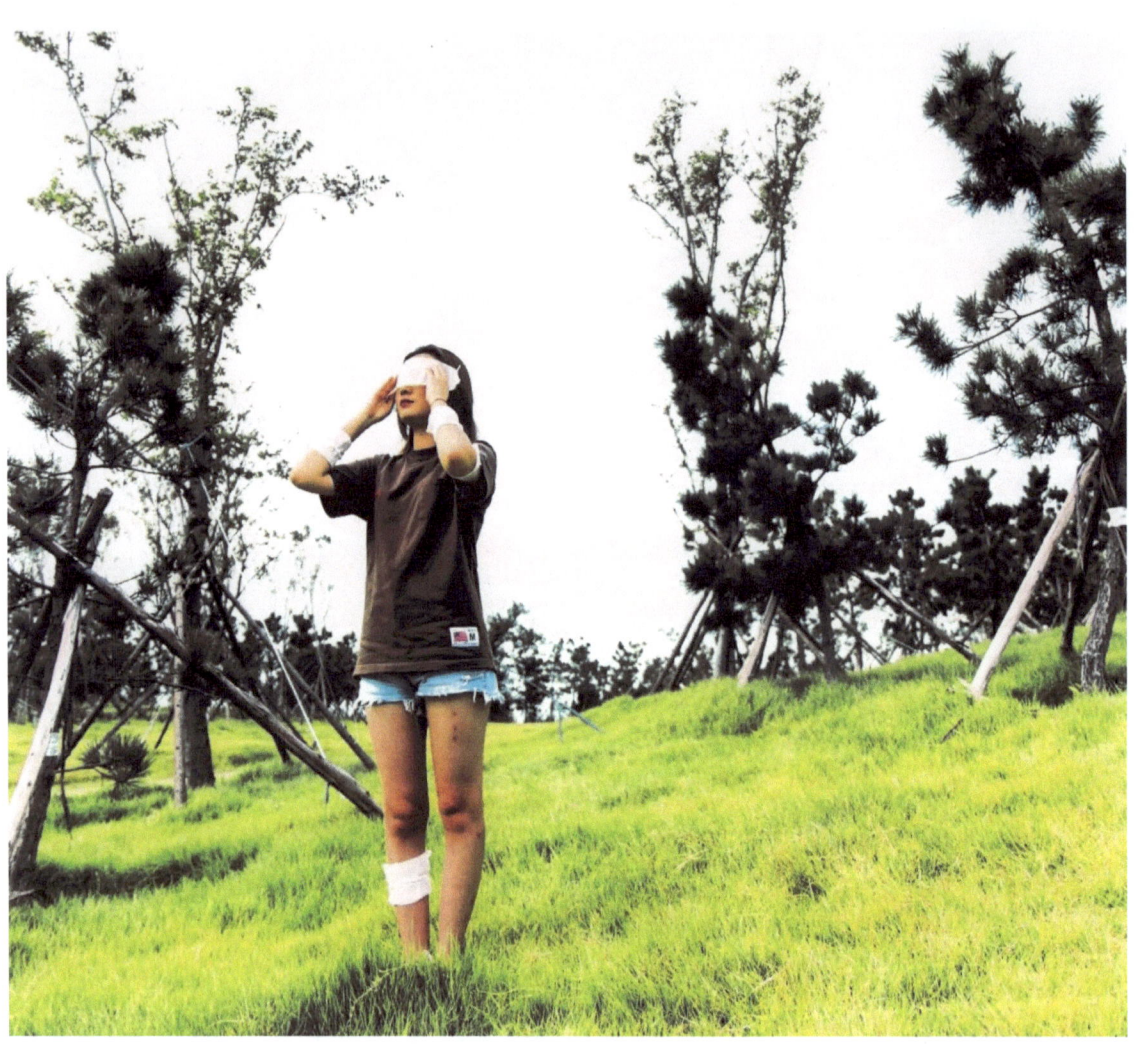

Wounded Tree——for the United Nations International Year of Plant Health 2020, performance art, 2019

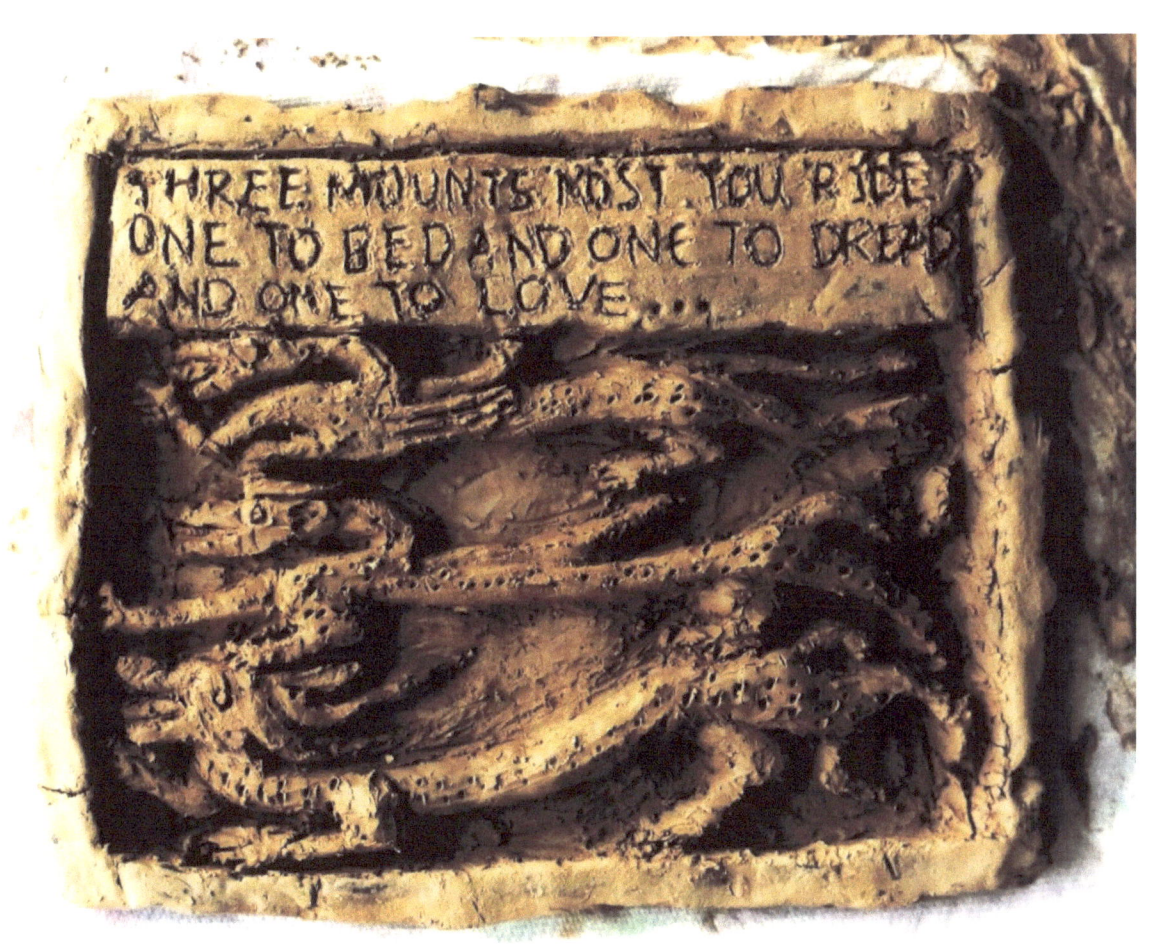

Three Mounts——from George R. R. Martin's A Song of Ice and Fire: A Clash of Kings, clay, 2019

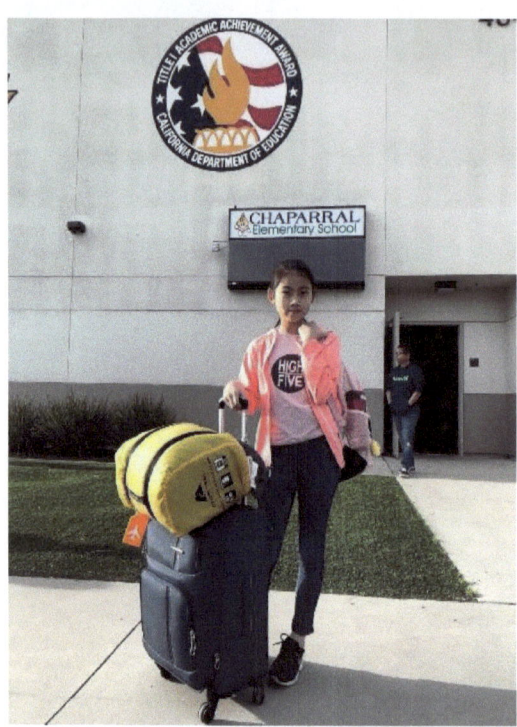

JINGYI YANG

Robert O. Townsend Junior High, USA

Silver Award for Art, 3rd Liberty Awards, International Society of Young Artists, USA, 2020-21
Bronze Award for Art, 2nd Liberty Awards, International Society of Young Artists, USA, 2019
Bronze Award for Art, 1st Liberty Awards, International Society of Young Artists, USA, 2018

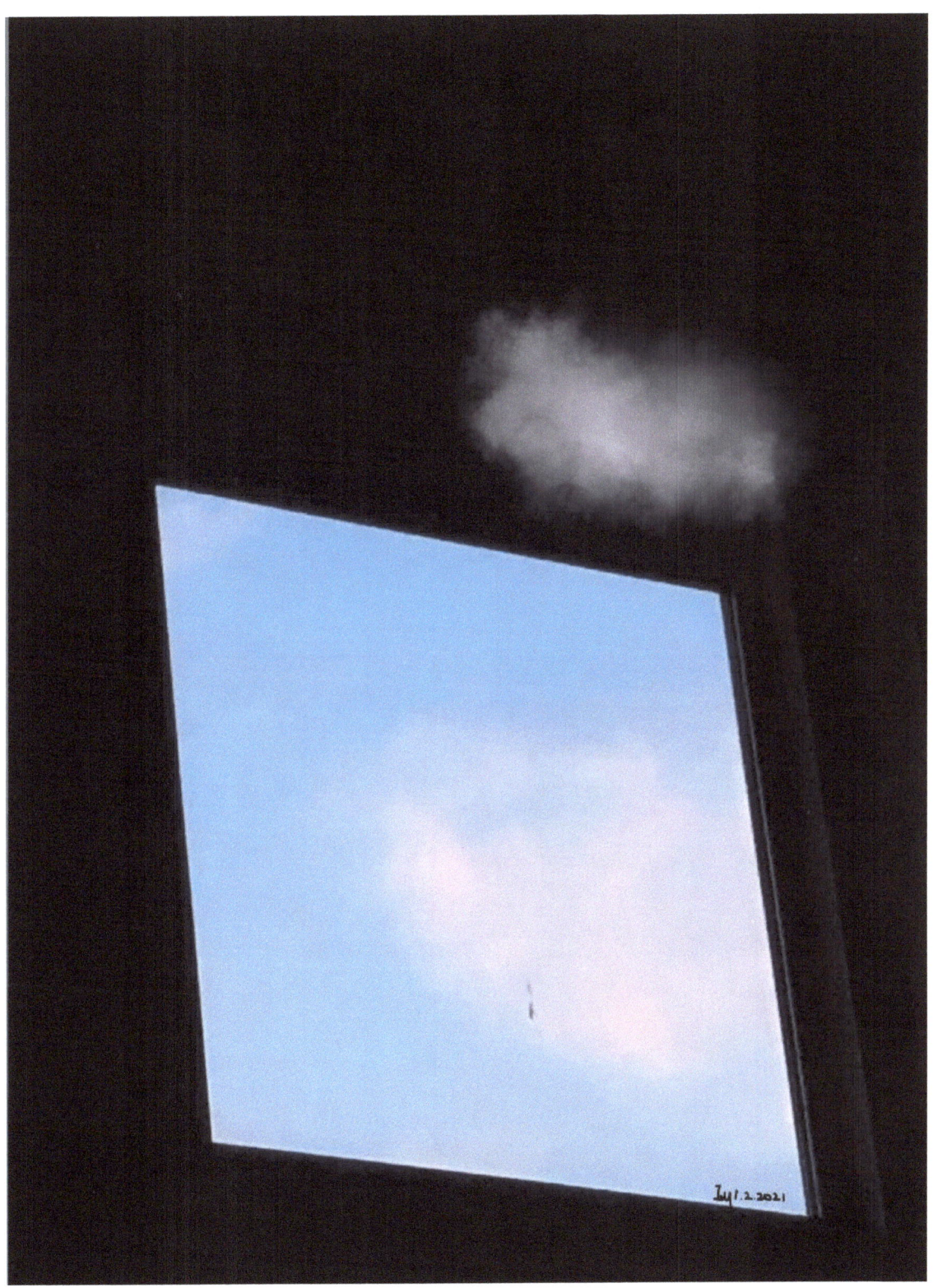

Companion, photo and digital, 2020

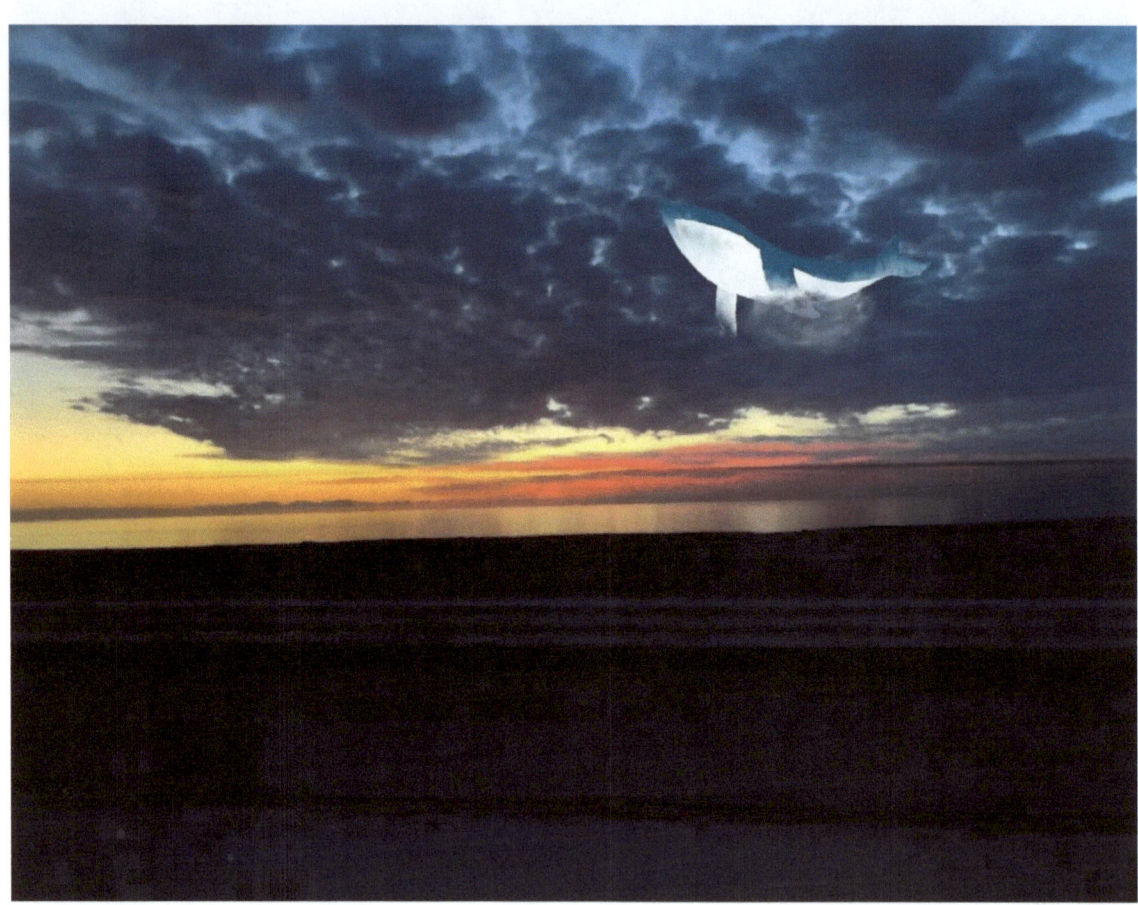

Roaming Whale, photo and digital, 2021

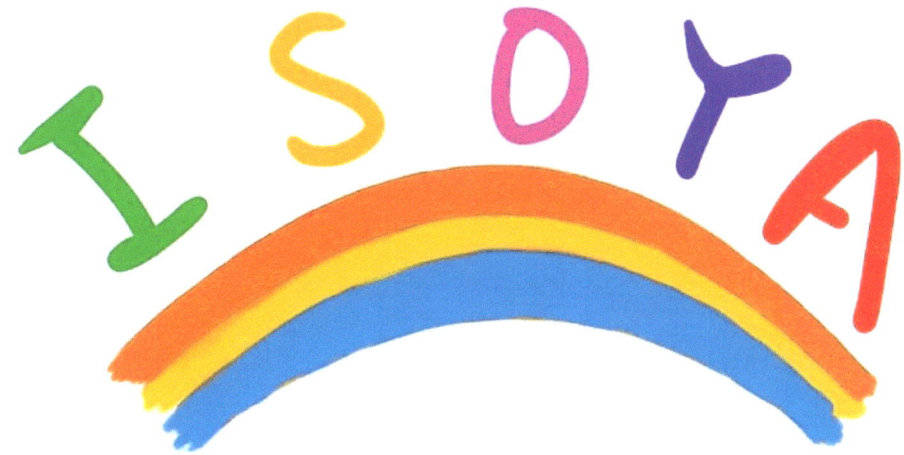

The Logo of International Society of Young Artist, digital, 2021

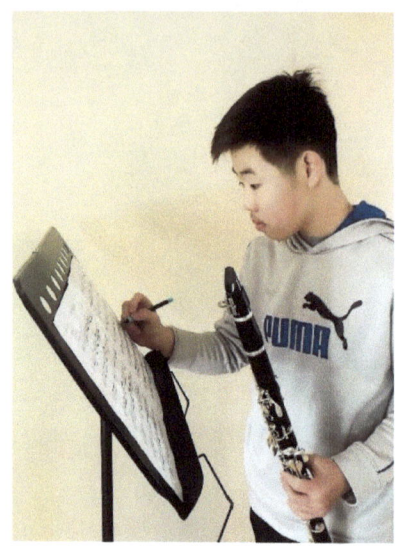

JUNKAI GONG

Princeton High School, USA

Bronze Award for Art, 3rd Liberty Awards, International Society of Young Artists, 2020
1st Place, Bridgewater-Raritan HS Forensics Speech& Debate Tournament, Novice Lincoln Douglas Debate, USA, 2020
4th Place, FTHS Invitational Novice Lincoln Douglas, USA, 2020
Double Octofinalist, Princeton Classic Novice Lincoln Douglas Debate, USA, 2019
Outstanding Academic Excellence, President's Education Awards Program, USA, 2019
Bronze Award for Art, 2nd Liberty Awards, International Society of Young Artists, USA, 2019
Rising Star Award, 1st Liberty Awards, International Society of Young Artists, USA, 2018
2nd Prize, 13th "For Study" Cup Elementary and Secondary School Innovative Composition Contest, China, 2017
Special Gold Prize, Oral English skill, 12th "Star & Torch" National Junior English Talent Competition, China, 2016
1st Prize, 4th *Evening News* Union Cup Cross-Strait Junior with-the-Topic Composition Contest, China, 2016
Election to Chinese Young Talents Database, China, 2016

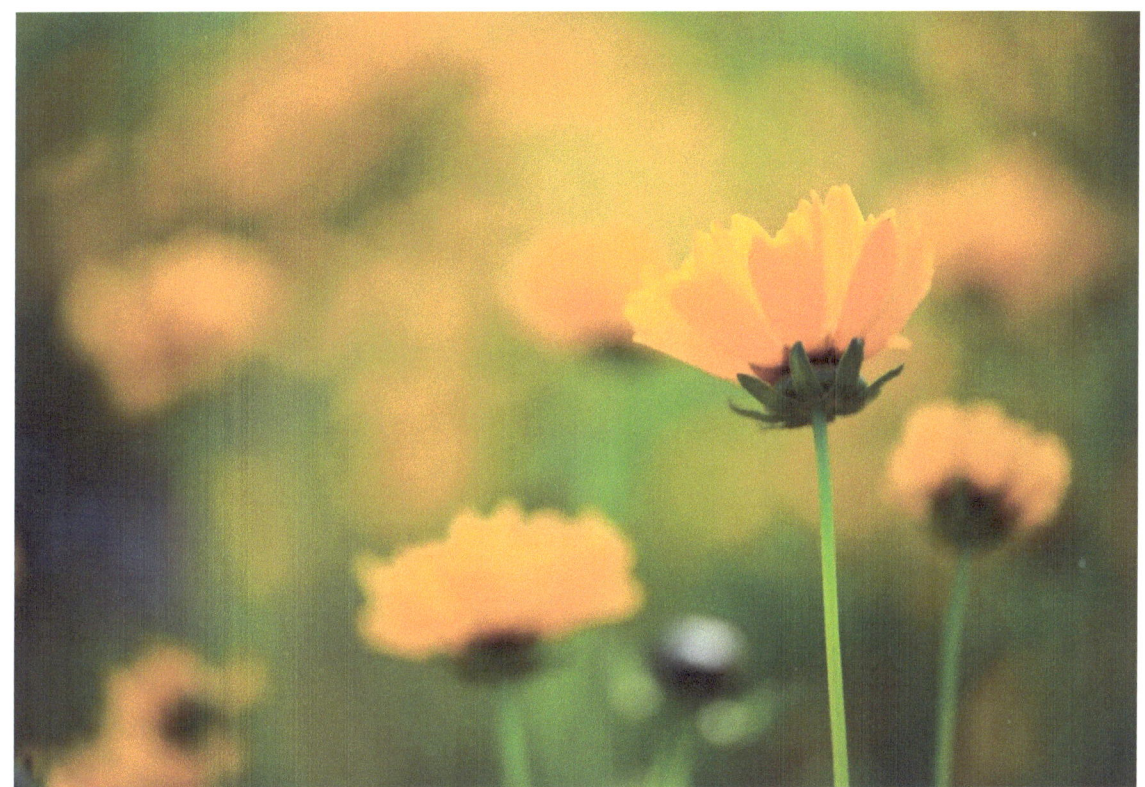

Blooming, photo, 2020

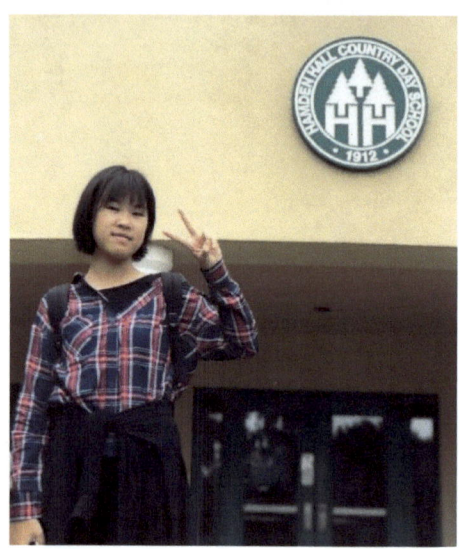

KUN WANG

Hamden Hall Country Day School, USA

Bronze Award for Art, 2nd Liberty Awards, International Society of Young Artists, USA, 2019
Bronze Award for Art, 1st Liberty Awards, International Society of Young Artists, USA, 2018

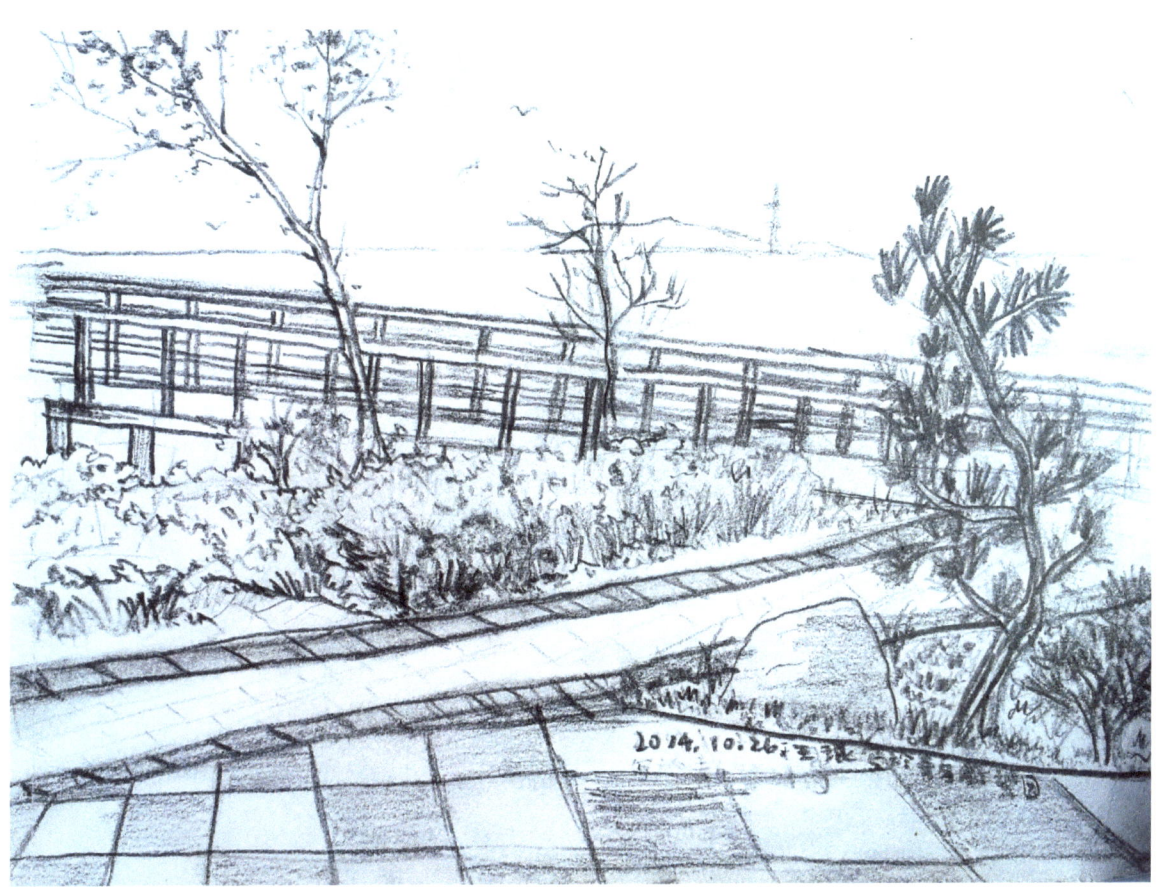

A Corner of Qingdao Sculpture Park, pencil on paper, 2014

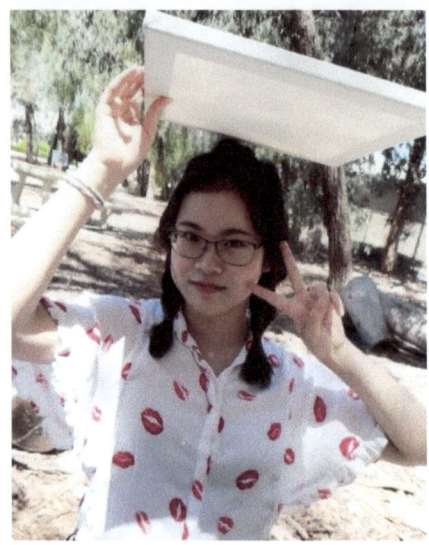

LEYI YANG

University of California, Santa Cruz, USA

Silver Award for Art, 3rd Liberty Awards, International Society of Young Artists, USA, 2020-21
Silver Award for Art, 2nd Liberty Awards, International Society of Young Artists, USA, 2019
Bronze Award for Art, 1st Liberty Awards, International Society of Young Artists, USA, 2018

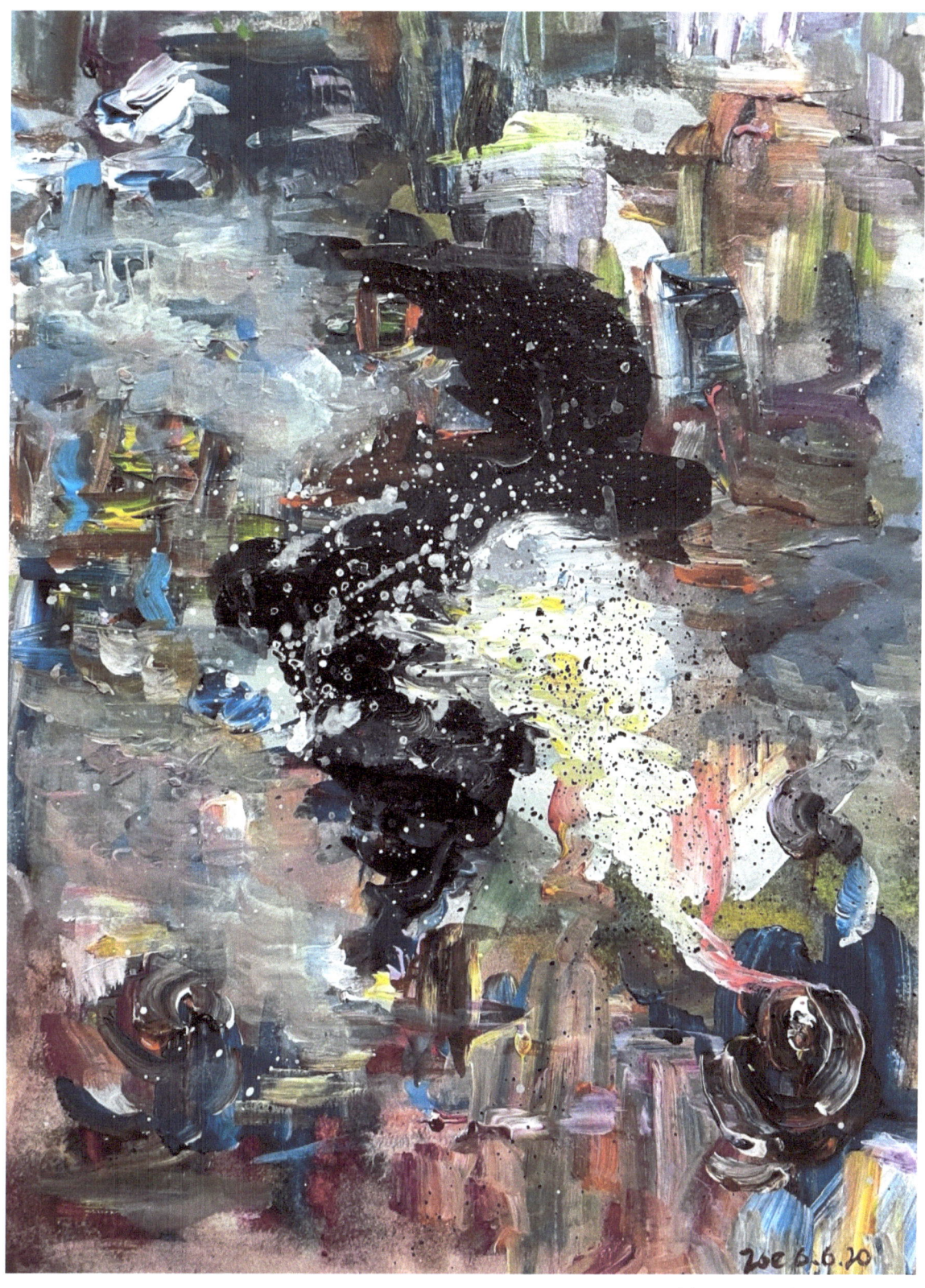

Lake's Dream, acrylic on paper, 2020

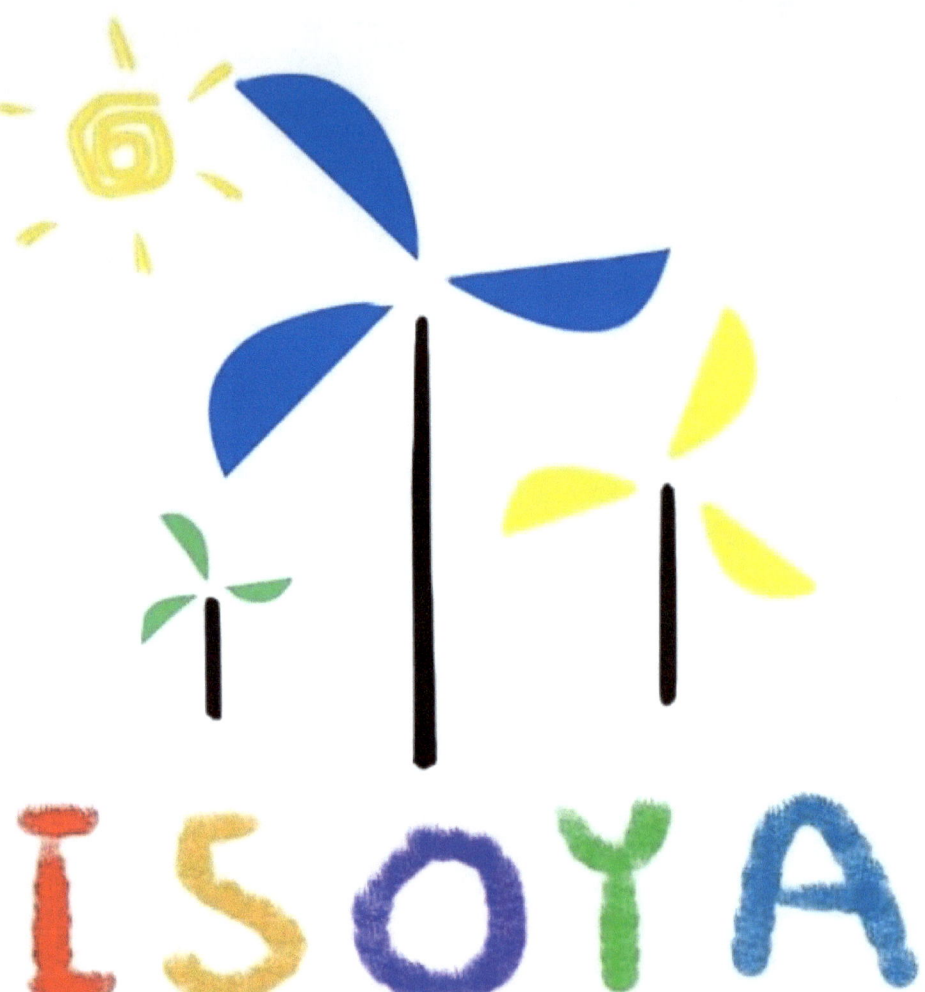

The Logo of International Society of Young Artist, digital, 2021

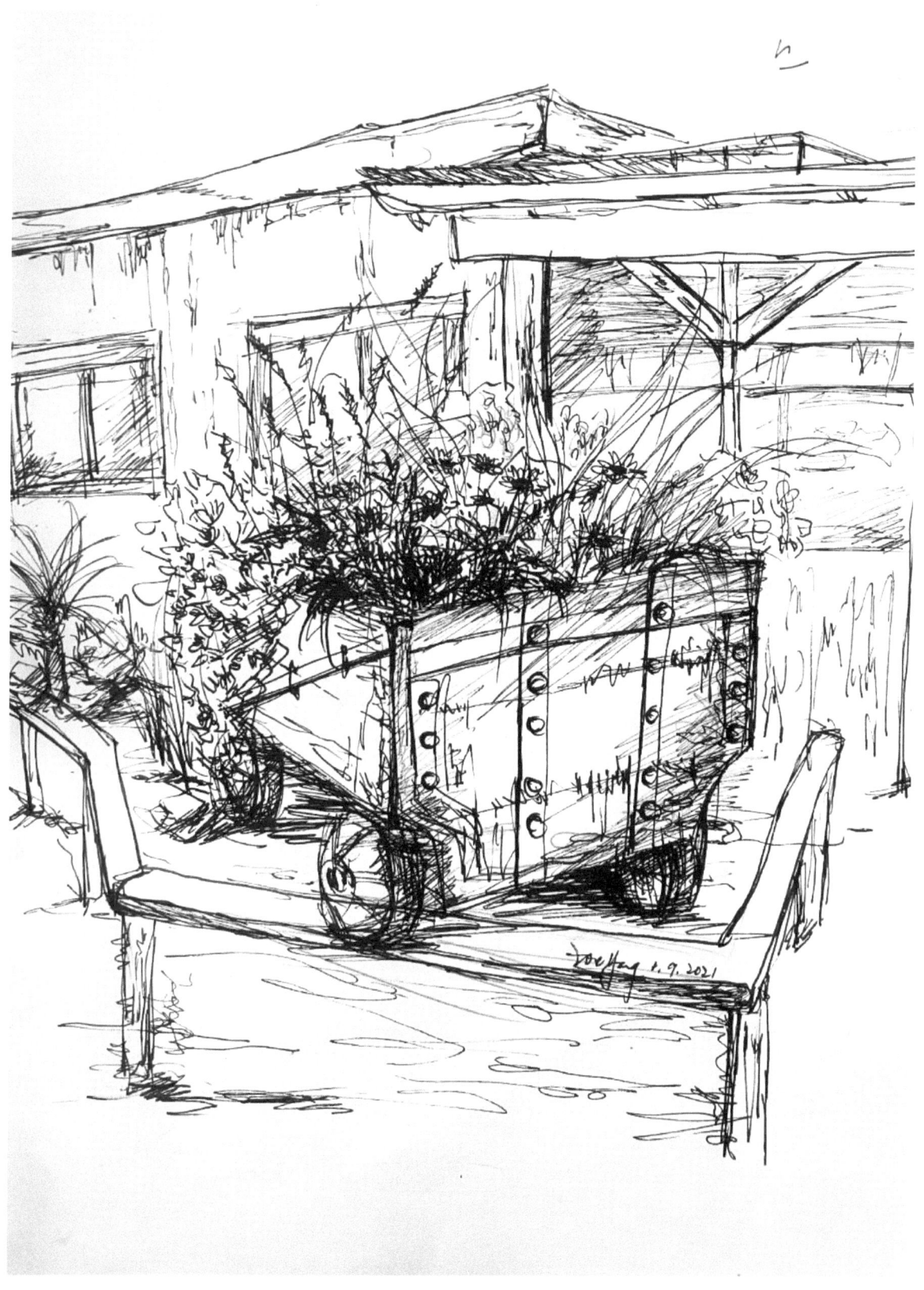

A Car Loaded with Lousy Grass, ink on paper, 2021

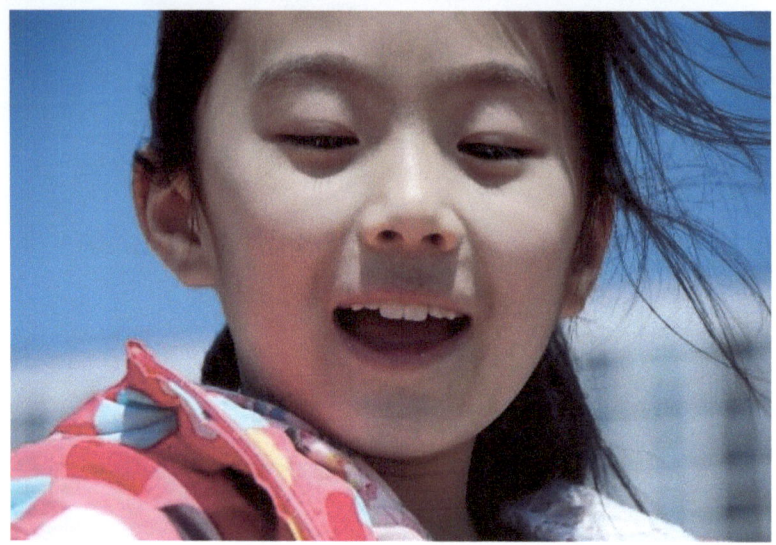

LIYU ZHANG

Qingdao No.9 High School, China

Rising Star Award, 1st Liberty Awards, International Society of Young Artists, USA, 2018

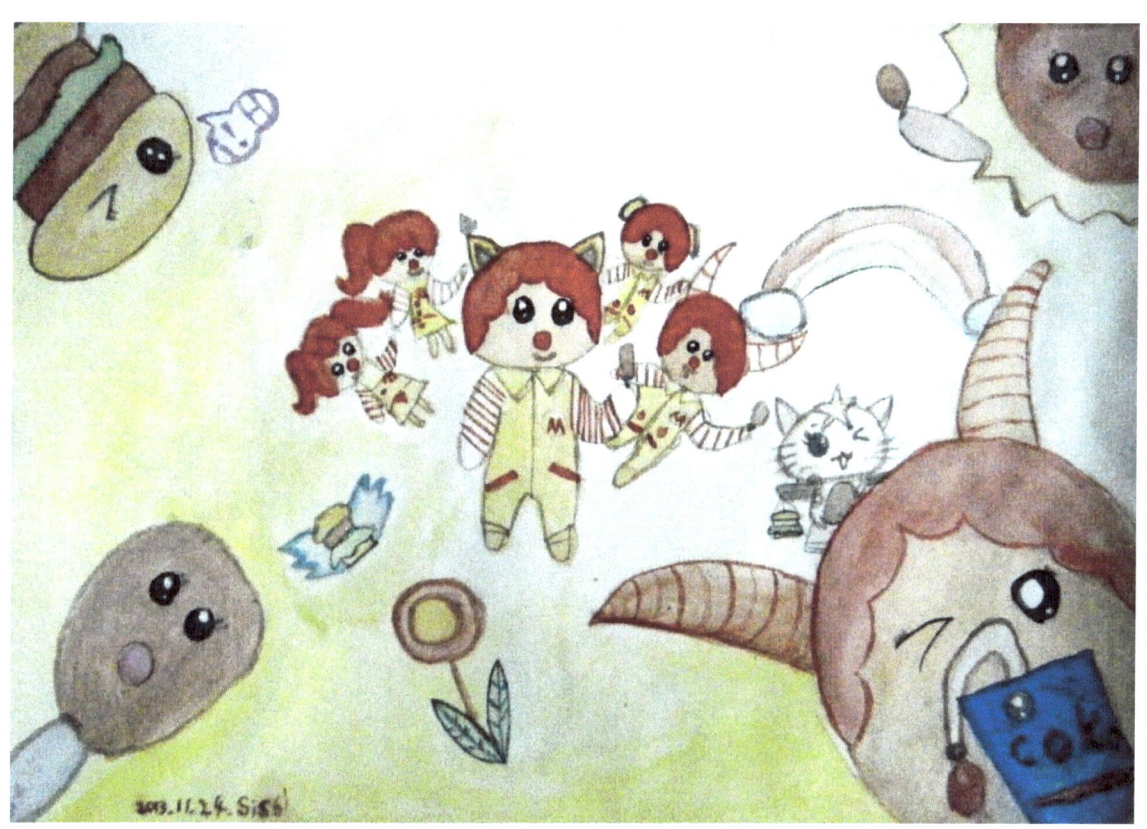

Joyous Day, gouache on paper, 2013

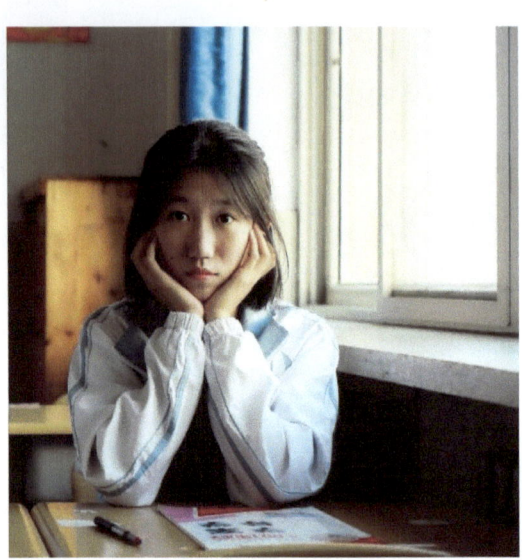

PEIYU WU

Qufu Normal University, China

Gold Award for Art, 2nd Liberty Awards, International Society of Young Artists, USA, 2019
Rising Star Award, 1st Liberty Awards, International Society of Young Artists, USA, 2018
Bronze Medal, 6th National University & Middle School Student Marine Culture Design Contest, 2017
2nd Prize, International Space Settlement Design Competition (China), 2016

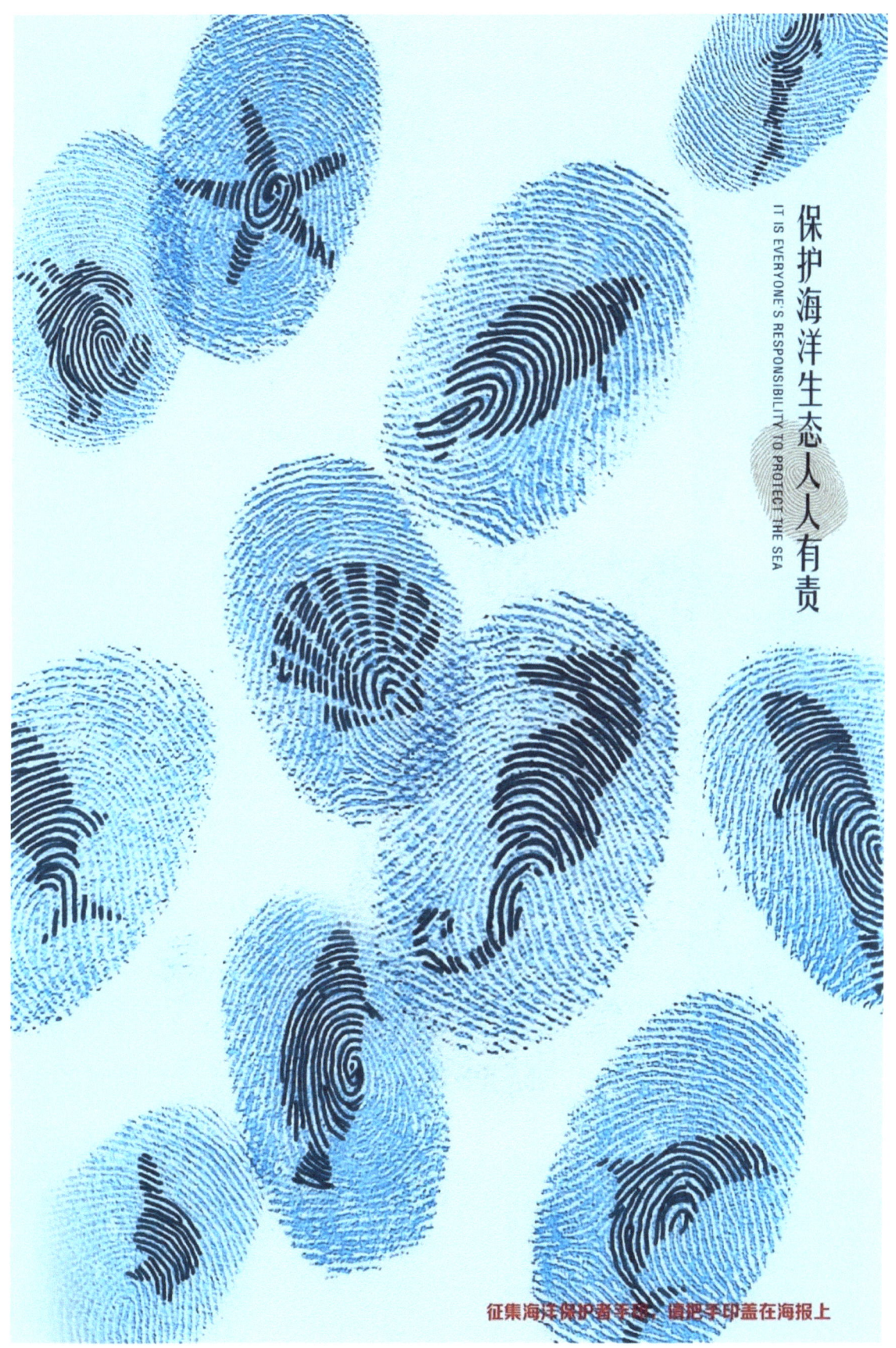

Public Service Advertising: *Protect the Ocean*, digital, 2017

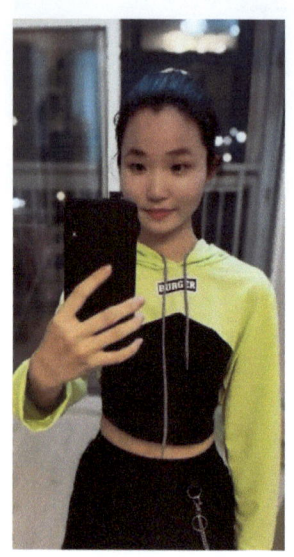

QINGXIA SONG

Qingdao No.58 High School, China

Gold Award for Art, 3rd Liberty Awards, International Society of Young Artists, USA, 2020-21
Silver Award for Art, 2nd Liberty Awards, International Society of Young Artists, USA, 2019
Silver Award for Art, 1st Liberty Awards, International Society of Young Artists, USA, 2018
Silver Award, "The Colorful Peace" Art Project Honoring the 100th Anniversary of the WWI Armistice, International Society of Young Artists, USA, 2018
3rd Prize, ACT National Youth English Proficiency Demonstration and Communication Show, China, 2016
2nd Prize, ACT National Youth English Proficiency Demonstration and Communication Show of Qingdao, China, 2016

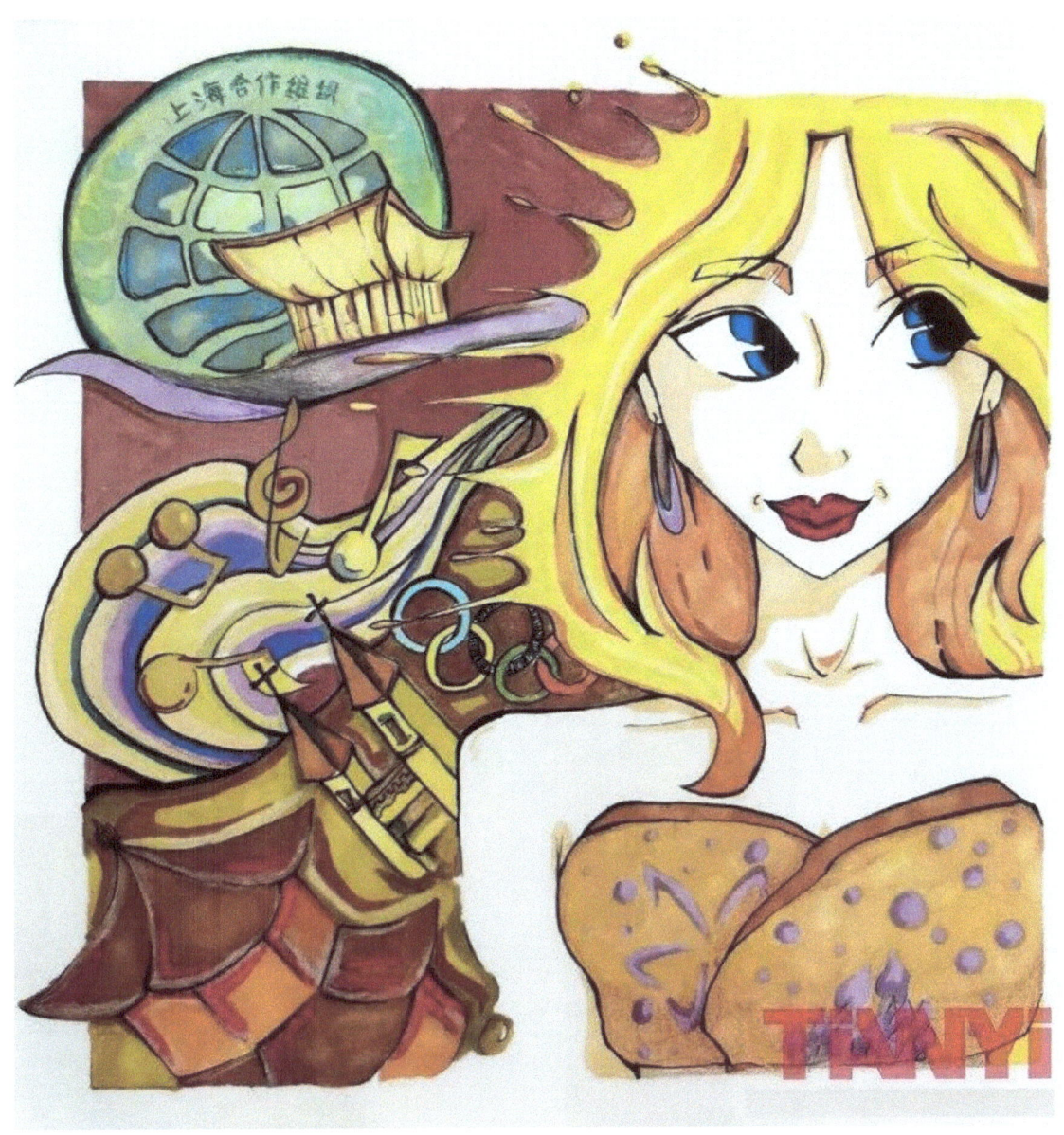

My Fashion Qingdao, marker on paper, 2020

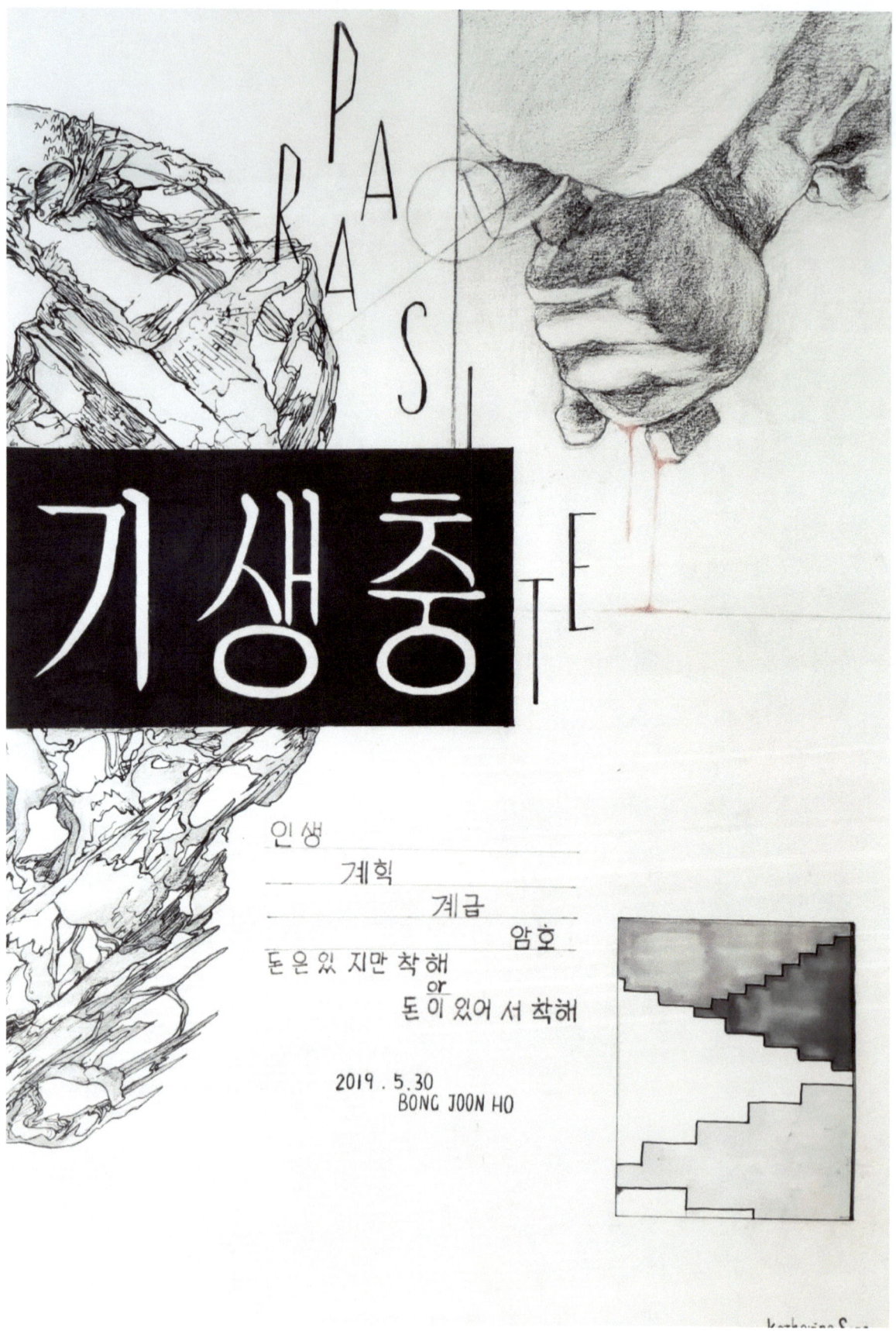

Movie Poster: *Parasite*, pencil and ink on paper, 2020

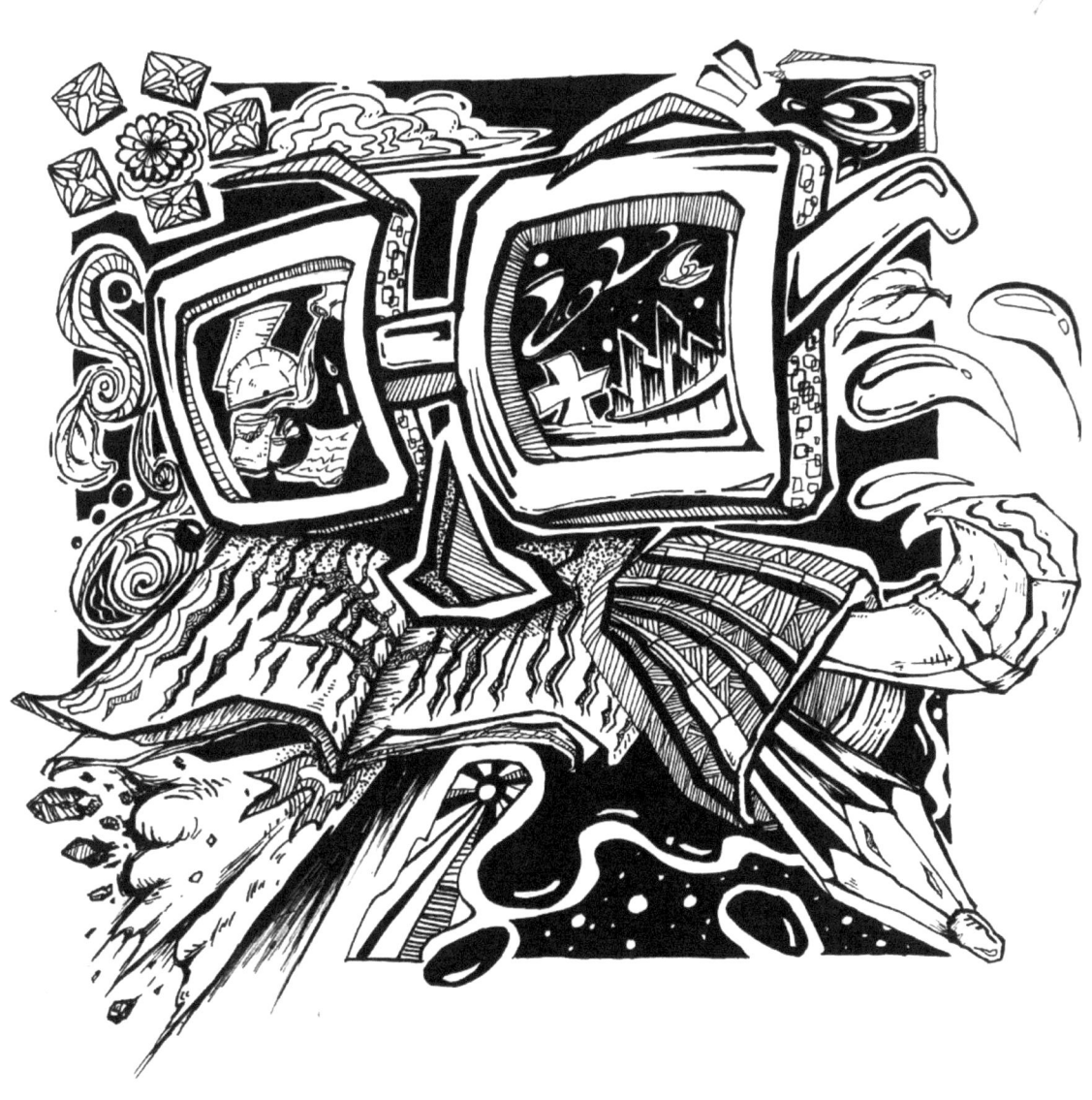

My Future, ink on paper, 2020

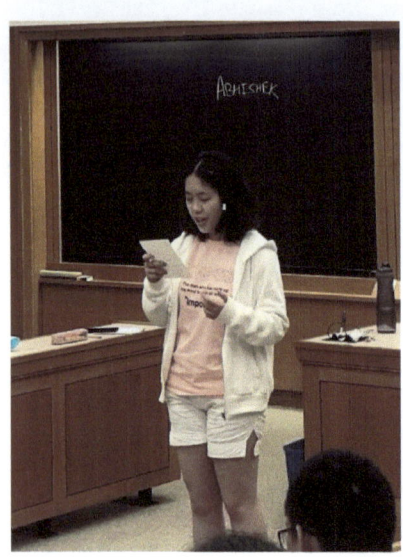

RONG HONG

Qingdao No. 1 High School, China

Bronze Award for Art, 3rd Liberty Awards, International Society of Young Artists, USA, 2020-21
Gold Award for Art, 2nd Liberty Awards, International Society of Young Artists, USA, 2019
Rising Star Award, 1st Liberty Awards, International Society of Young Artists, USA, 2018

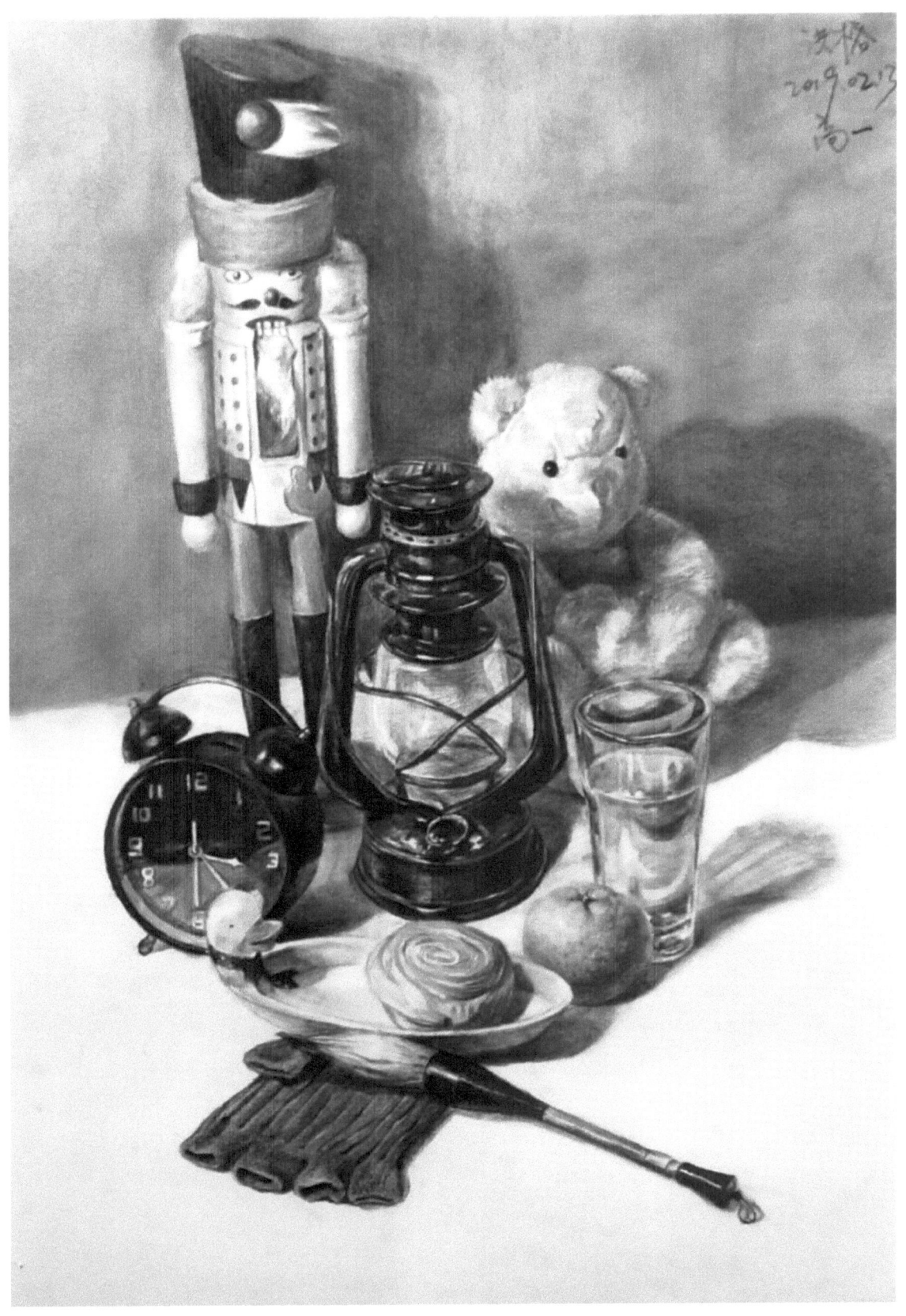

Still Life with a Kerosene Lamp, pencil on paper, 2019

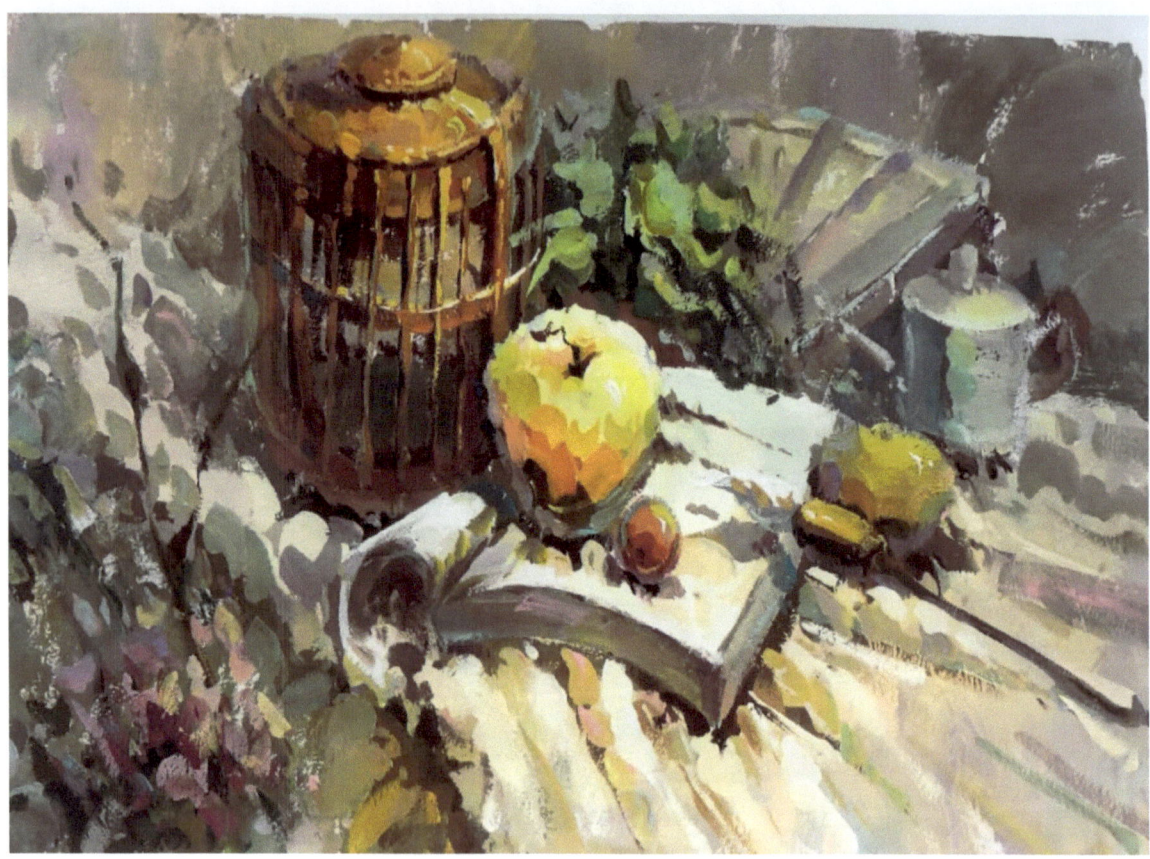

Still Life with a Book, gouache on paper, 2020

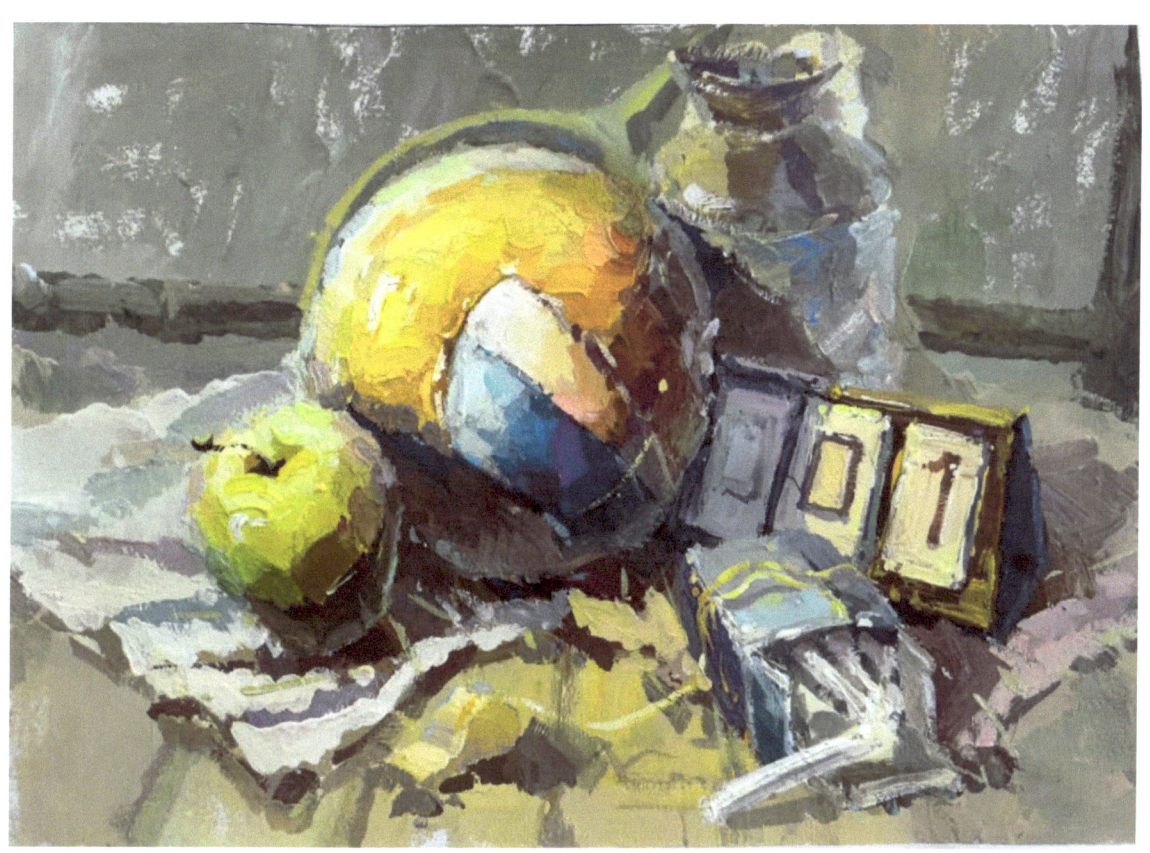

Still Life with a Scoreboard, gouache on paper, 2020

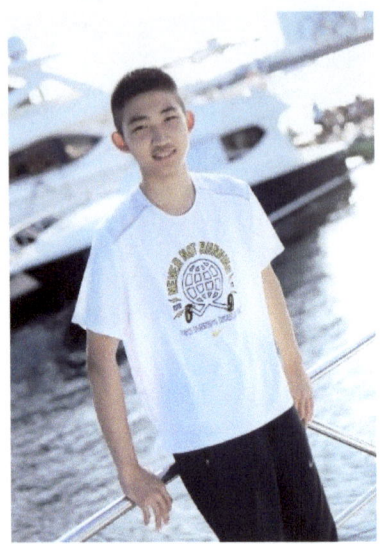

RUI LI

Qingdao University Affiliated Middle School, China

Bronze Award for Art, 2nd Liberty Awards, International Society of Young Artists, USA, 2019
Rising Star Award, 1st Liberty Awards, International Society of Young Artists, USA, 2018

Qingdao Hongdao Road, ink on paper, 2018

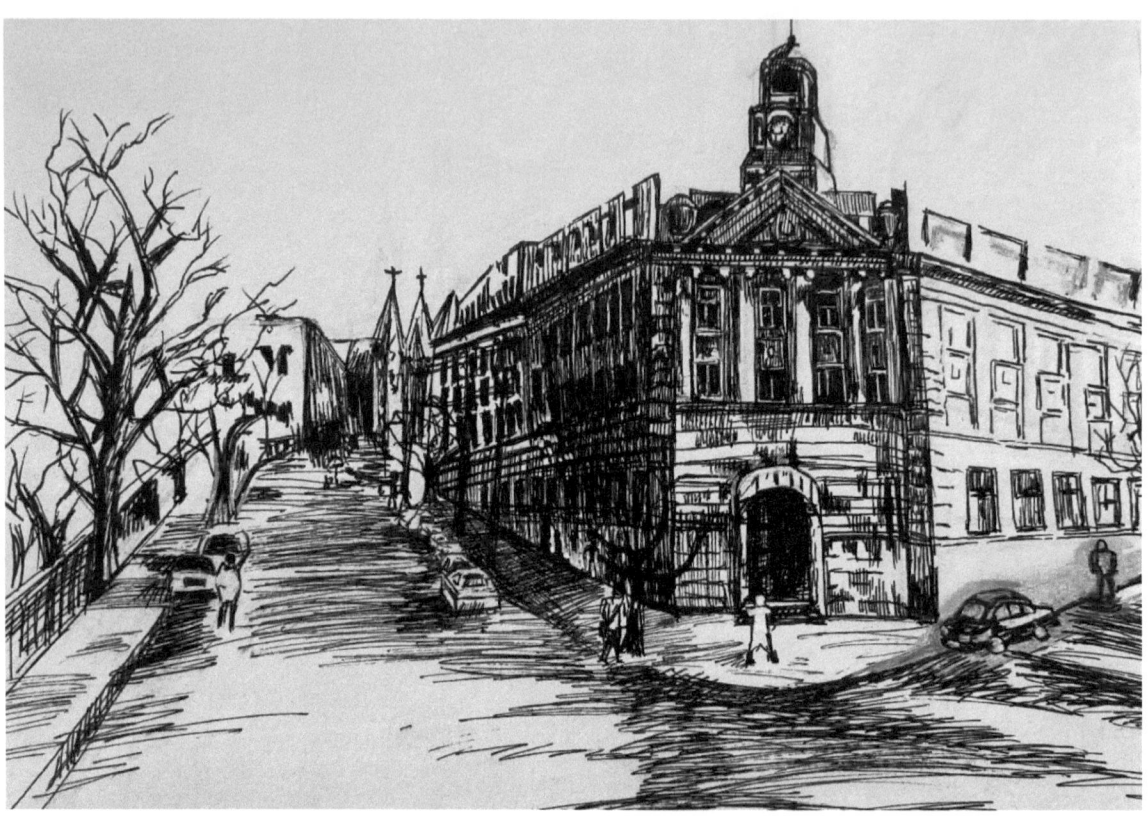

Old Building of Qingdao Jincheng Bank, ink on paper, 2018

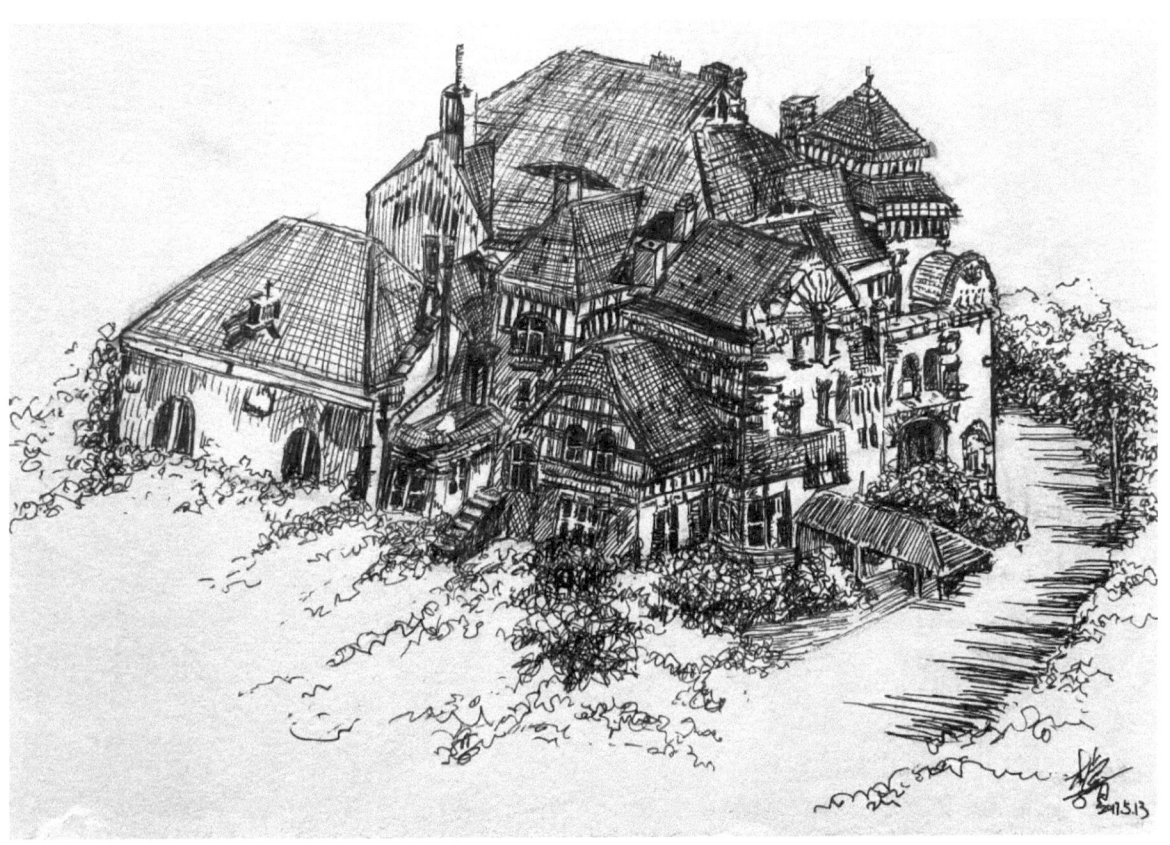

A Guesthouse in Qingdao, ink on paper, 2018

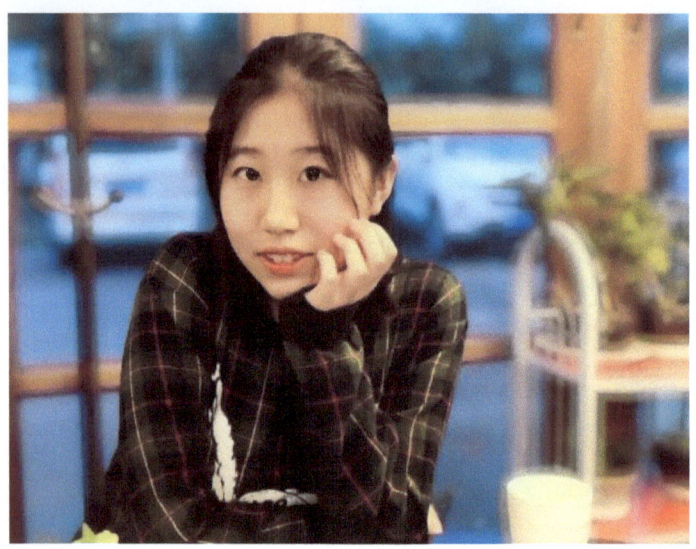

SHUO PANG

Shandong University, China

Silver Award for Art, 3rd Liberty Awards, International Society of Young Artists, USA, 2020-21
Rising Star Award, 2nd Liberty Awards, International Society of Young Artists, USA, 2019
Rising Star Award, 1st Liberty Awards, International Society of Young Artists, USA, 2018
Honor Student of Qingdao, Qingdao Bureau of Education, China, 2017
Excellent Student Leader of Qingdao, Qingdao Bureau of Education, China, 2017

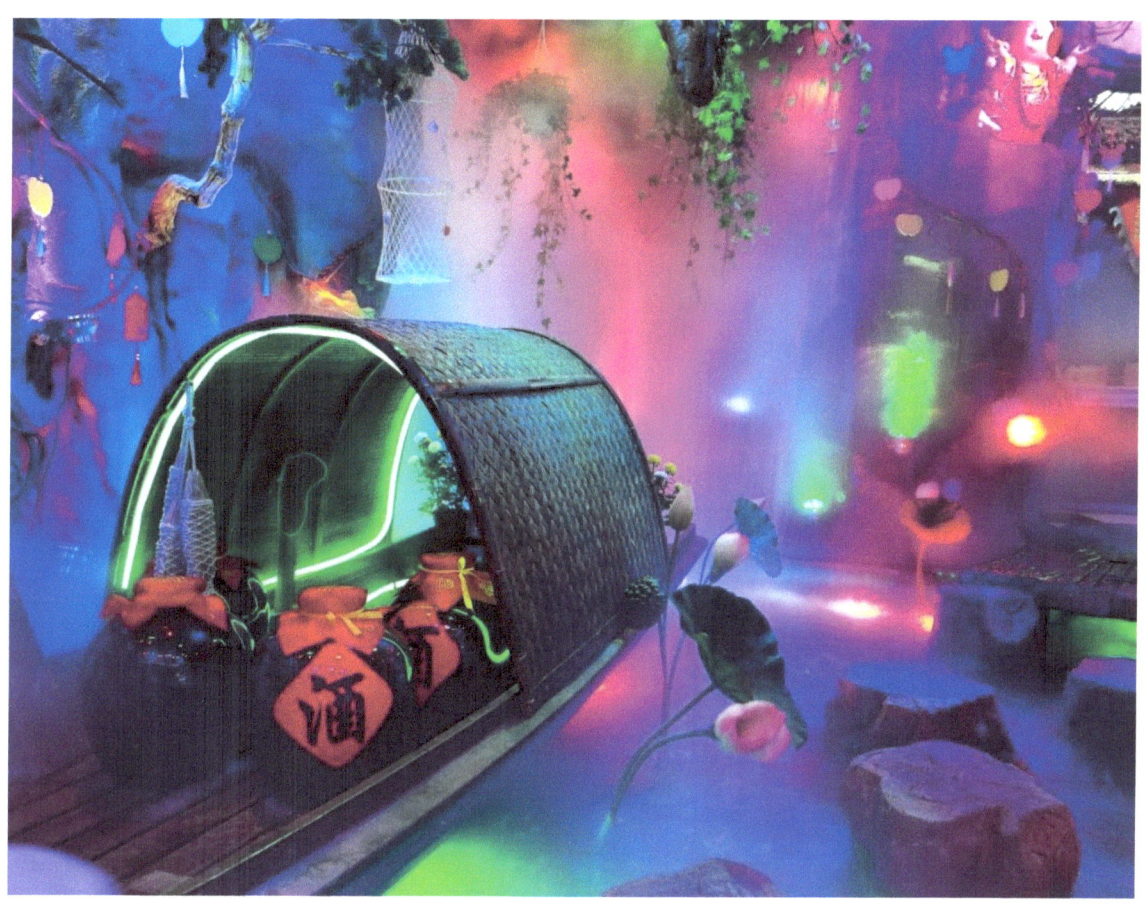

Jinan Furong Street, photo, 2021

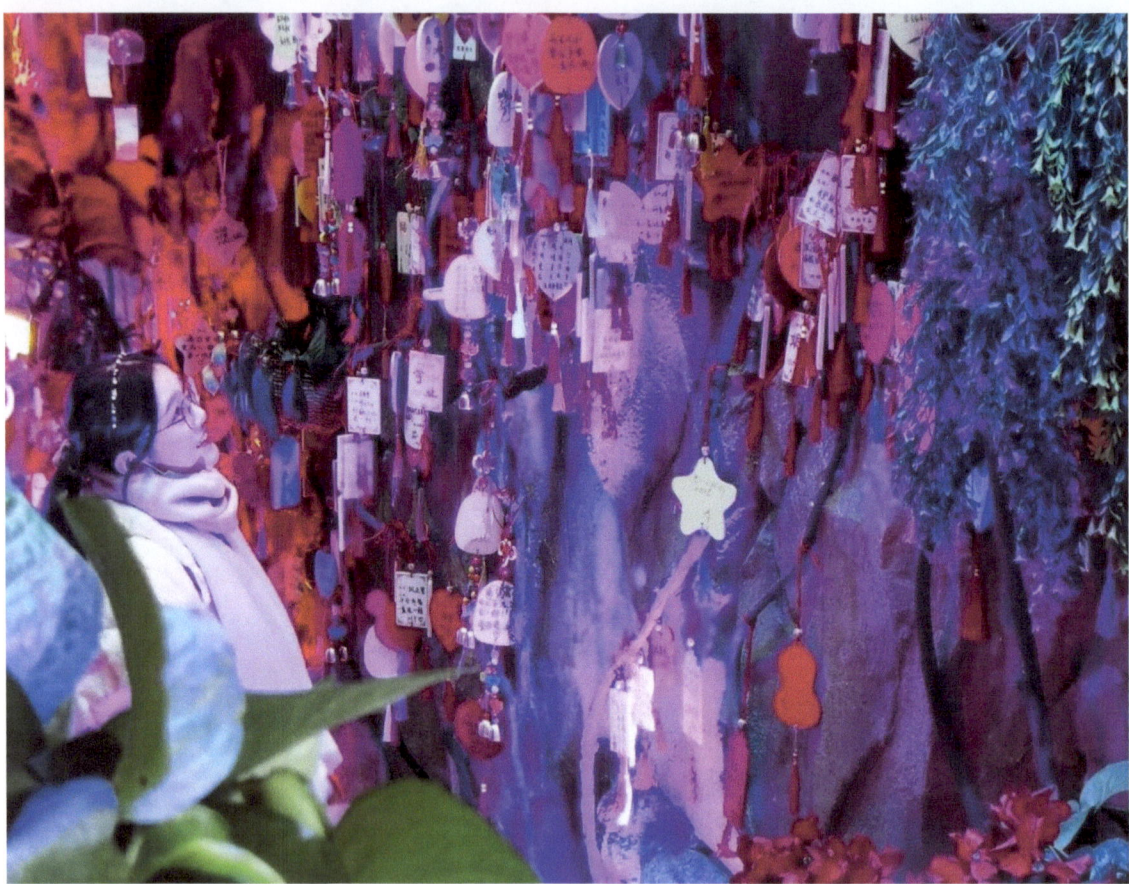

Jinan Furong Cave, photo, 2021

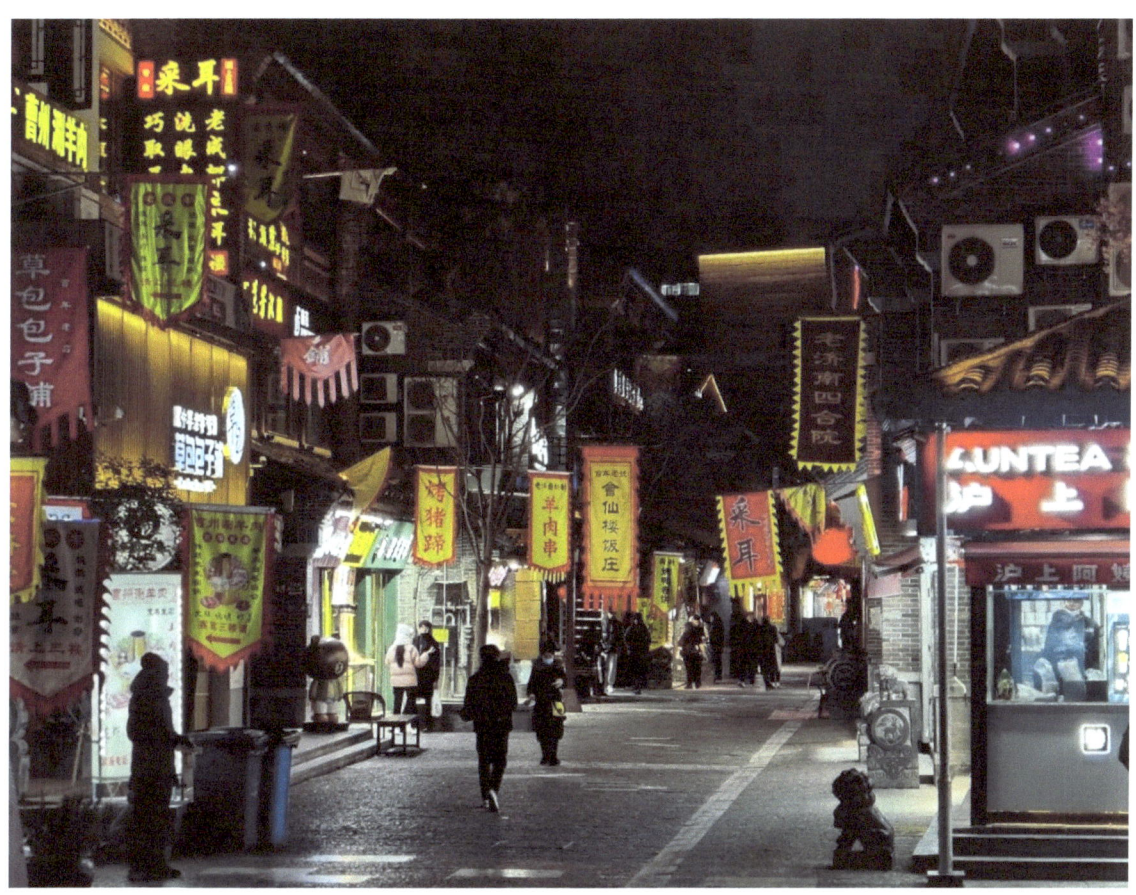

Jinan Kuanhou Street, photo, 2021

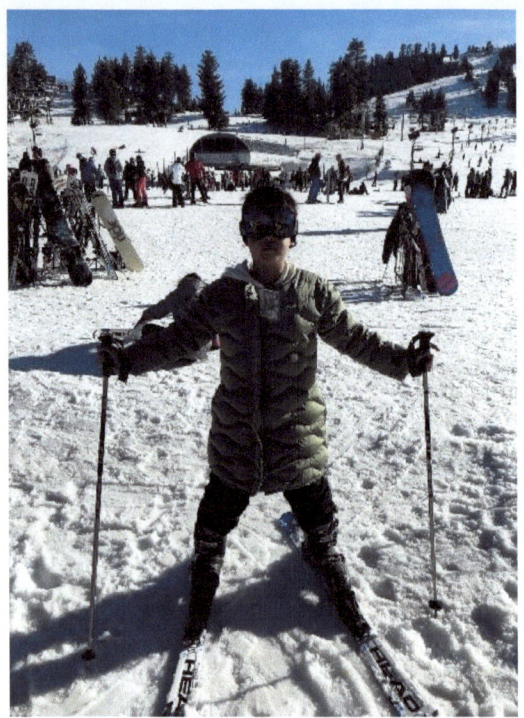

TIMOTHY X. WU

Chaparral Elementary School, USA

Bronze Award for Art, 3rd Liberty Awards, International Society of Young Artists, USA, 2020-21
Bronze Award for Art, 2nd Liberty Awards, International Society of Young Artists, USA, 2019
Bronze Award for Art, 1st Liberty Awards, International Society of Young Artists, USA, 2018

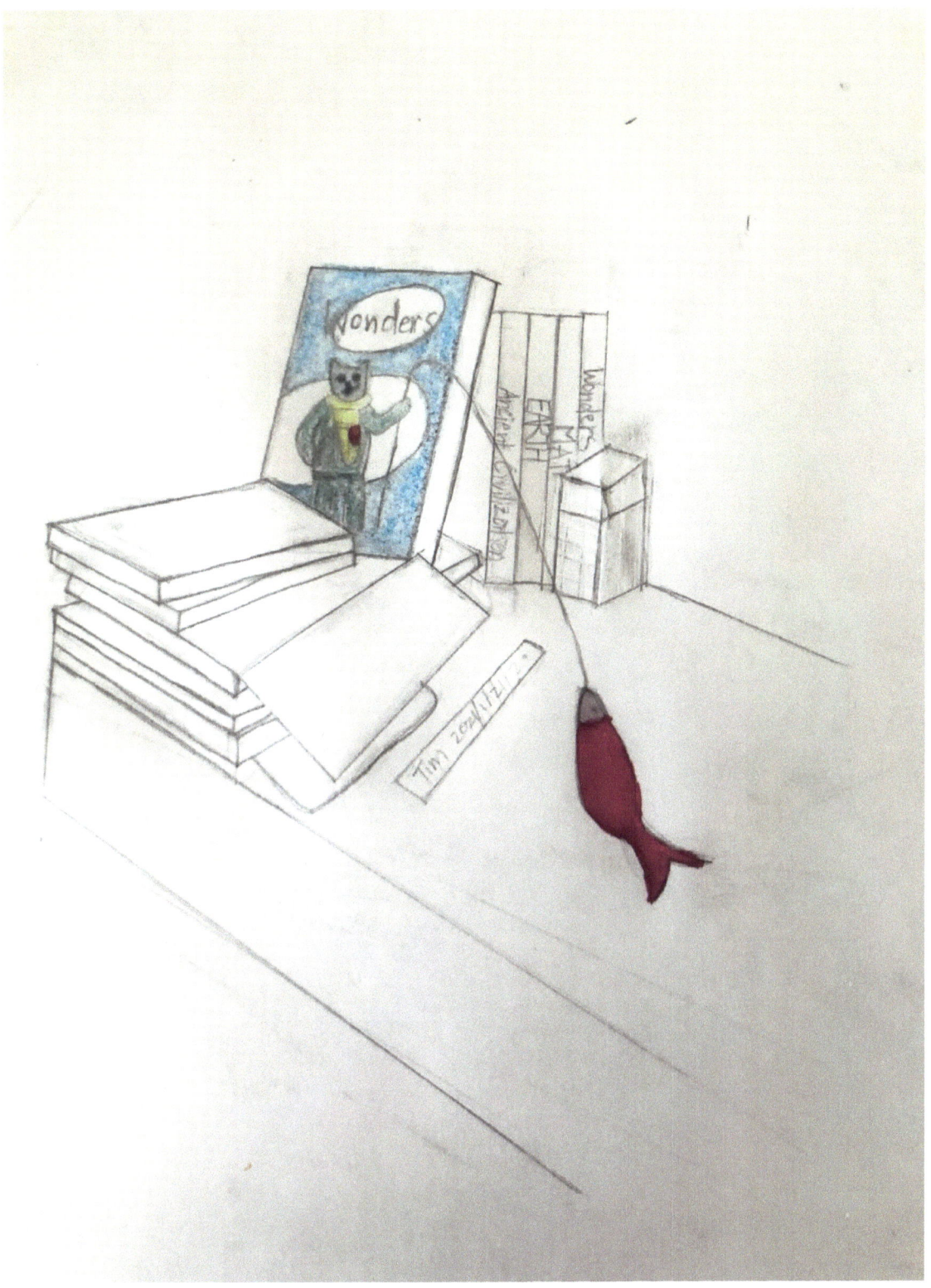

A Corner of Tim's Table, pencil, marker and colored pencil on paper, 2021

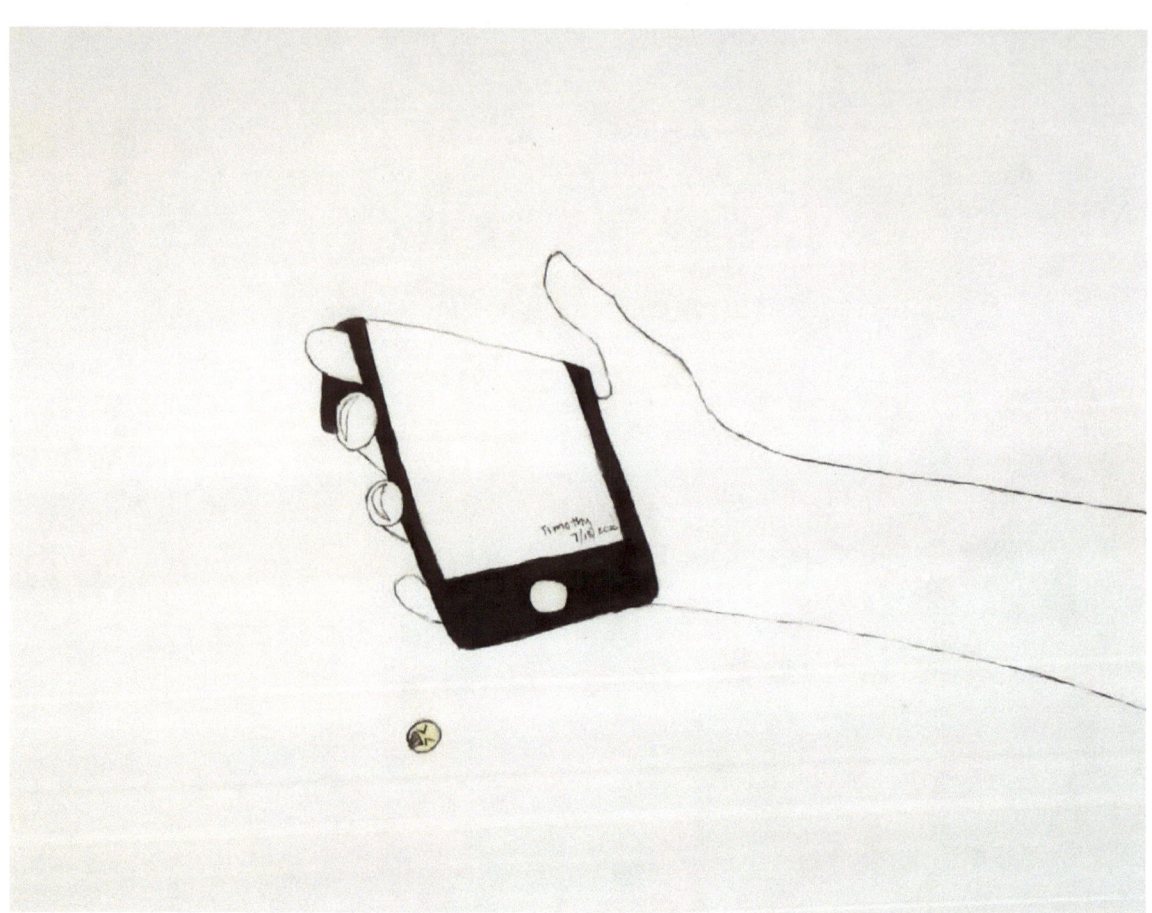

Soft Cell Phone, ink and colored pencil on paper, 2020

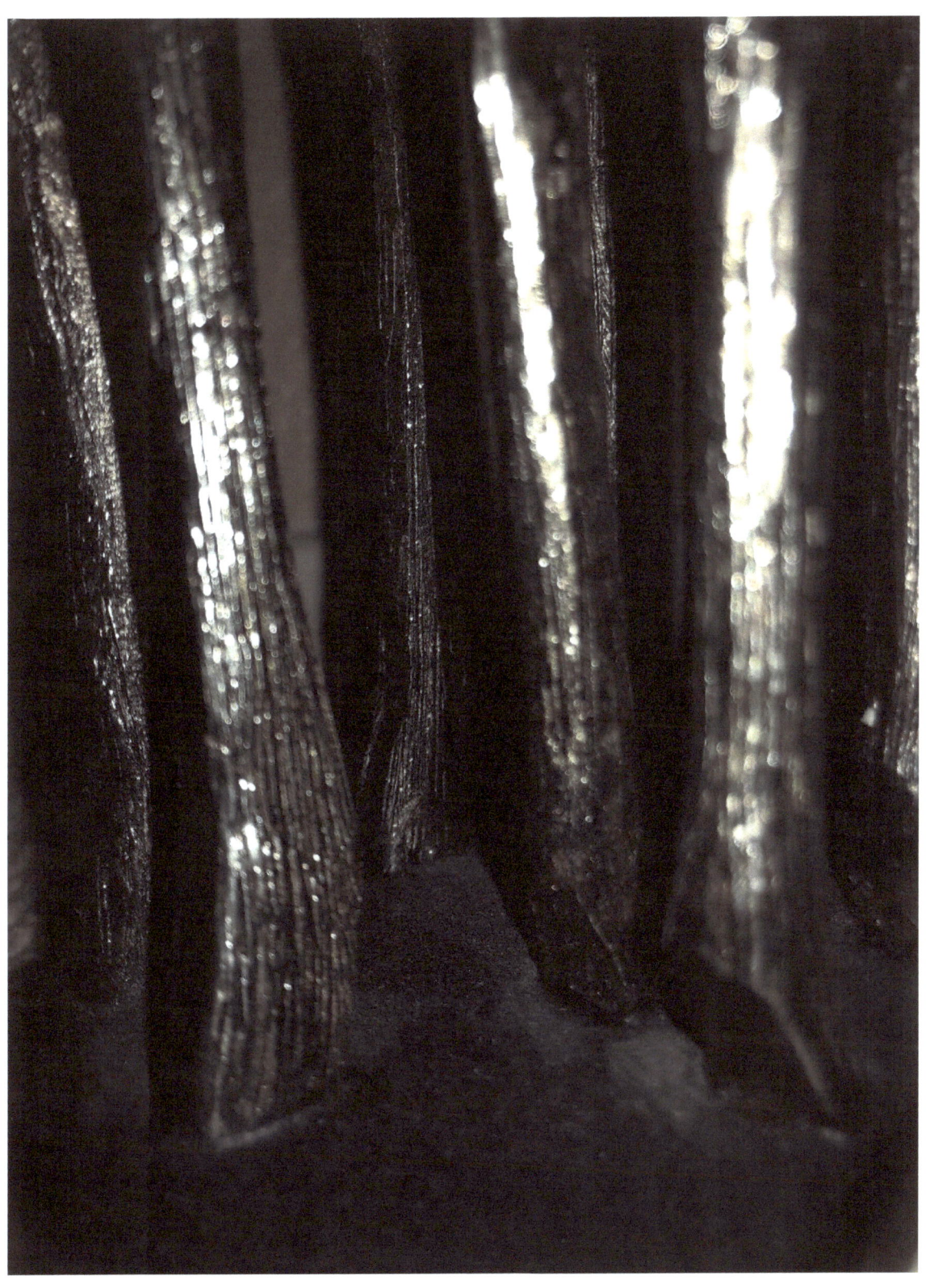

Metal Forest, photo, 2021

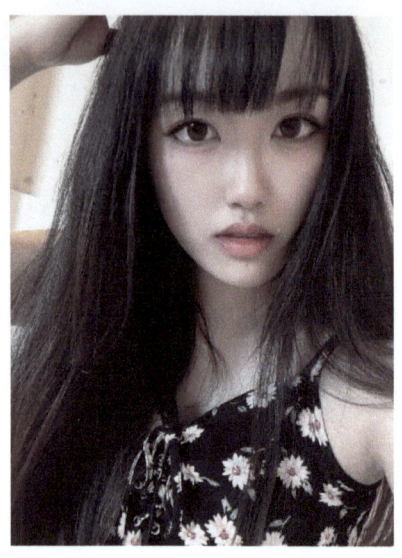

WANCHEN ZHANG

Georg-August-Universität Göttingen, Germany

Bronze Award for Art, 3rd Liberty Awards, International Society of Young Artists, USA, 2020-21
Bronze Award for Art, 1st Liberty Awards, International Society of Young Artists, USA, 2018

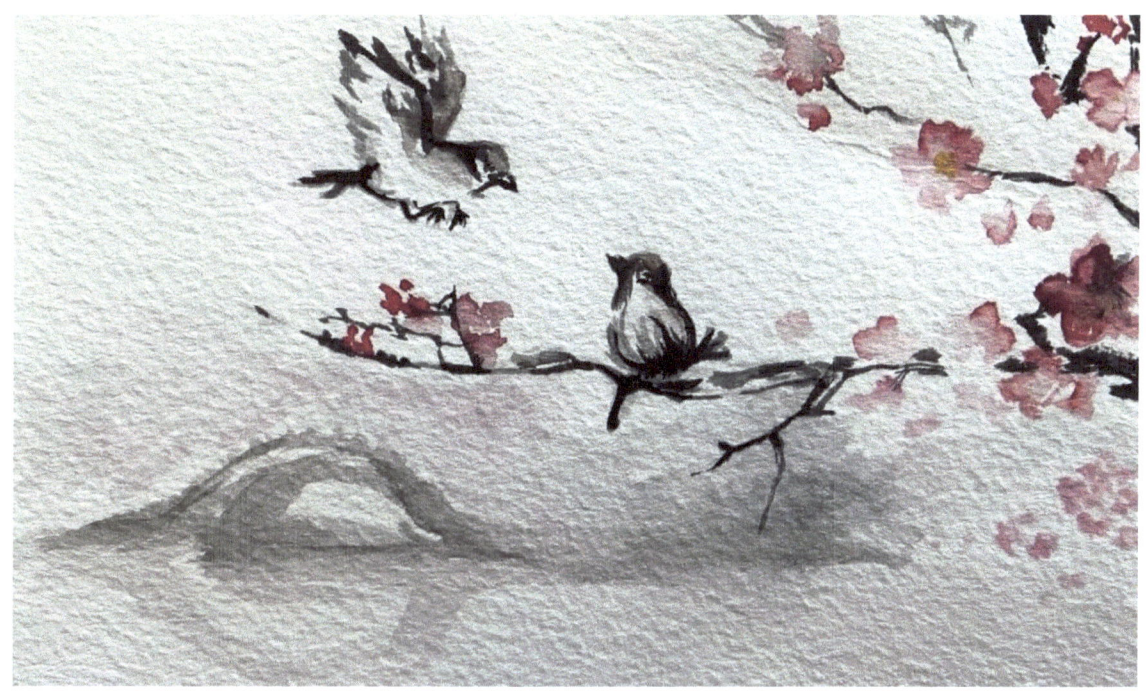

Springtime, ink and watercolor on paper, 2020

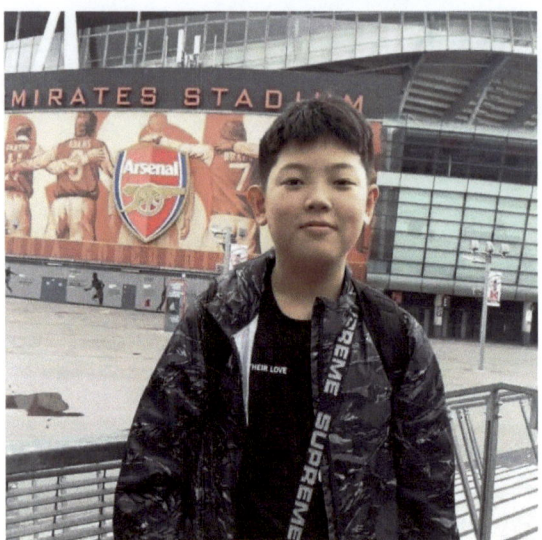

XIKAI XU

Qingdao University Affiliated Middle School, China

Bronze Award for Art, 2nd Liberty Awards, International Society of Young Artists, USA, 2019

Bronze Award for Art, 1st Liberty Awards, International Society of Young Artists, USA, 2018

Bronze Award, "The Colorful Peace" Art Project Honoring the 100th Anniversary of the WWI Armistice, International Society of Young Artists, USA, 2018

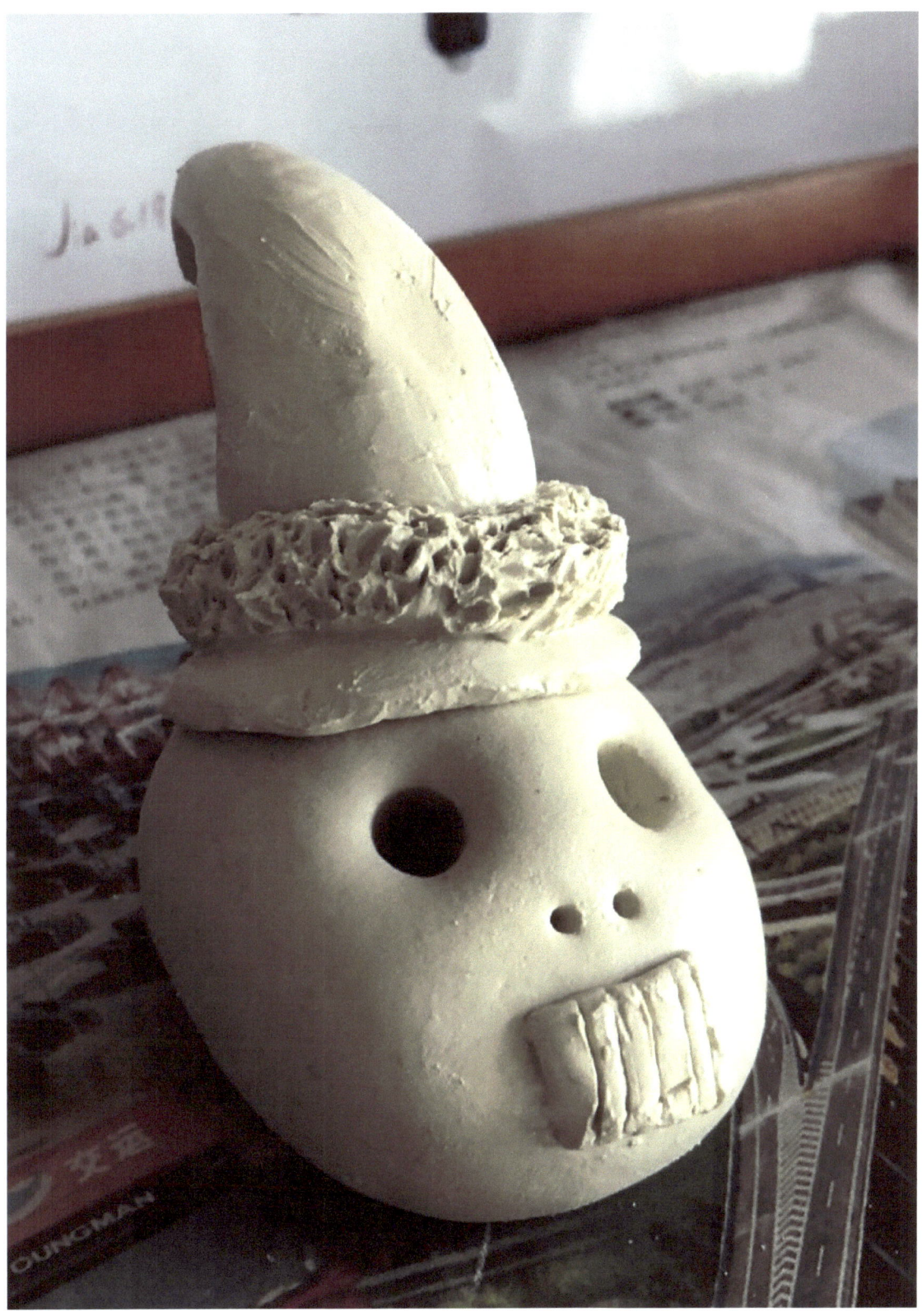

Wizard, clay, 2018

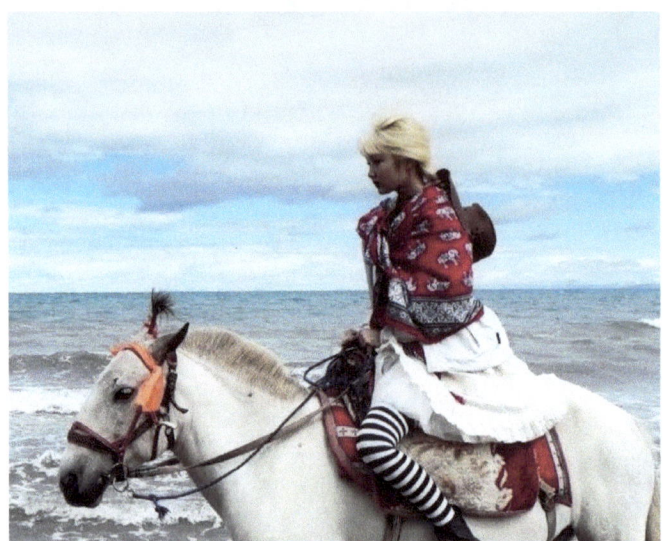

XIN WEN

Qingdao No.58 High School, China

Gold Award for Art, 3rd Liberty Awards, International Society of Young Artists, USA, 2020-21
Bronze Award for Art, 1st Liberty Awards, International Society of Young Artists, USA, 2018
Excellent Performance, 8th "China Meets Europe" Art Festival in 2018, Austria, 2018
1st Prize, Simulated Remote-Controlled Helicopter Crossing Contest, Qingdao Junior Aeromodelling Competition, China, 2018
1st Prize, Guzheng, 6th Annual Qiluqing Campus Student Talent Show Contest, China, 2017

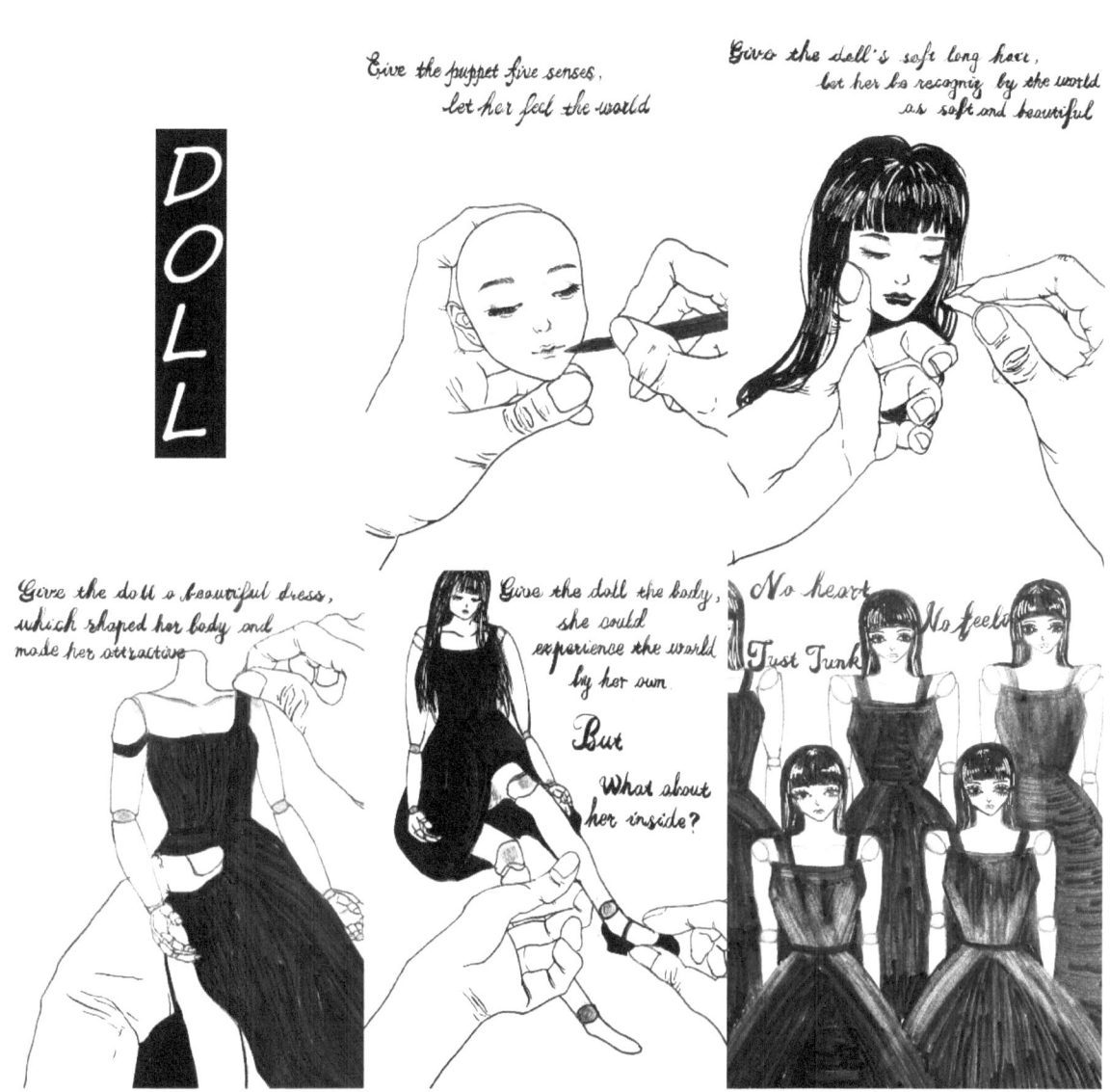

Doll, marker and pen on paper, 2020

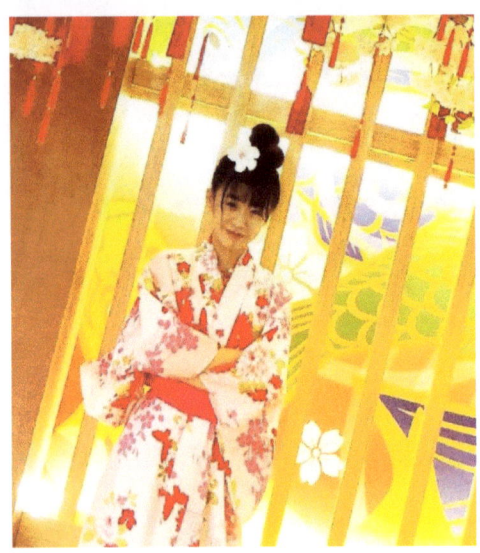

XUNYAN KUANG

Ruben S. Ayala High School, USA

Gold Award for Art, 3rd Liberty Awards, International Society of Young Artists, USA, 2020-21
Person of the Year 2019, International Society of Young Artists, USA, 2019
Gold Award for Art, 2nd Liberty Awards, International Society of Young Artists, USA, 2019
Bronze Award for Art, 1st Liberty Awards, International Society of Young Artists, USA, 2018

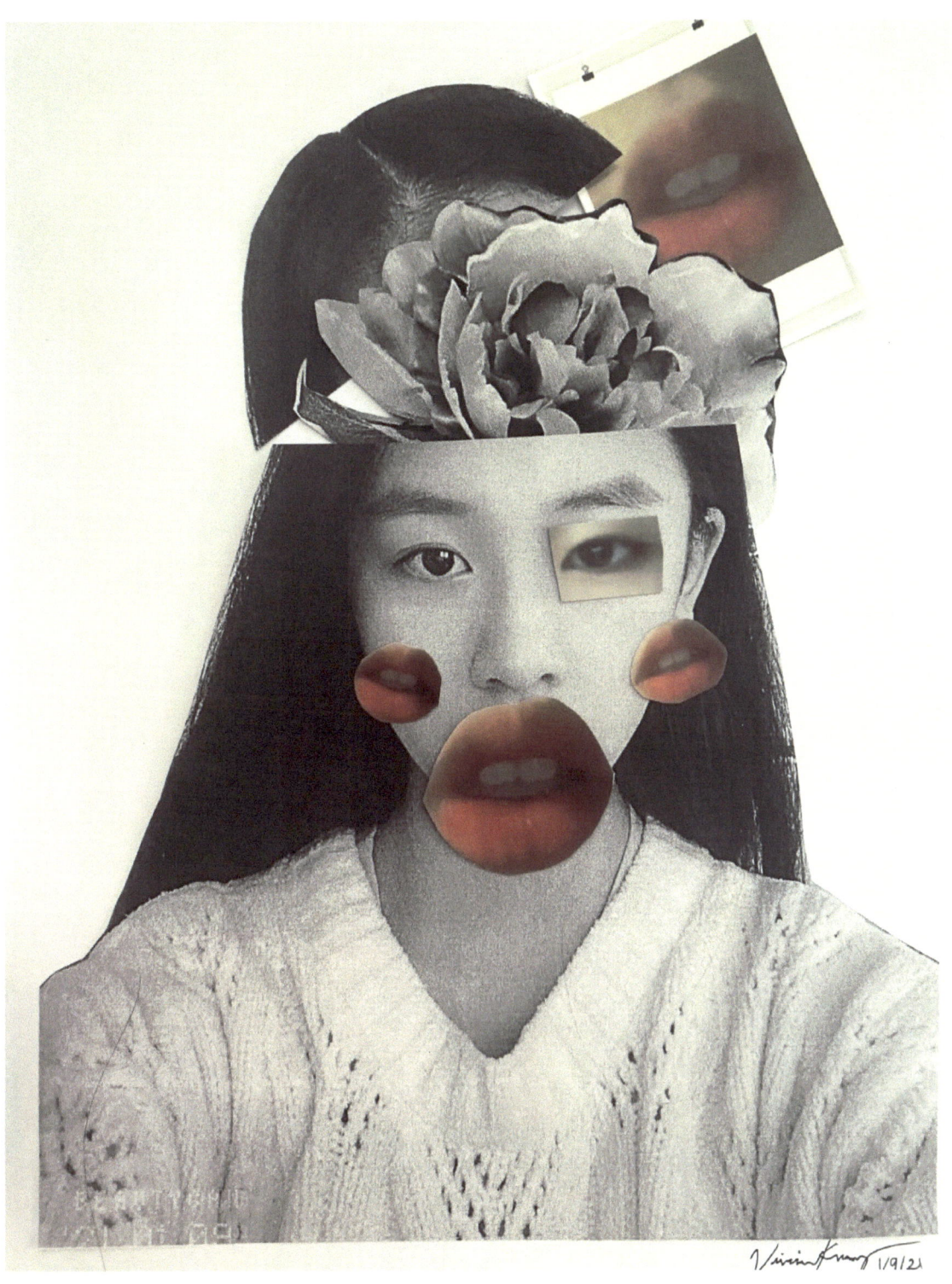

Chatter, photo and mix media, 2021

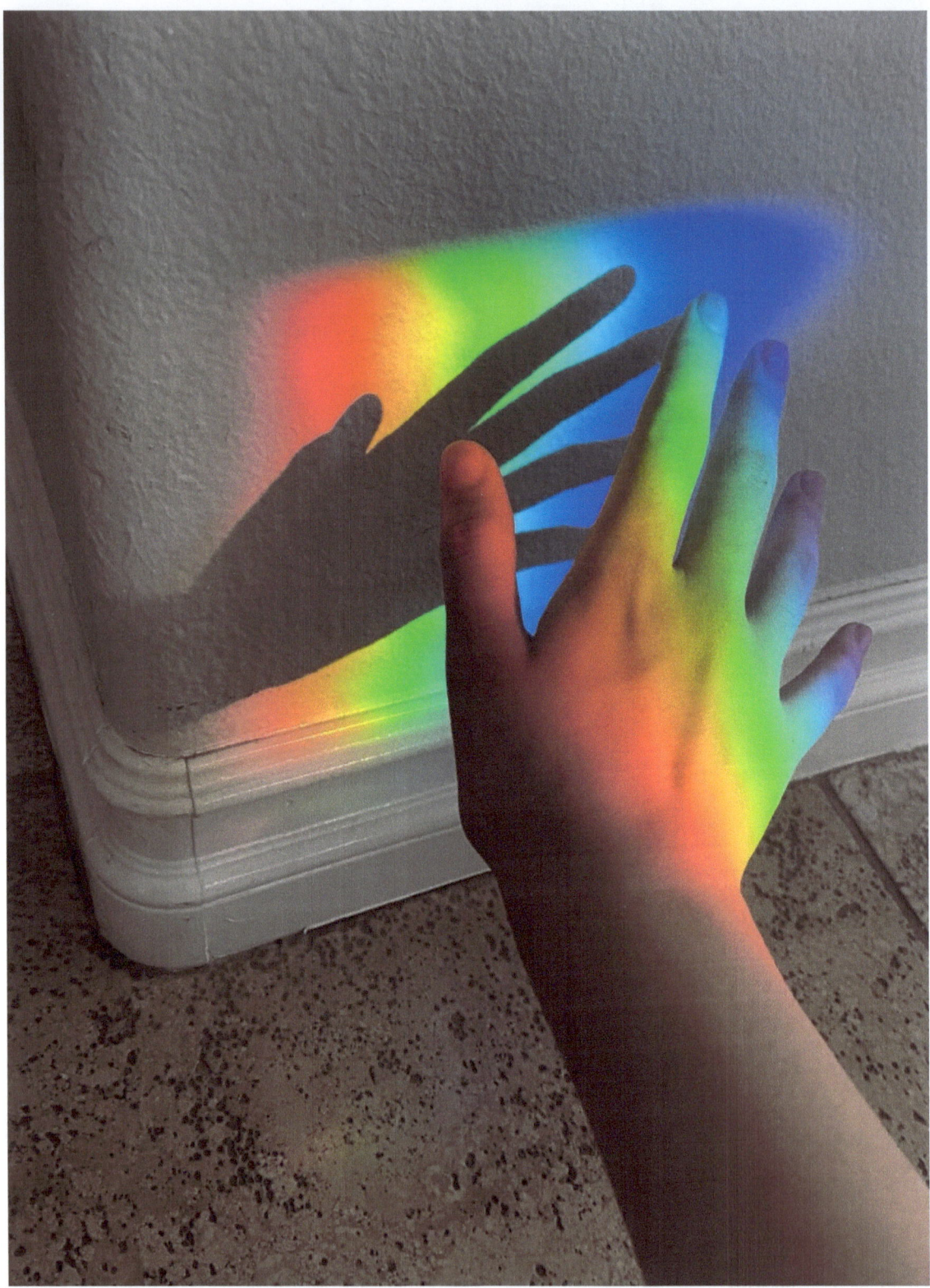

Untouchable, performance, 2020

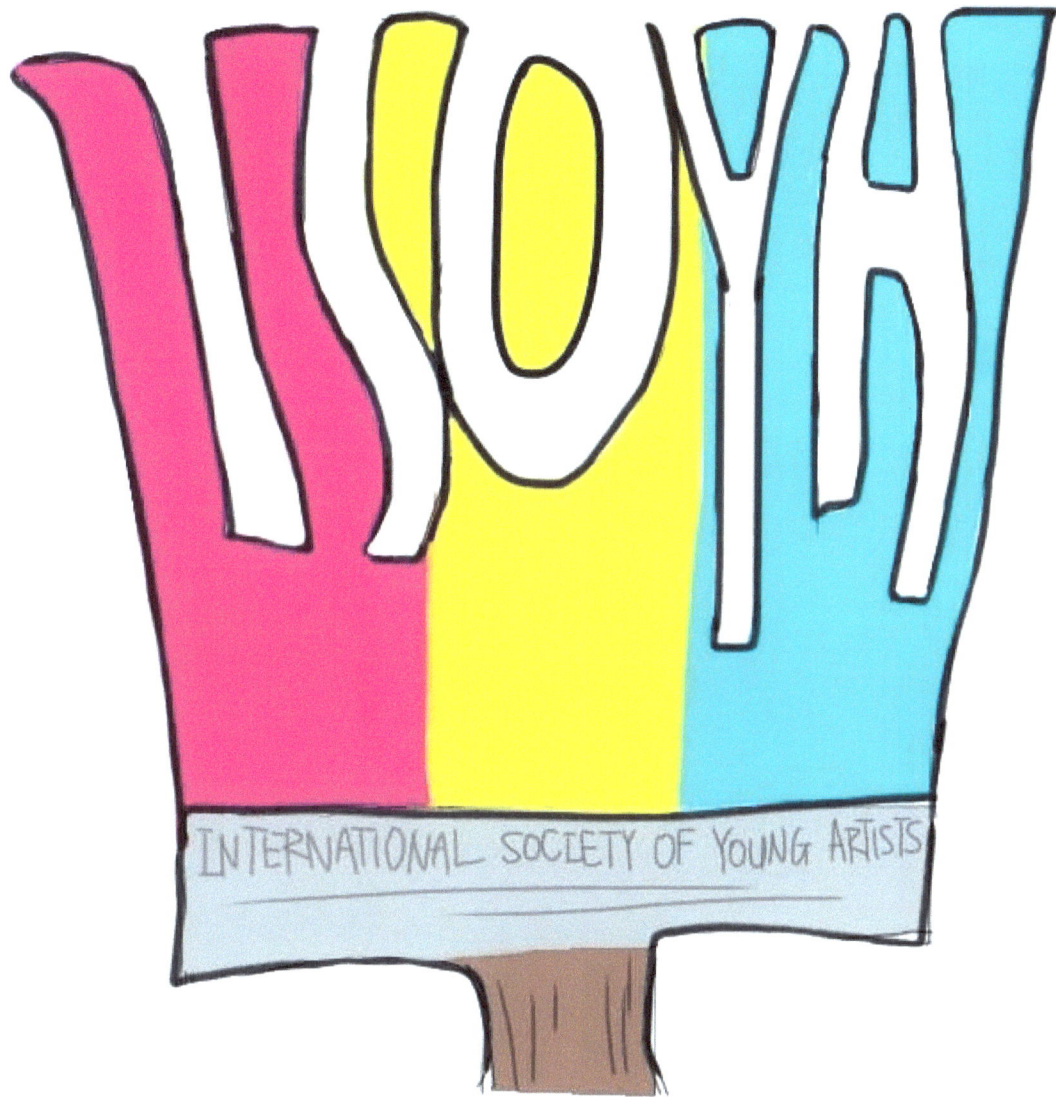

The Logo of International Society of Young Artist, digital, 2021

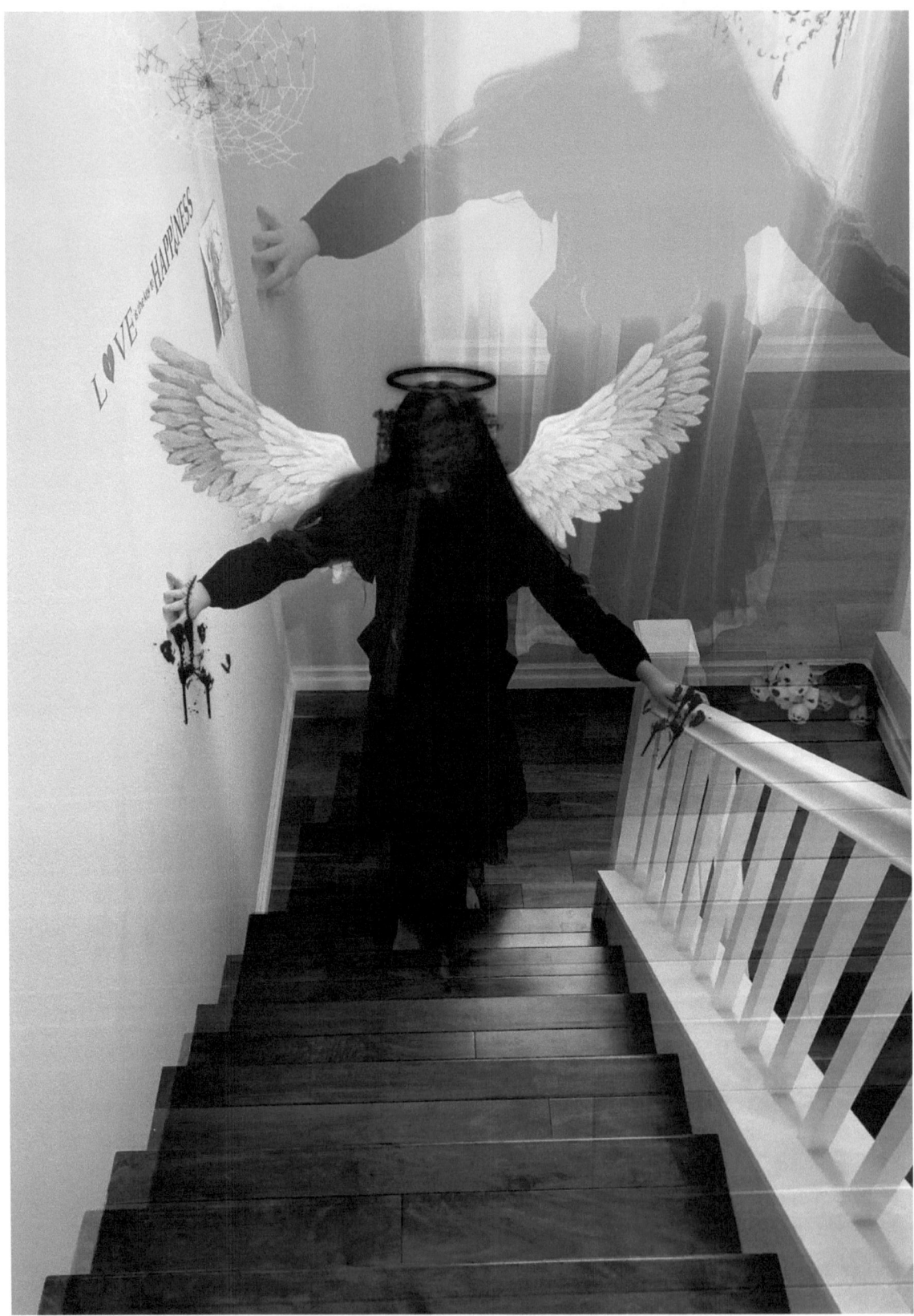

Unknown, performance, 2020

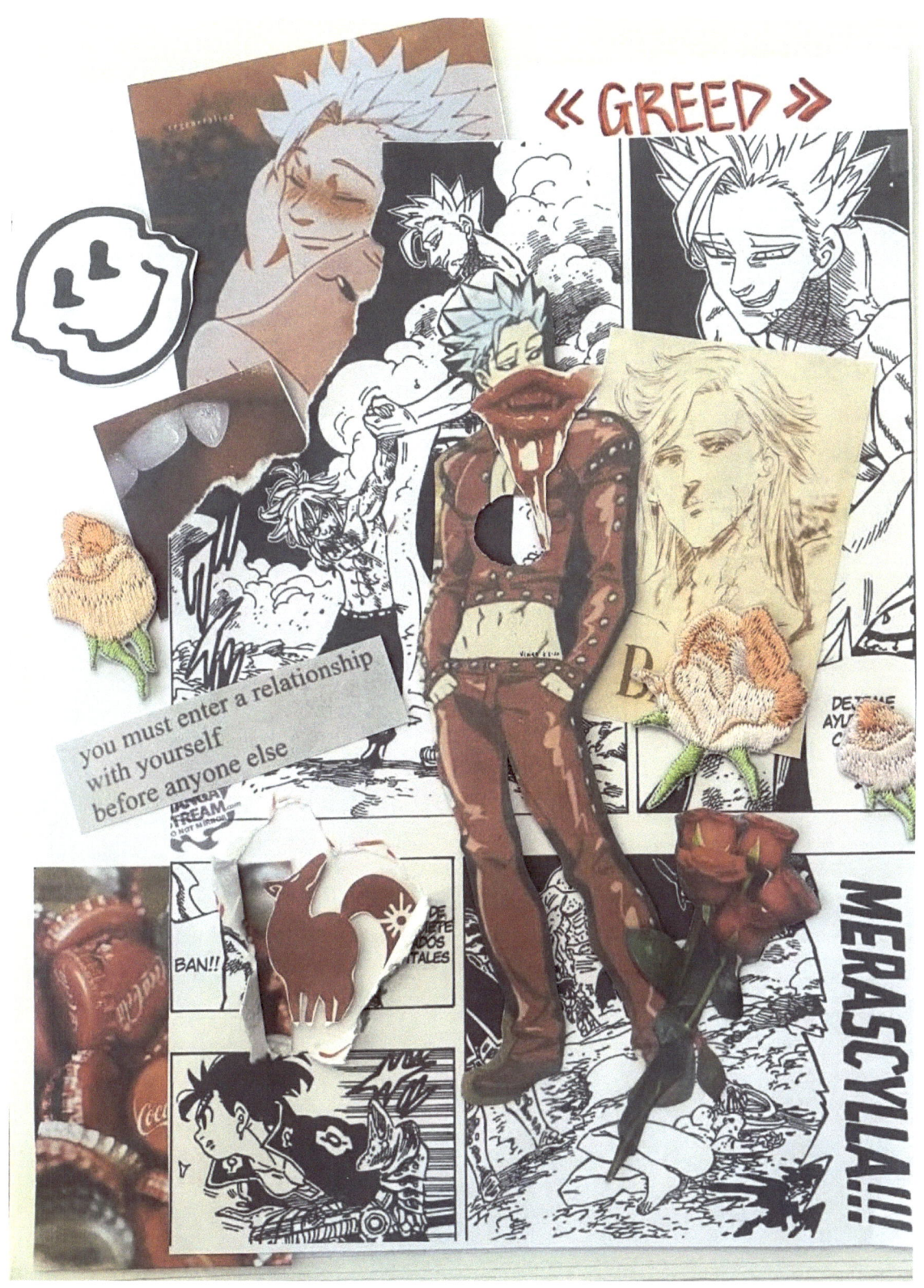

Fox Sin of Greed, mix media, 2020

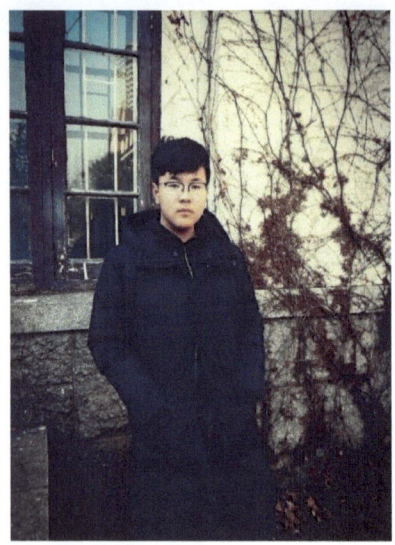

YIFEI WANG

Qingdao No. 1 High School, China

Gold Award for Art, 3rd Liberty Awards, International Society of Young Artists, USA, 2020-21
Bronze Award for Art, 2nd Liberty Awards, International Society of Young Artists, USA, 2019
Bronze Award for Art, 1st Liberty Awards, International Society of Young Artists, USA, 2018

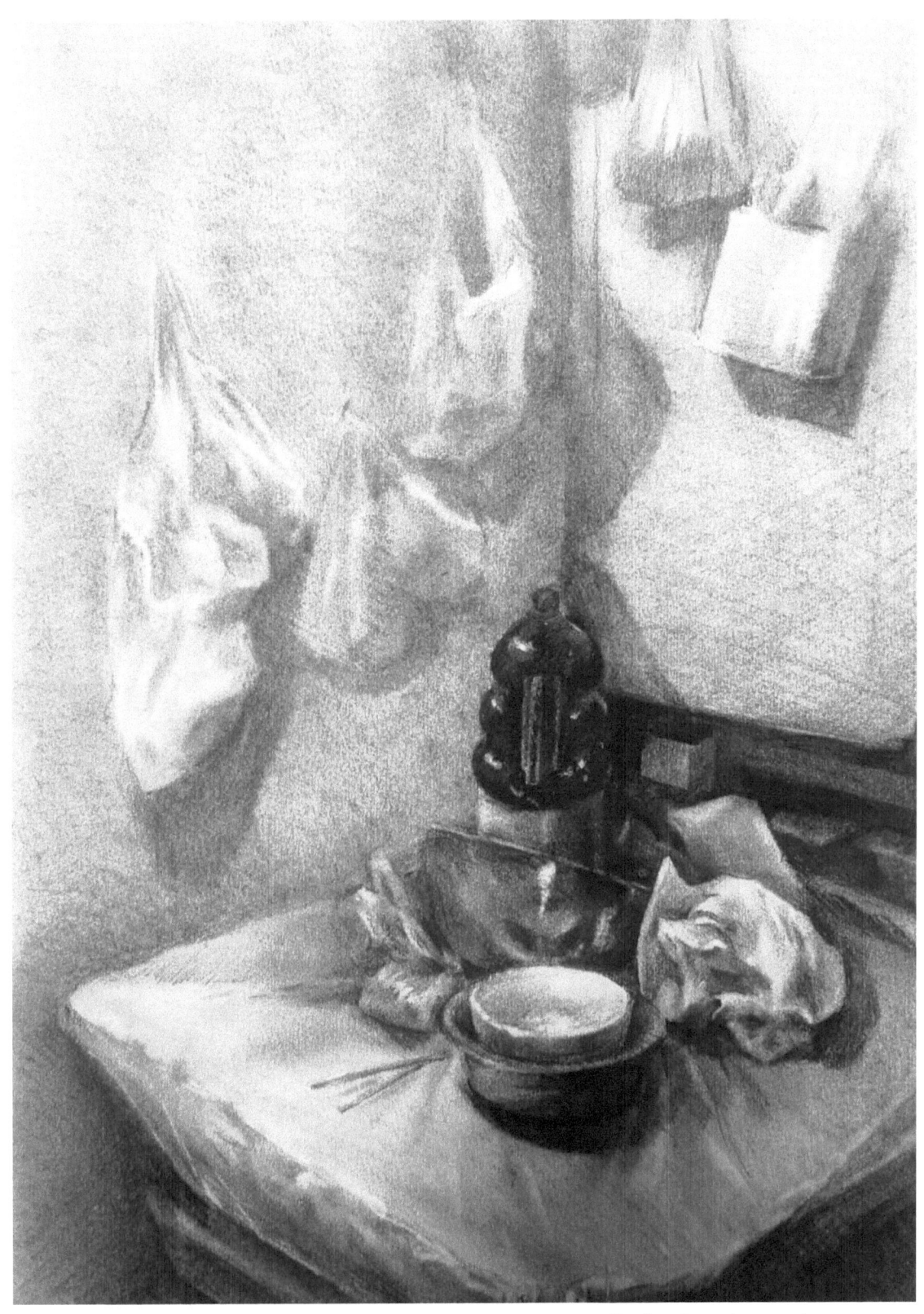

Still Life in the Kitchen, pencil on paper, 2020

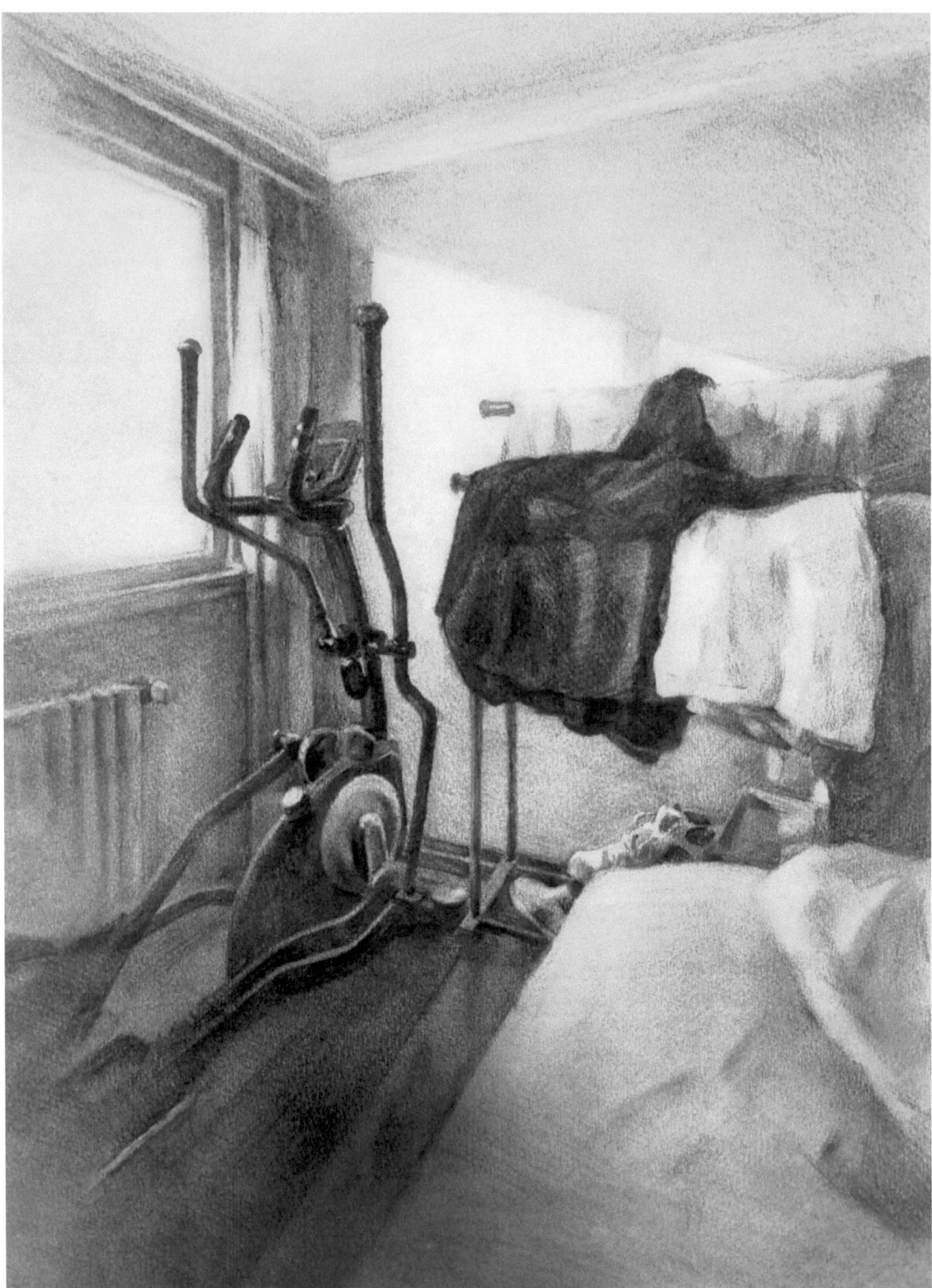

Corner of the Bedroom, pencil on paper, 2020

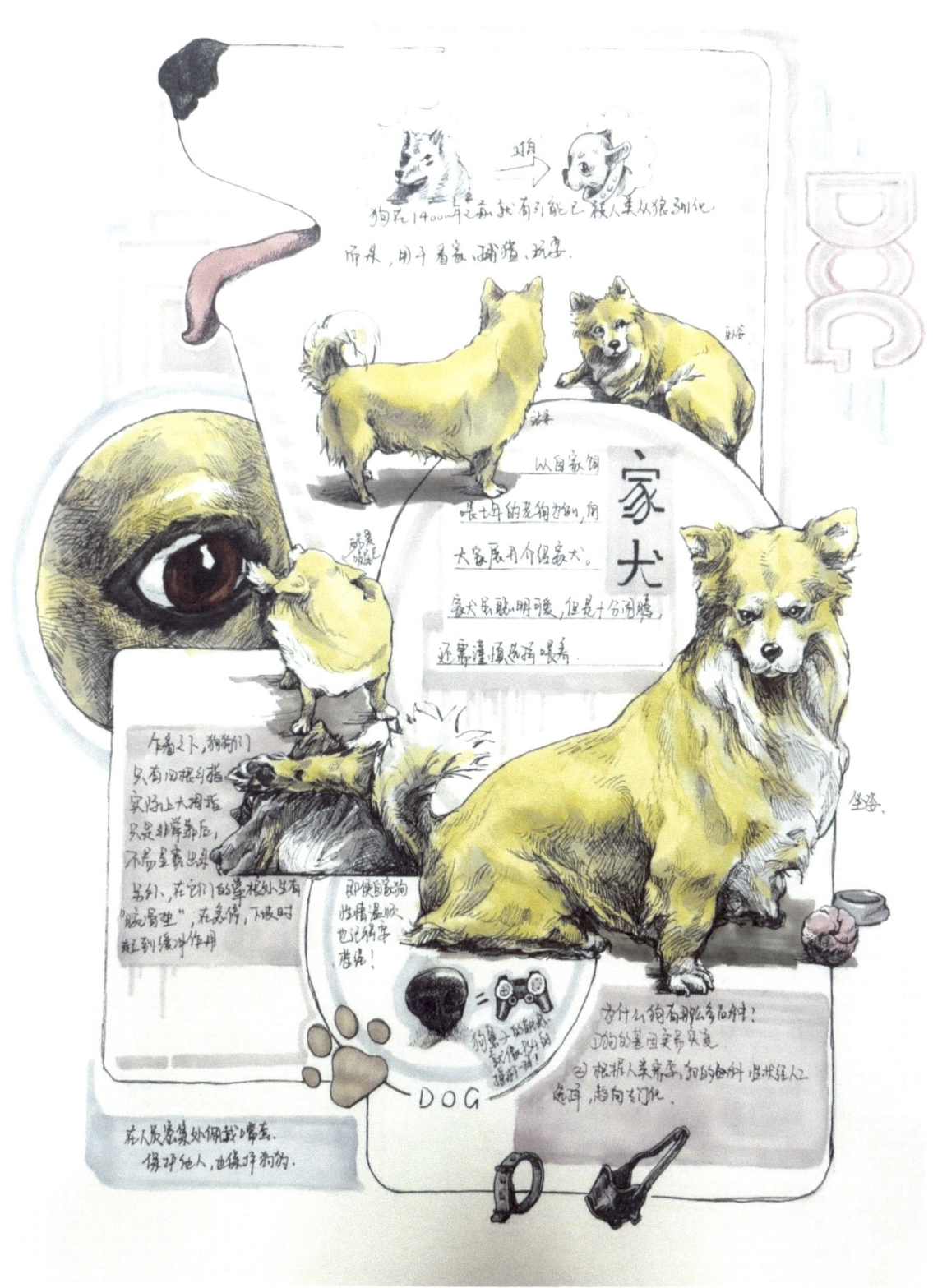

Dog, watercolor brush pen on paper, 2020

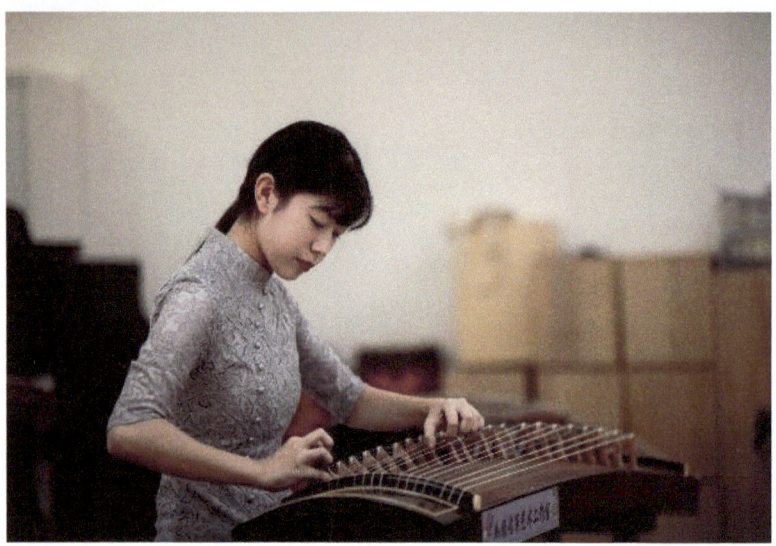

YIHAN ZHANG

Ocean University of China Affiliated Middle School, China

Gold Award for Art, 2nd Liberty Awards, International Society of Young Artists, USA, 2019
Rising Star Award, 1st Liberty Awards, International Society of Young Artists, USA, 2018
National 2nd Prize, Guzheng, 2nd Music Creates Future International Youth Talent Plan, China, 2018
1st Prize, Guzheng, 2nd Music Creates Future International Youth Talent Plan of Shandong, China, 2018
Gold Medal, Guzheng, National Juvenile Art Show by Central Conservatory of Music, China, 2017

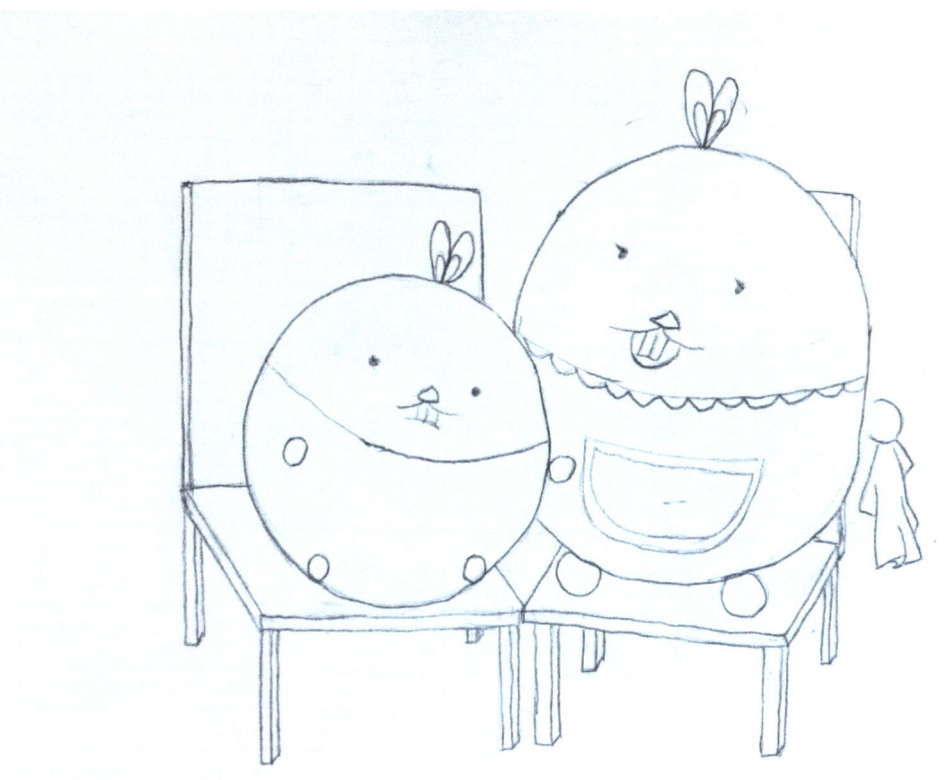

Selection from *The Chubby Bunny*, pencil on paper, 2018

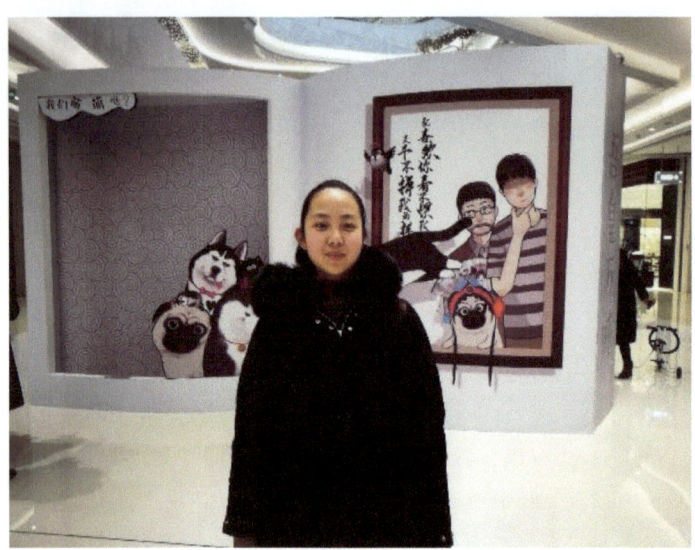

YU JIANG

Qingdao No.58 High School, China

Silver Award for Art, 3rd Liberty Awards, International Society of Young Artists, USA, 2020-21
Bronze Award for Art, 2nd Liberty Awards, International Society of Young Artists, USA, 2019
Gold Award for Art, 1st Liberty Awards, International Society of Young Artists, USA, 2018

Description of design: *This Logo represents the vigorous teenagers from Qingdao No.58 High School, Class of 2019 enrollment, block 9, who are full of vigor, like the sun at 9 o'clock in the morning. They are determined to succeed in China National College Entrance Examination, which will star at 9 a.m.*

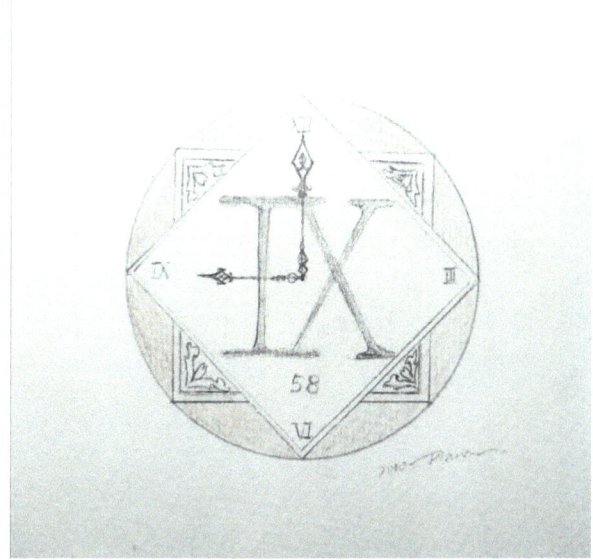

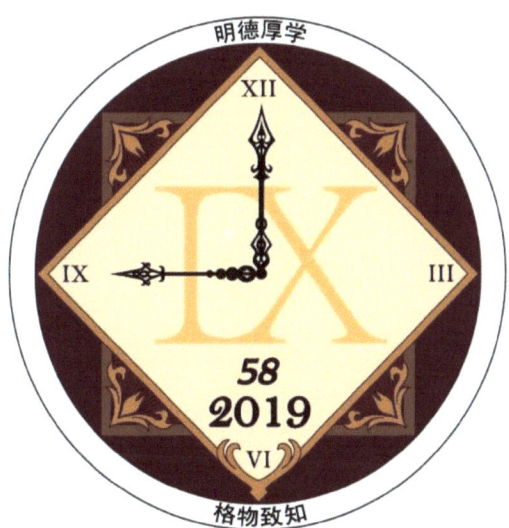

Class Logo of Qingdao No.58 High School, Class of 2019 Enrollment, Block 9
Pencil on paper (manuscript) & digital (effect picture), 2020

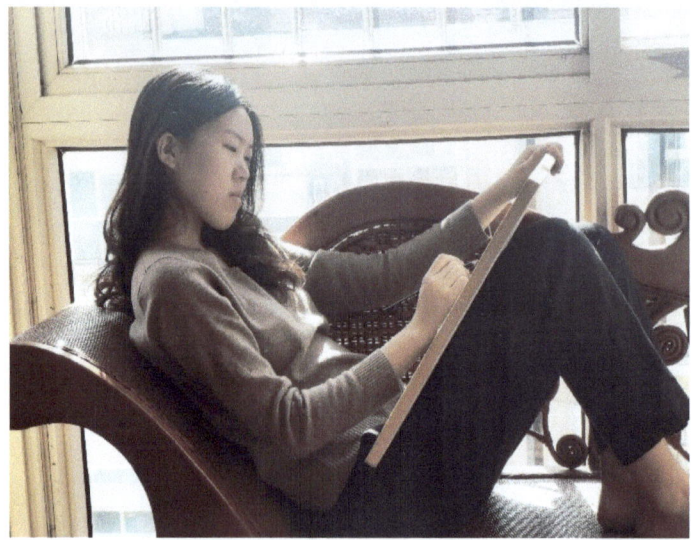

YUE LIU

Qingdao No.58 High School, China

Gold Award for Art, 3rd Liberty Awards, International Society of Young Artists, USA, 2020-21

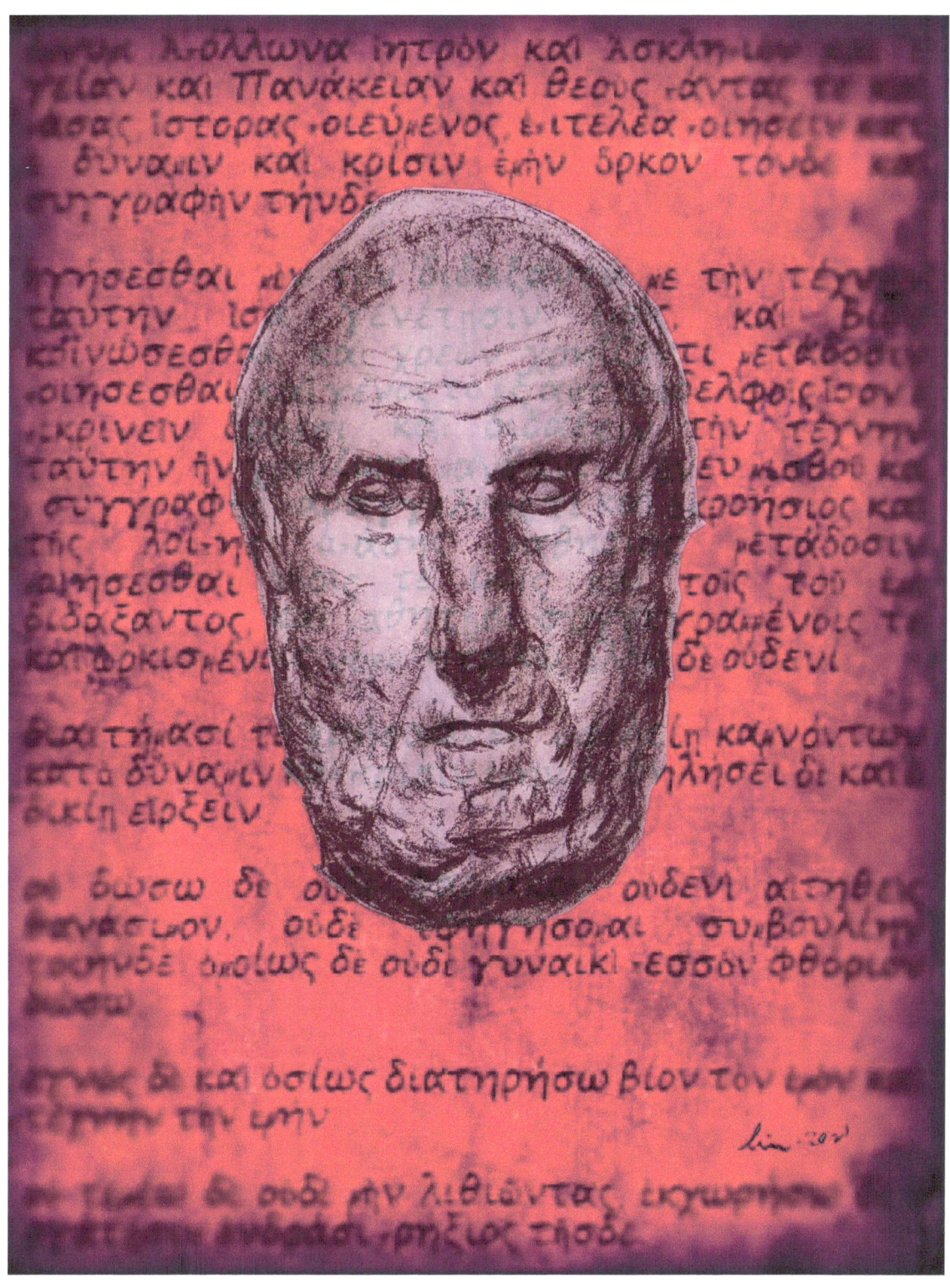

Hippocratic Oath, charcoal stick on paper & digital, 2021

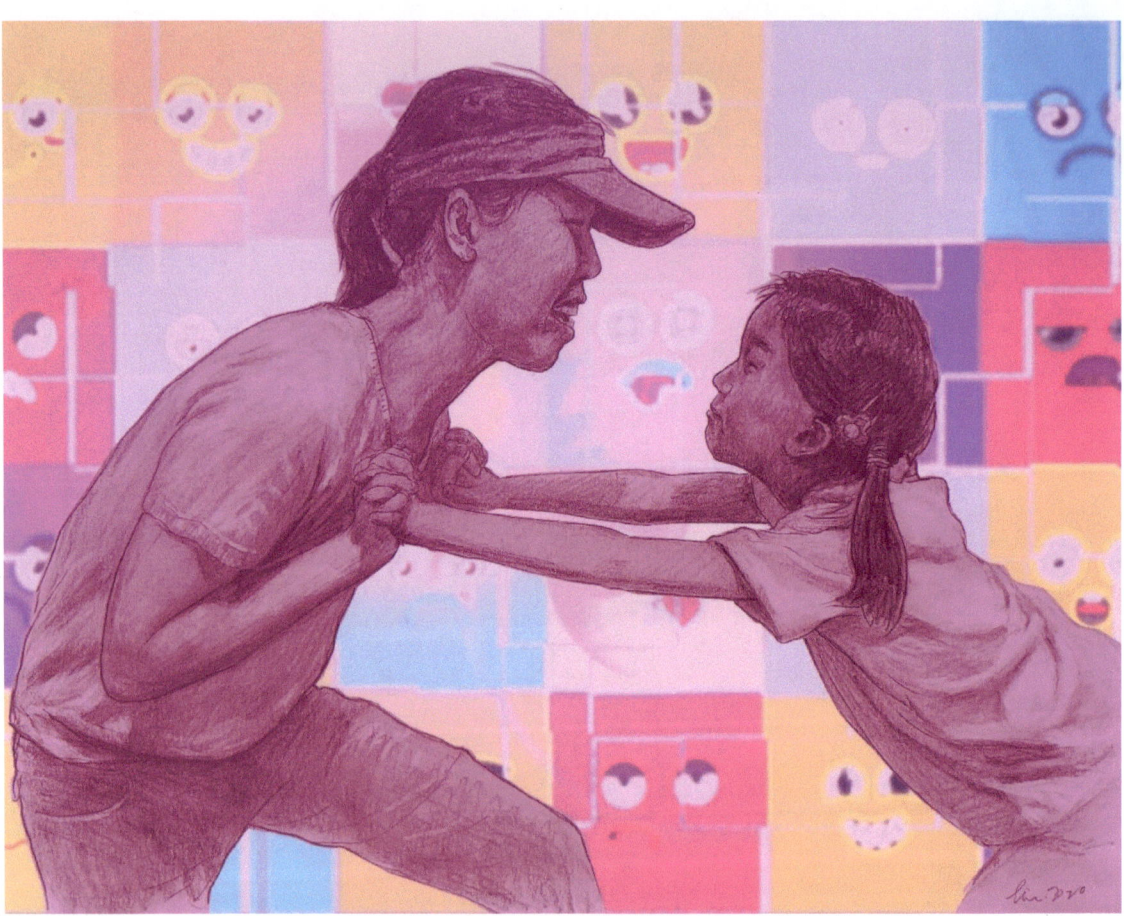

My Childhood, pencil on paper & digital, 2020

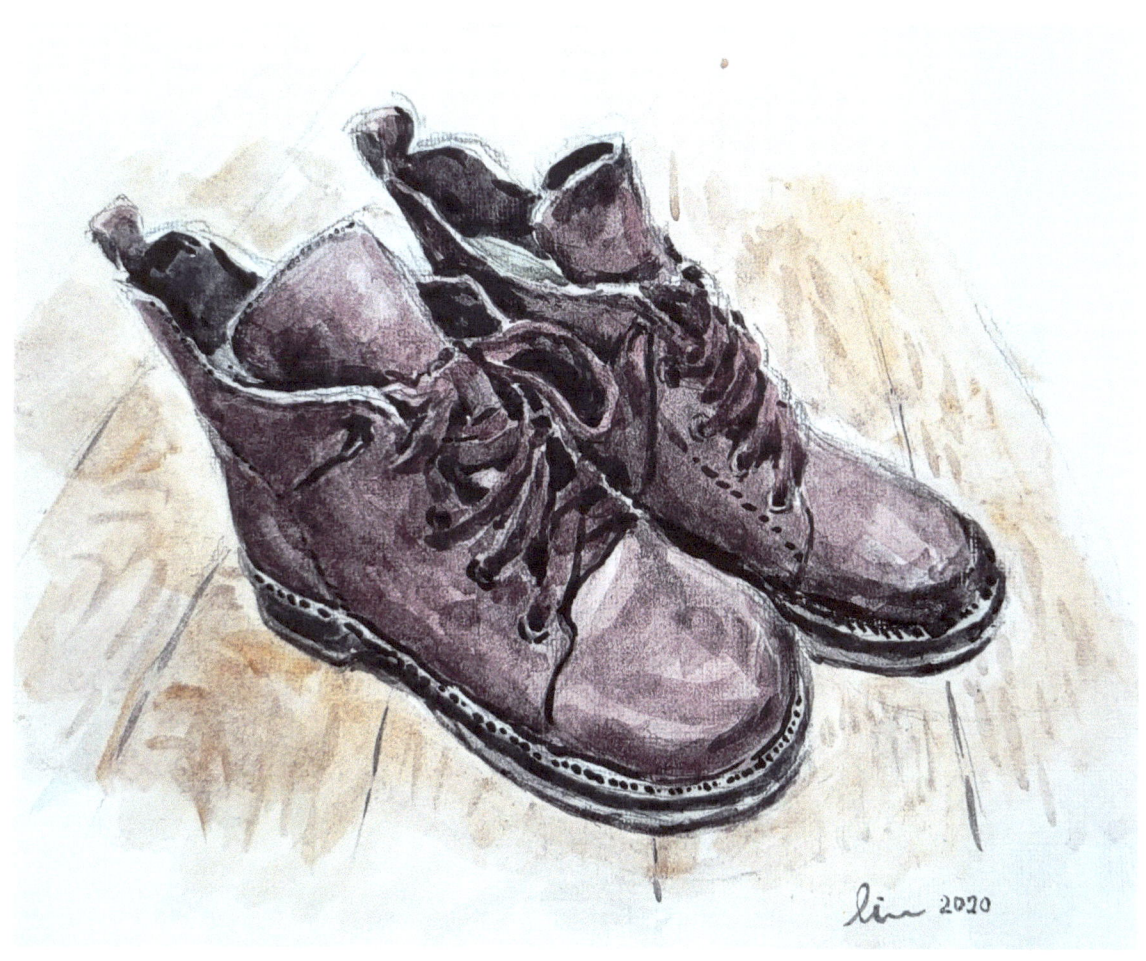

My Boots, acrylic on paper, 2020

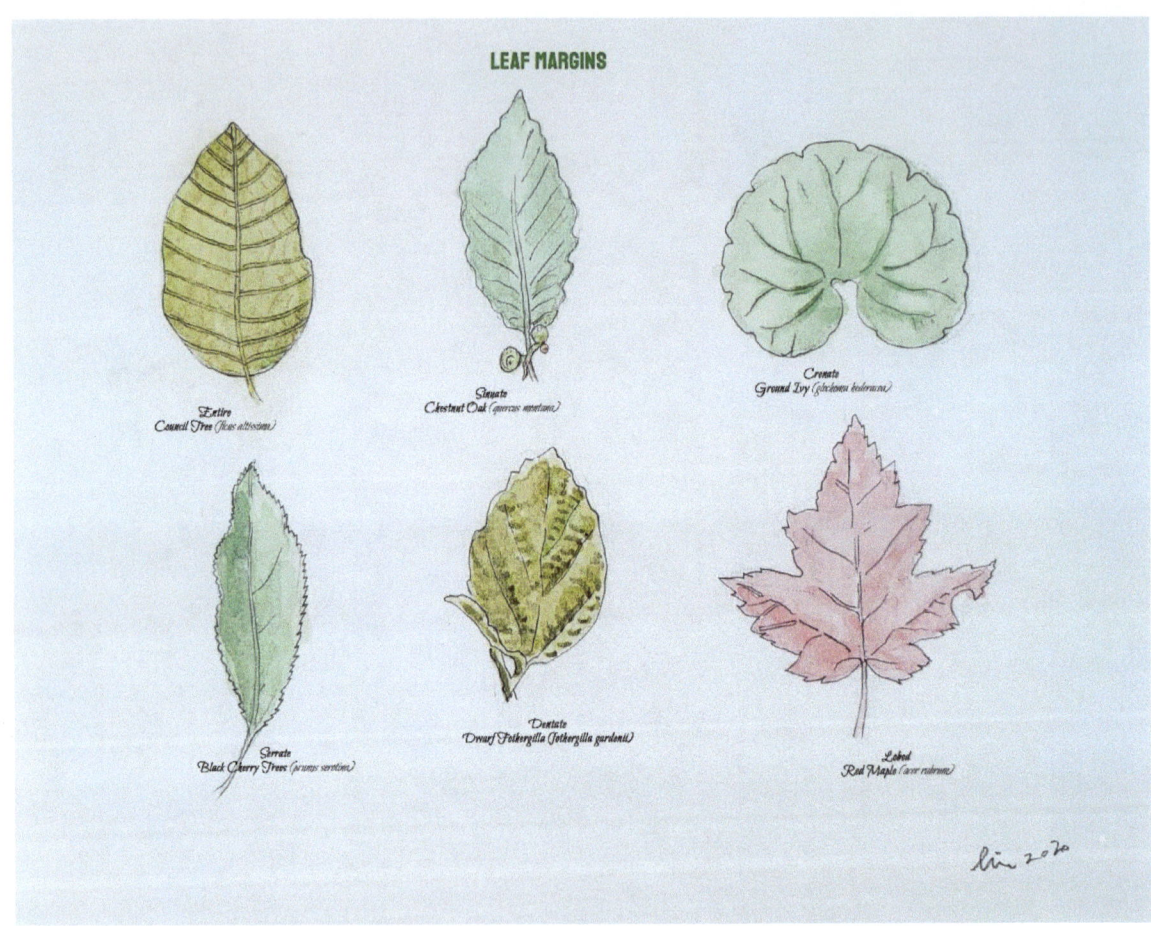

Leaf Margins, pencil and acrylic on paper, 2020

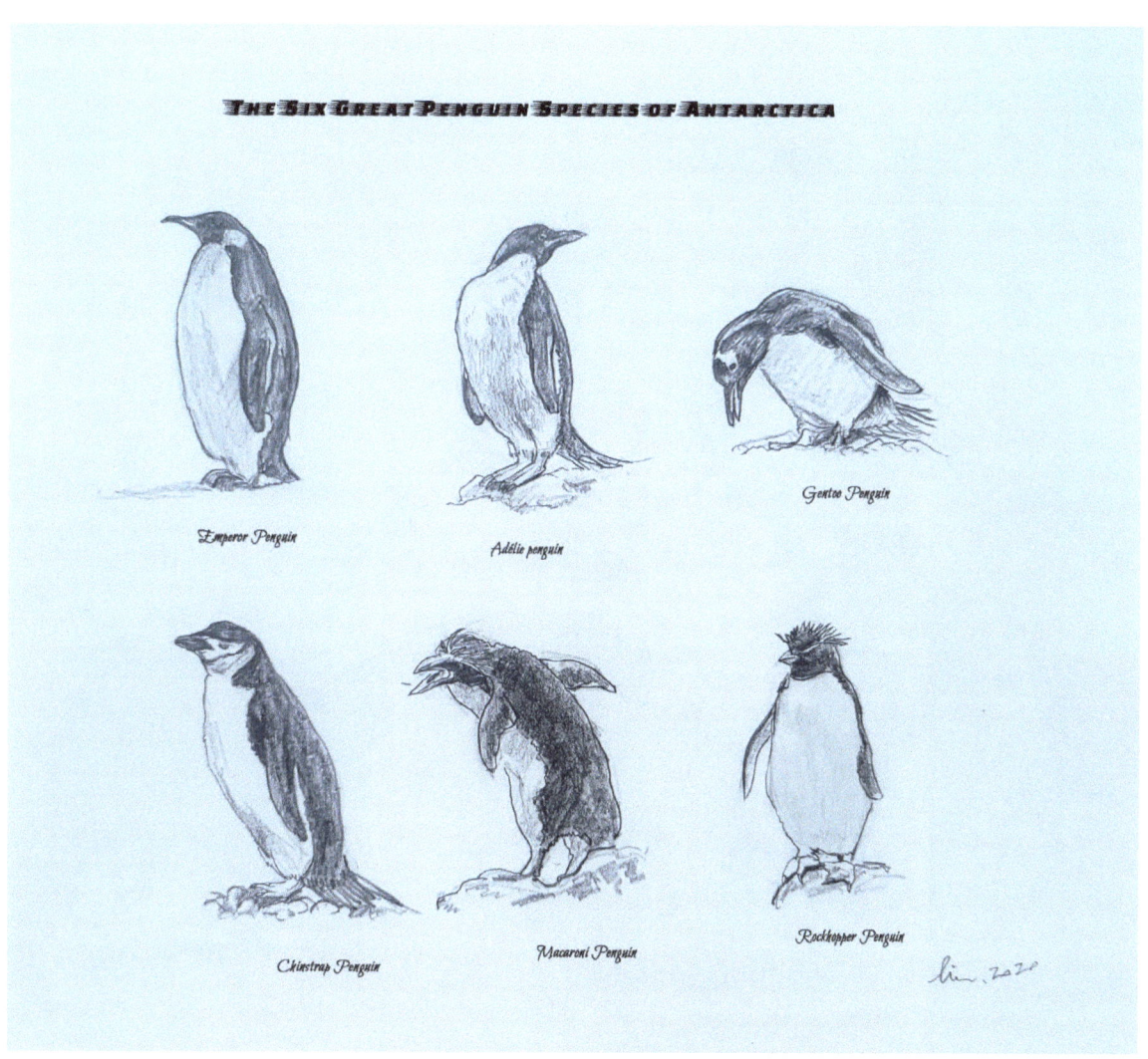

The Six Great Penguin Species of Antarctica, pencil on paper, 2020

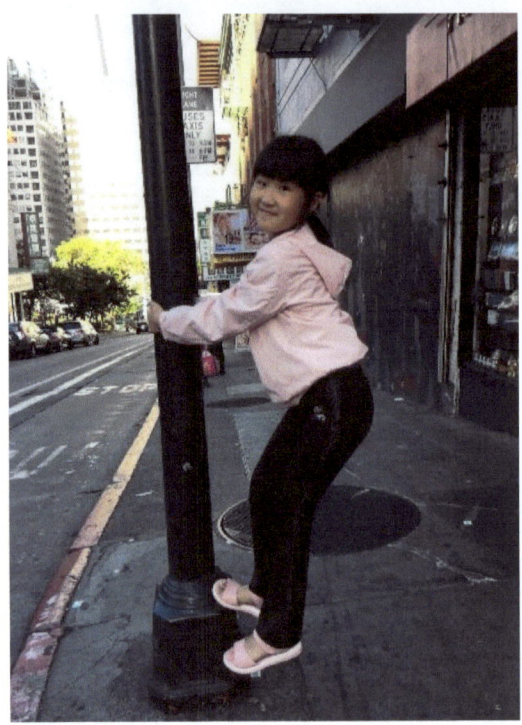

YUE WANG

Qingdao Cornerstone Bilingual School, China

Rising Star Award, 2nd Liberty Awards, International Society of Young Artists, USA, 2019
Rising Star Award, 1st Liberty Awards, International Society of Young Artists, USA, 2018

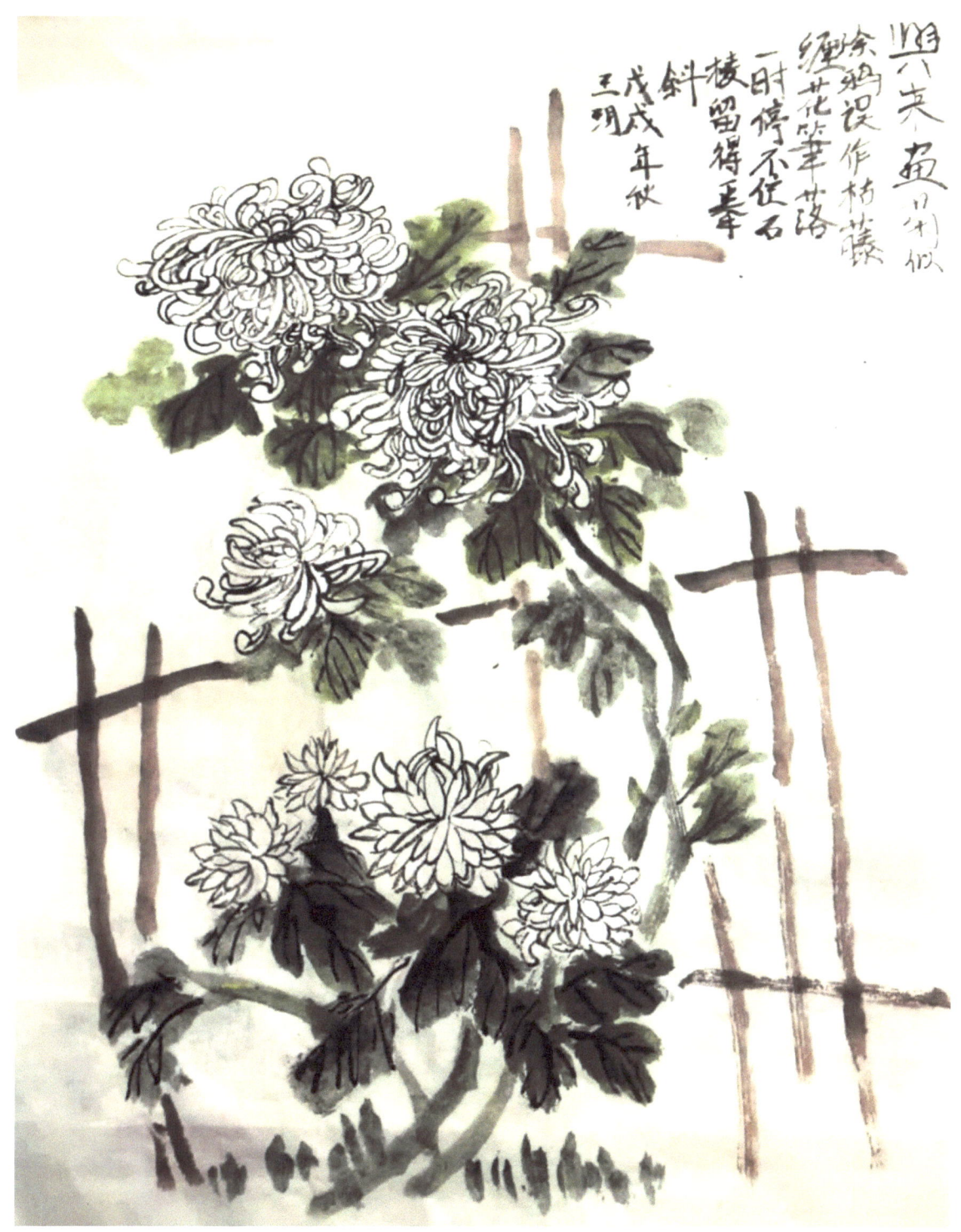

Chrysanthemum, Chinese painting pigment on rice paper, 2018

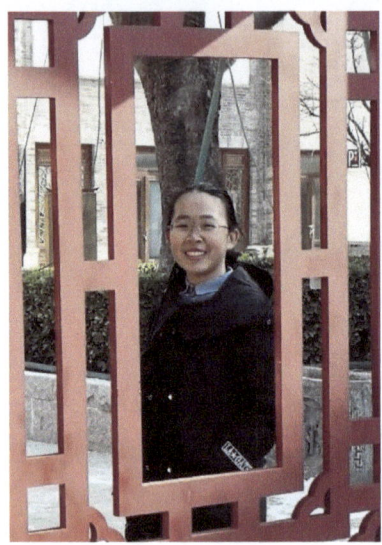

YUNING YANG

Qingdao University Affiliated Middle School, China

Bronze Award for Art, 2nd Liberty Awards, International Society of Young Artists, USA, 2019
Bronze Award for Art, 1st Liberty Awards, International Society of Young Artists, USA, 2018
3rd Prize, Painting, 22nd National Elementary and Secondary School Painting and Calligraphy Competition, 2017
3rd Prize, Painting, 6th Annual Qiluqing Campus Student Talent Show Contest, 2017

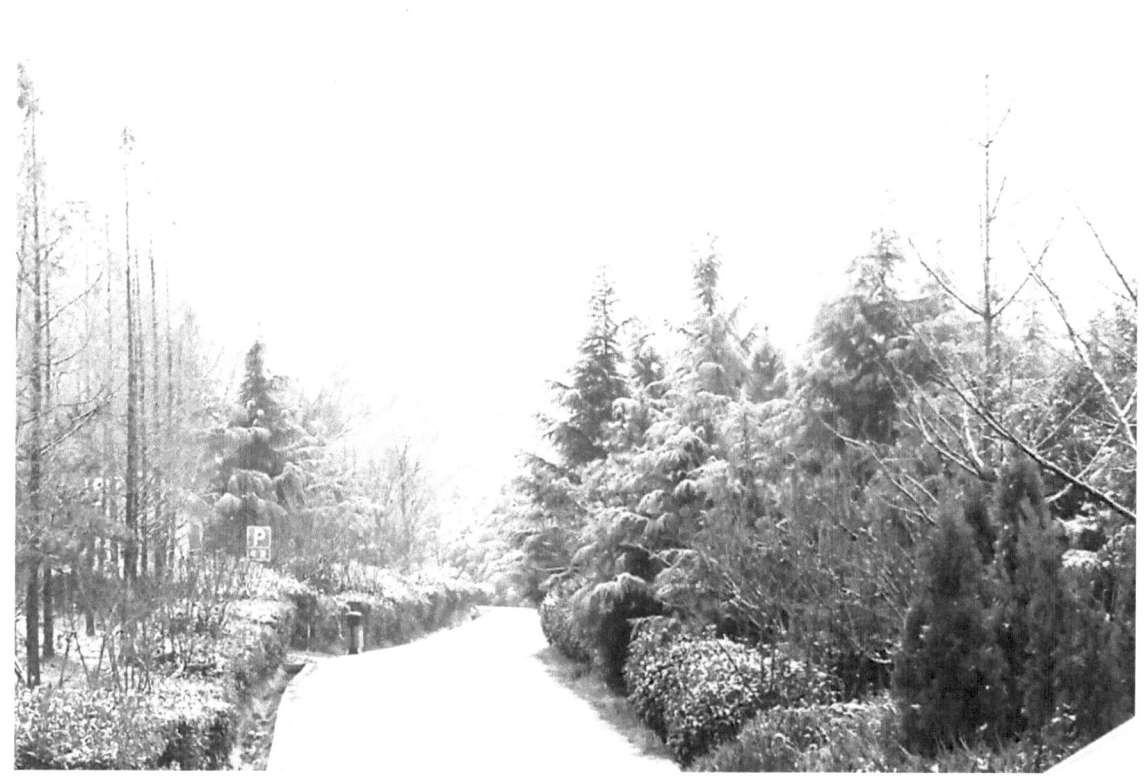

Mount Fu in the Snow, photo, 2018

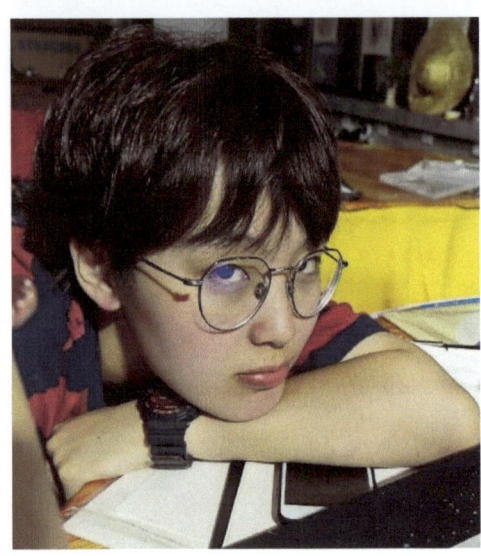

YUTING HE

Qingdao No.17 High School, China

Gold Award for Art, 3rd Liberty Awards, International Society of Young Artists, USA, 2020-21
Gold Award for Art, 2nd Liberty Awards, International Society of Young Artists, USA, 2019
Silver Award for Art, 1st Liberty Awards, International Society of Young Artists, USA, 2018
2nd Prize, National Middle School Students Mathematics Proficiency Contest of Qingdao, China, 2018
2nd Prize, National Middle School Students English Proficiency Competition, China, 2018
3rd Prize, 14th the Hope Cup National Composition Contest, China, 2017

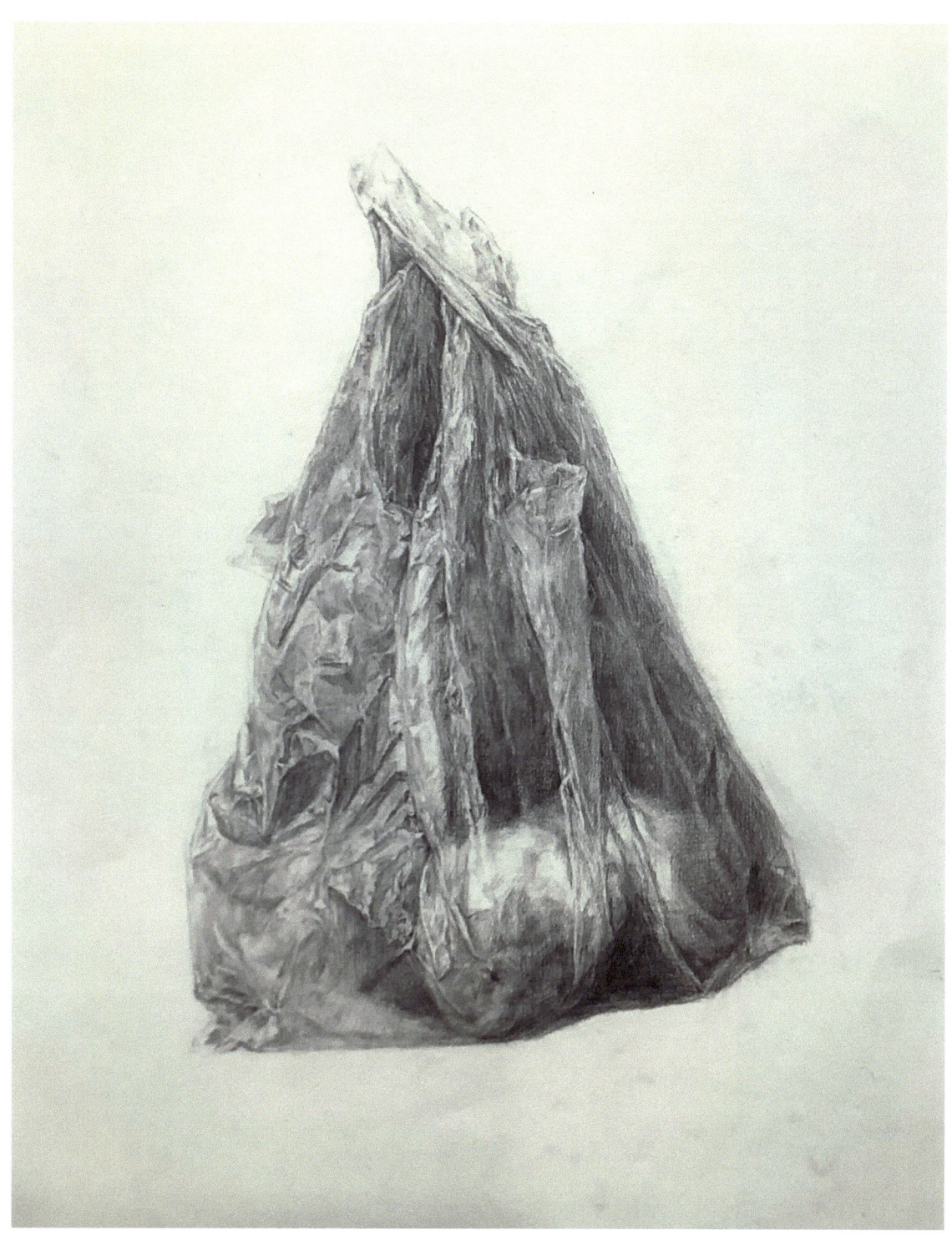

Some Fruits in a Plastic Bag, pencil on paper, 2020

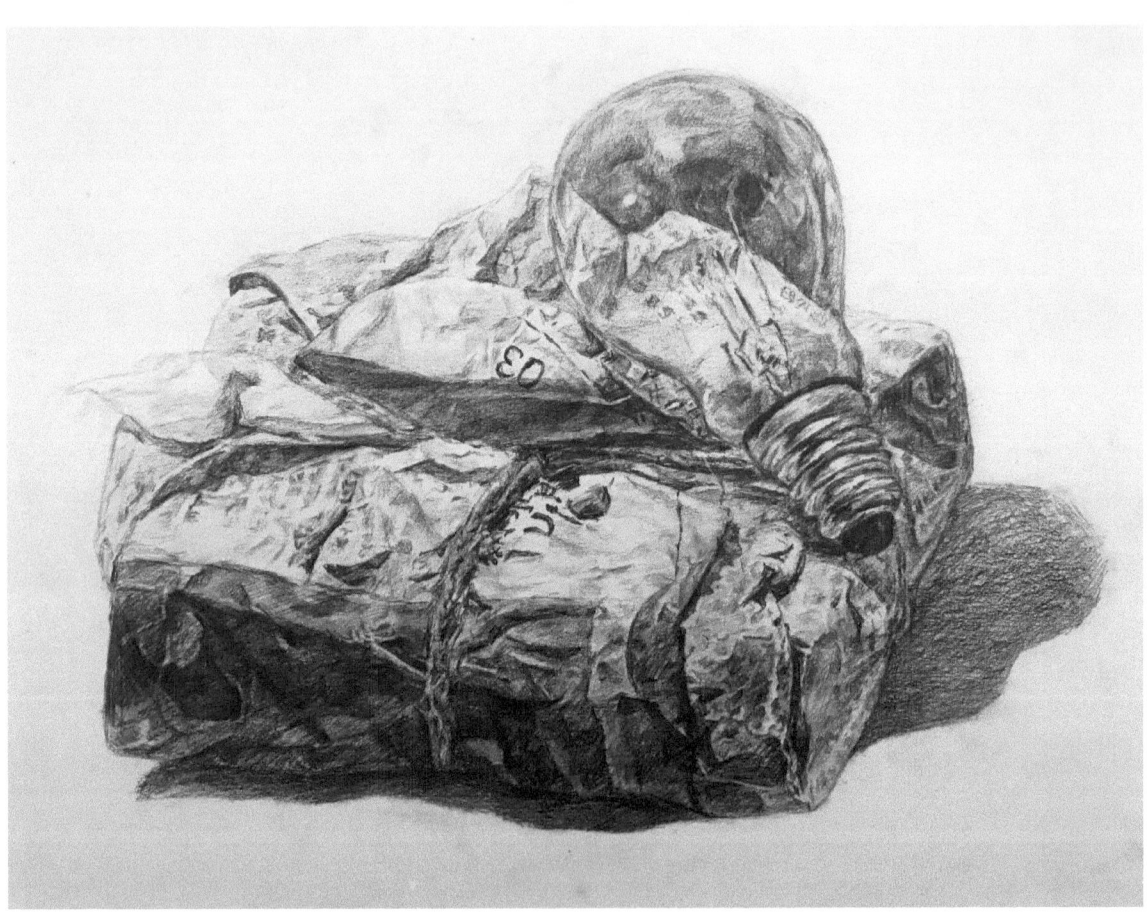

A Light Bulb and a Package, pencil on paper, 2020

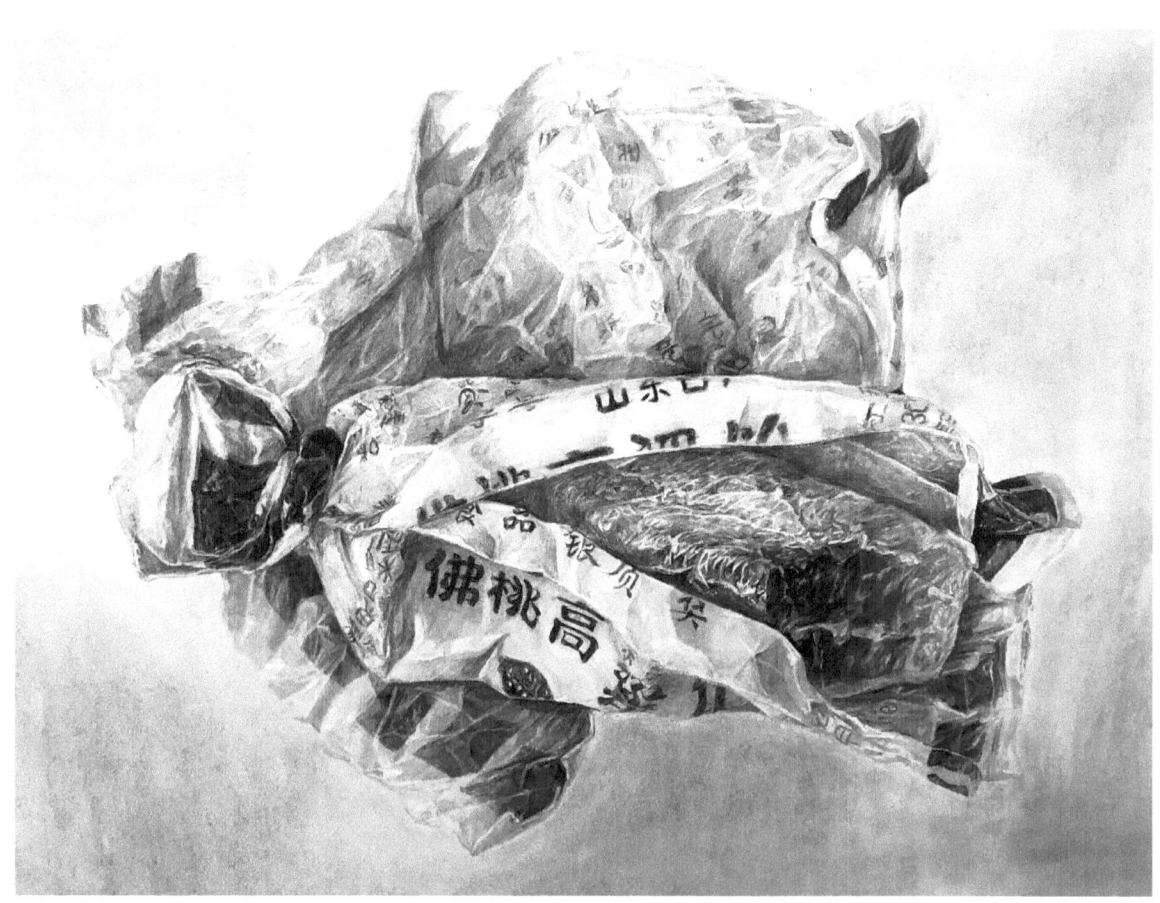

Sorghum Molasses, pencil on paper, 2020

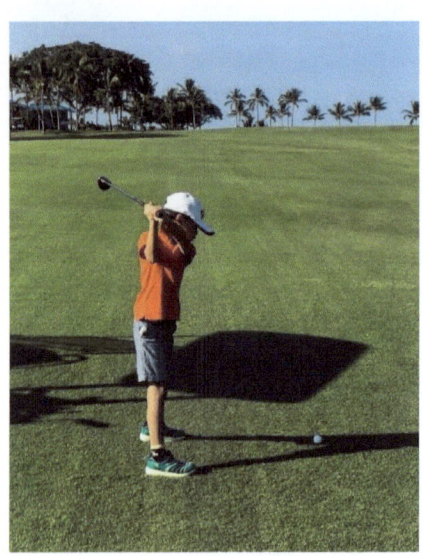

ZIQI MENG

Qingdao Baishan School, China

Silver Award for Art, 3rd Liberty Awards, International Society of Young Artists, USA, 2020-21
Bronze Award for Art, 2nd Liberty Awards, International Society of Young Artists, USA, 2019
Rising Star Award, 1st Liberty Awards, International Society of Young Artists, USA, 2018

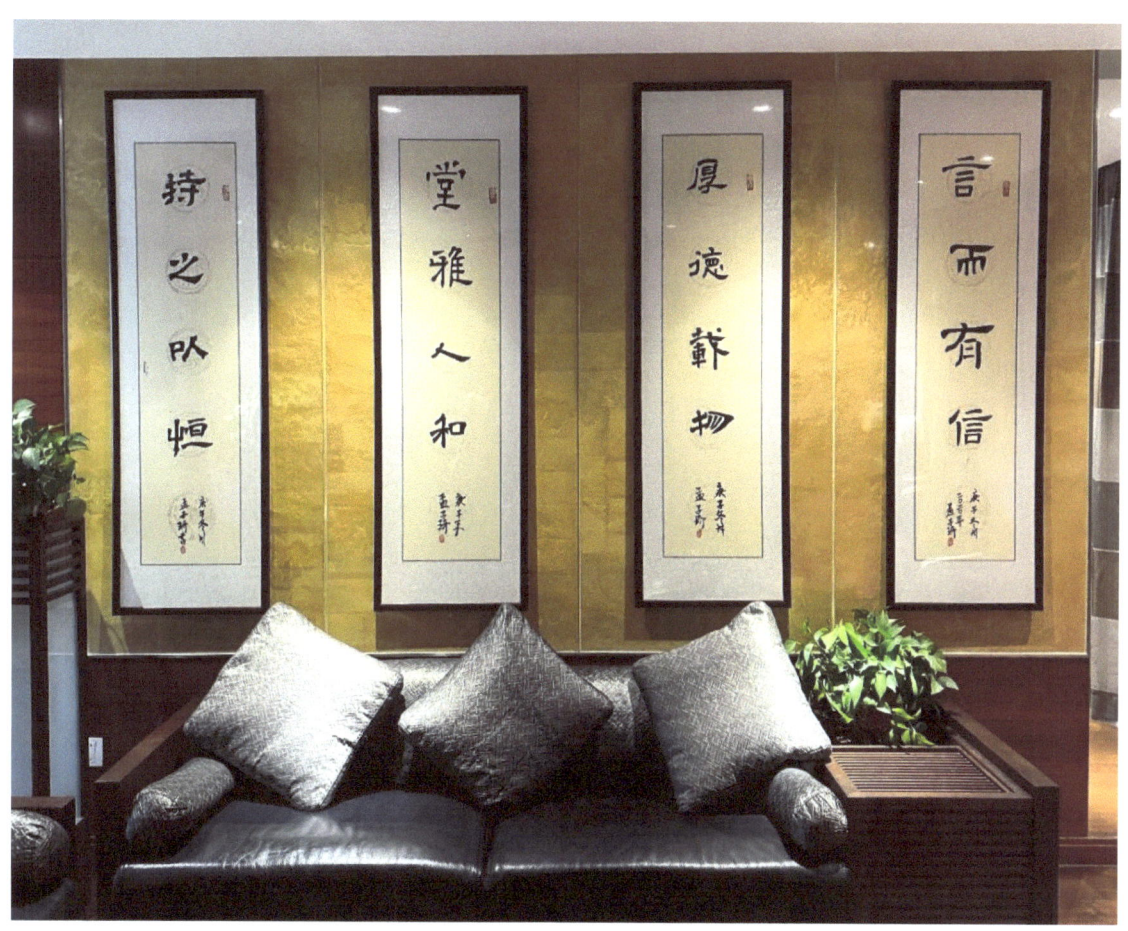

Hall Couplets, ink on rice paper, 2020

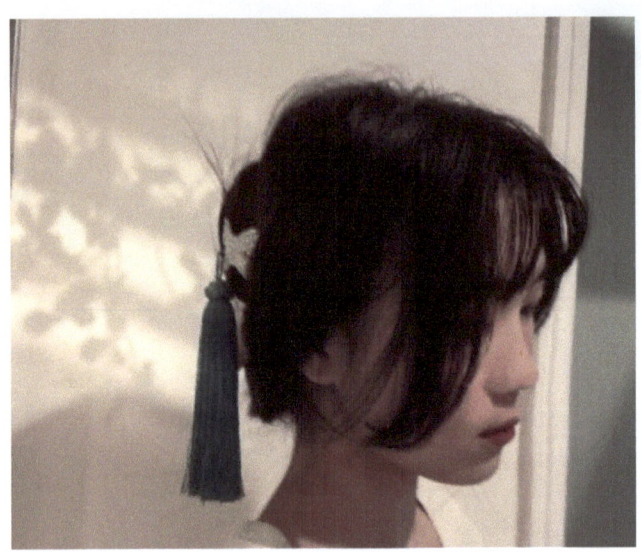

ZIYAN CHEN

Ruben S. Ayala High School, USA

Gold Award for Art, 3rd Liberty Awards, International Society of Young Artists, USA, 2020-21
Gold Award for Art, 2nd Liberty Awards, International Society of Young Artists, USA, 2019

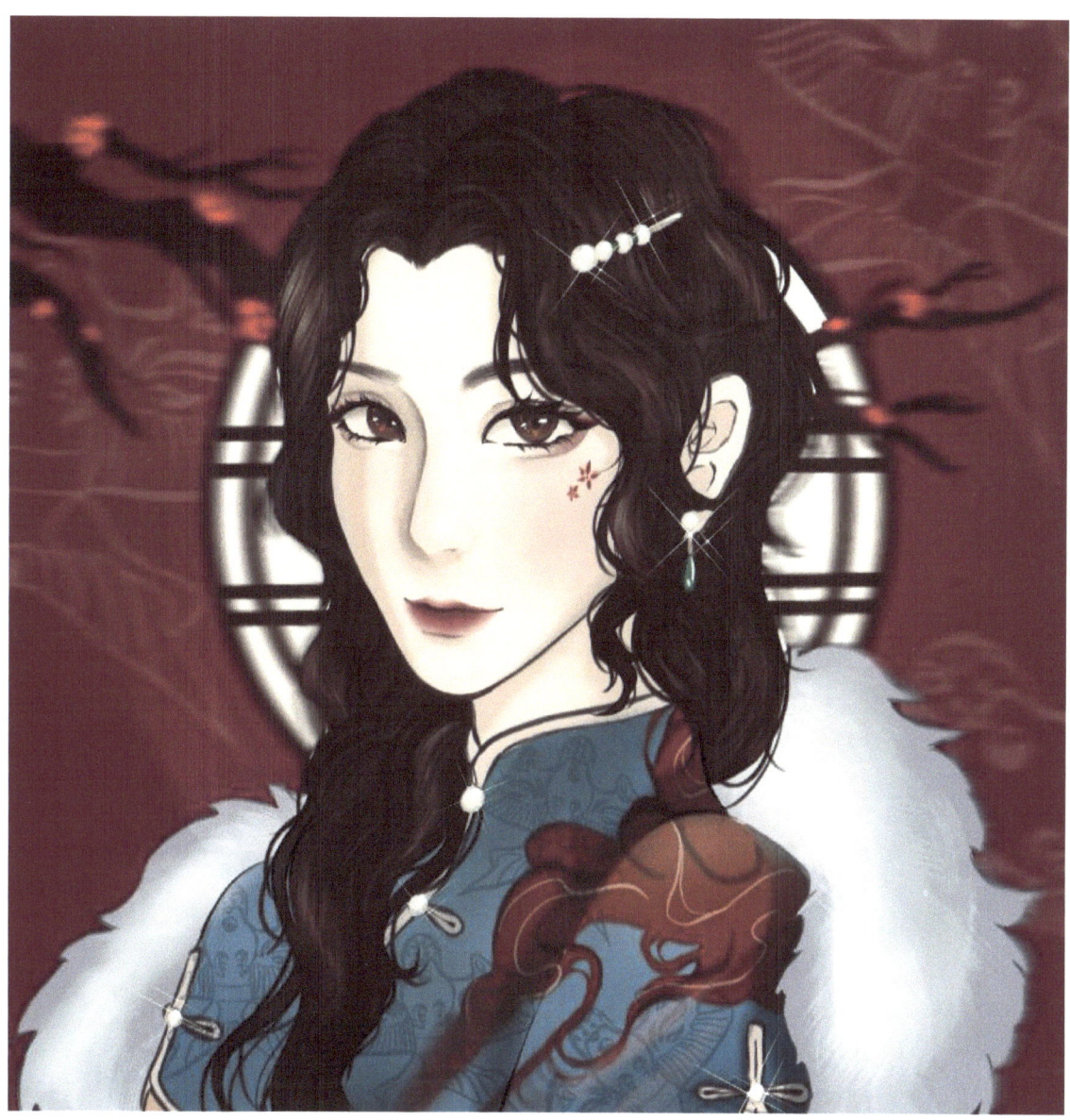

Nancy, digital, 2020

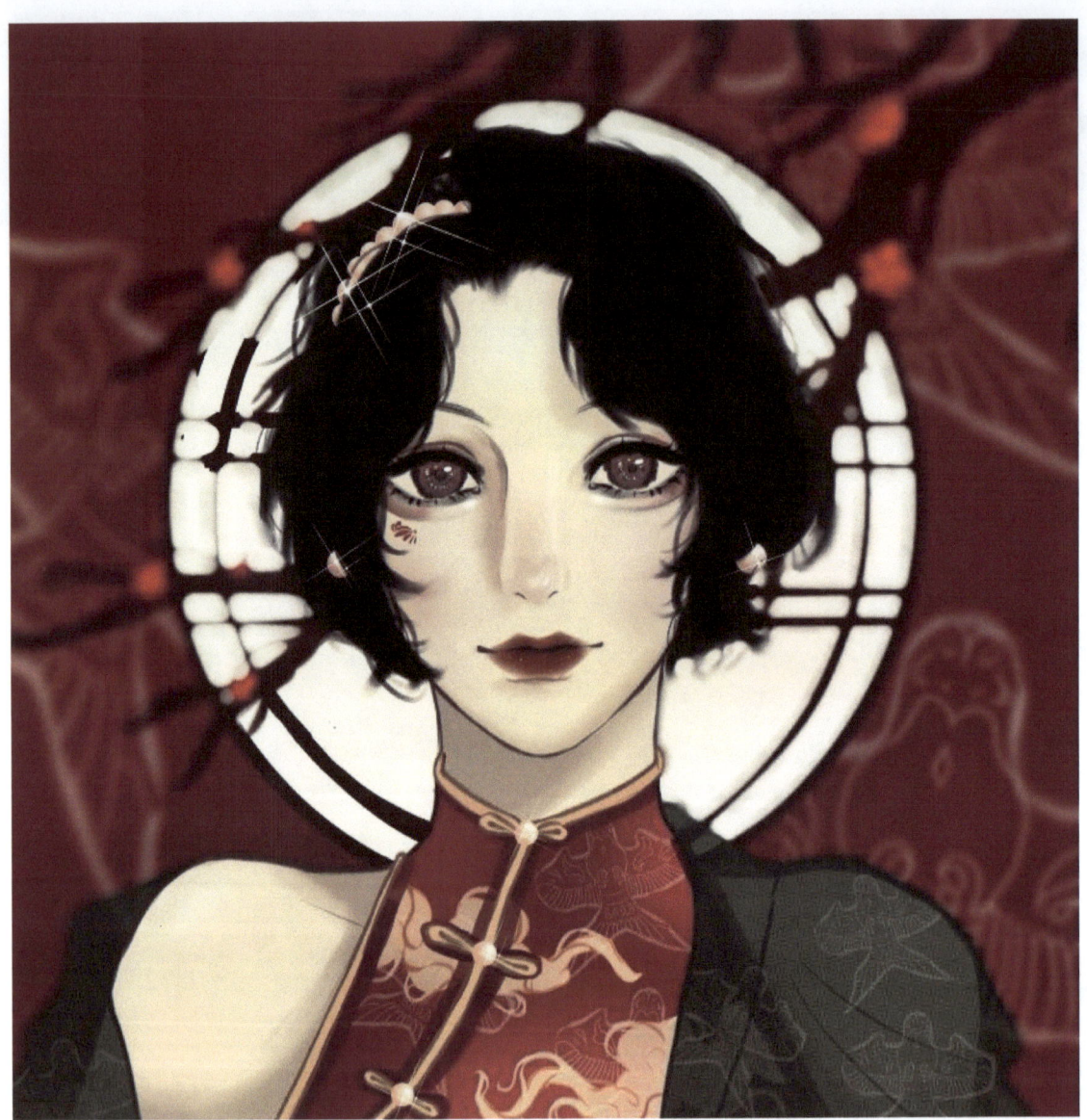
Selina, digital, 2020

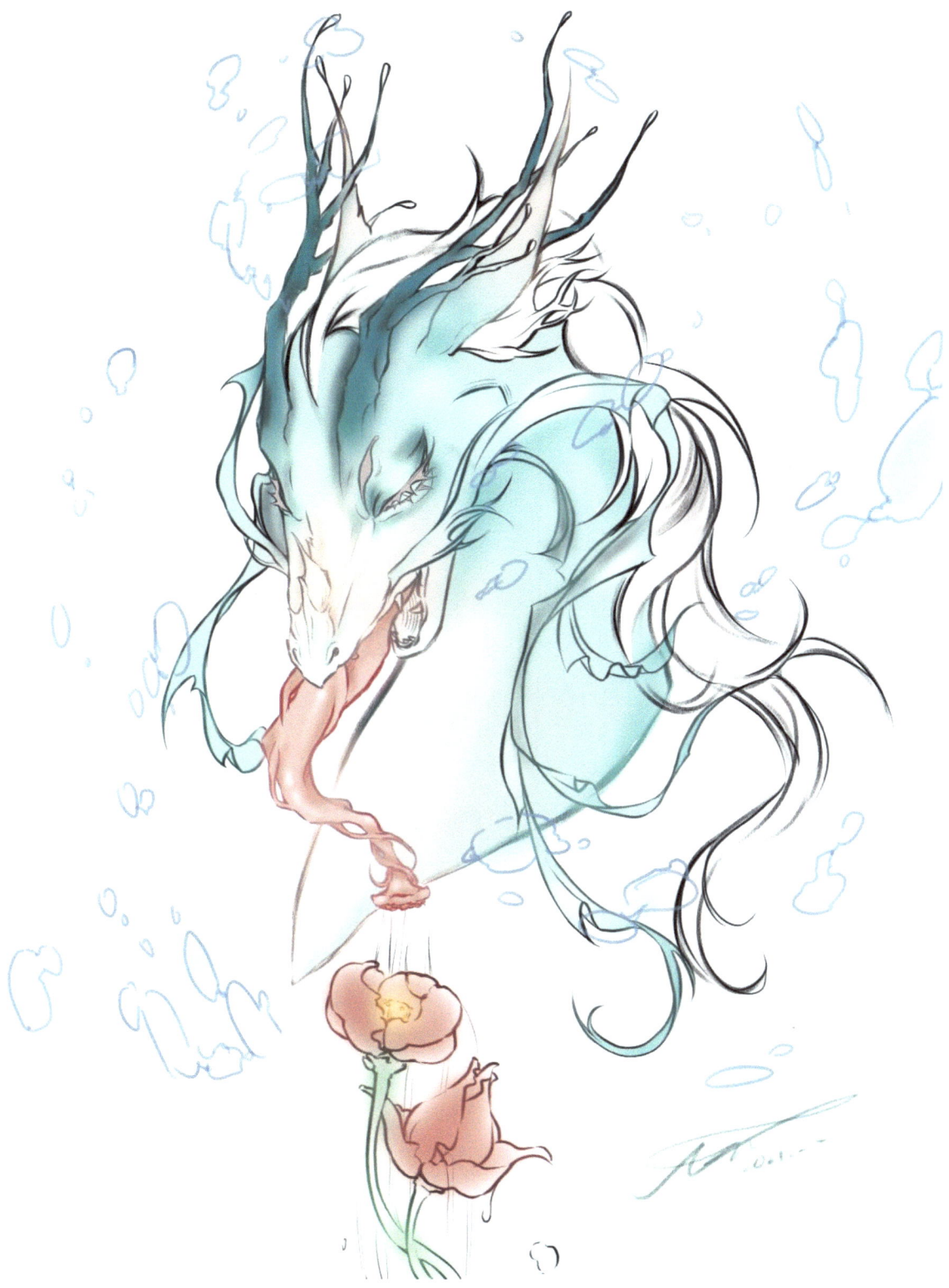

Love, digital, 2021

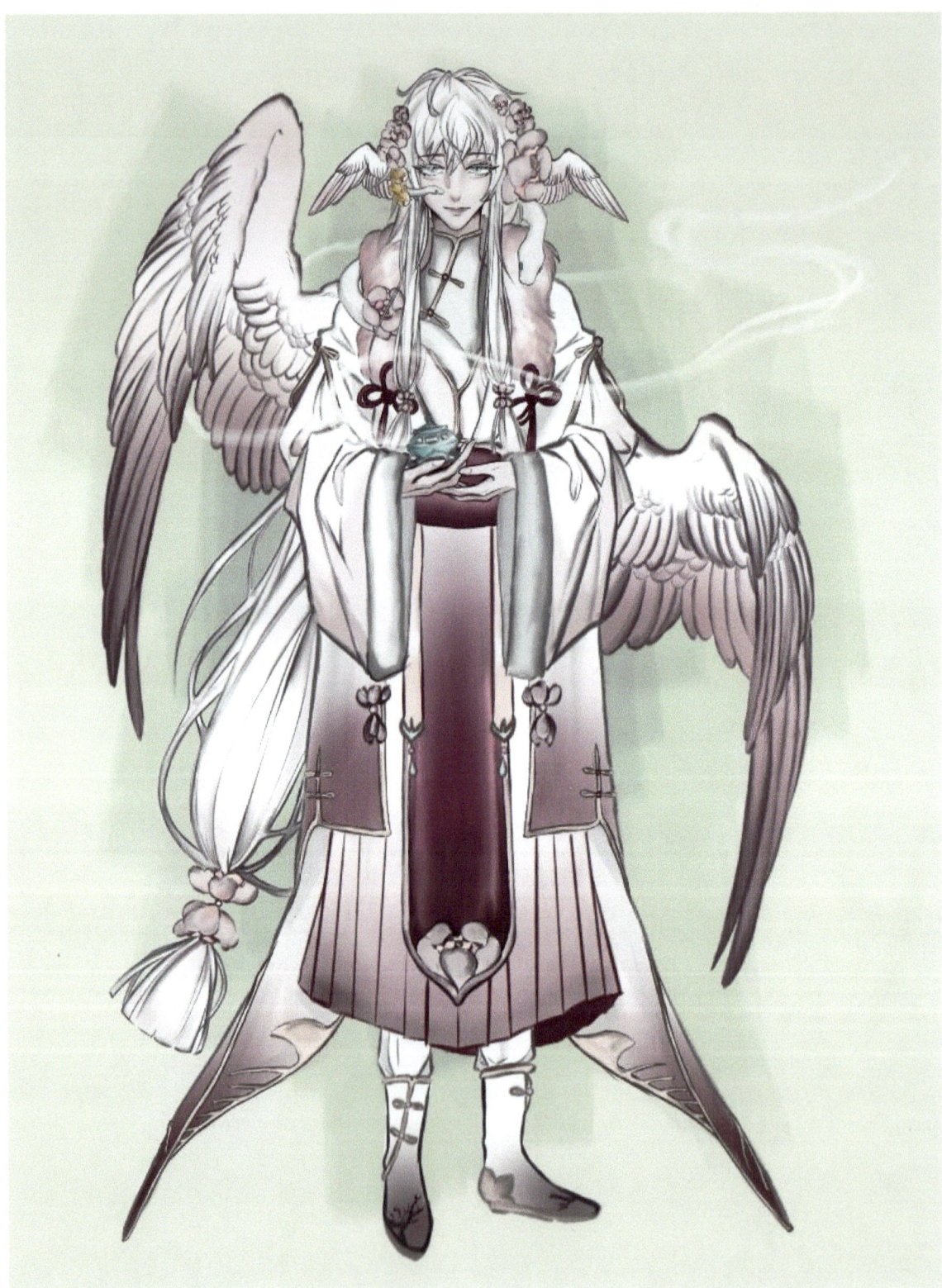

Spring, digital, 2020

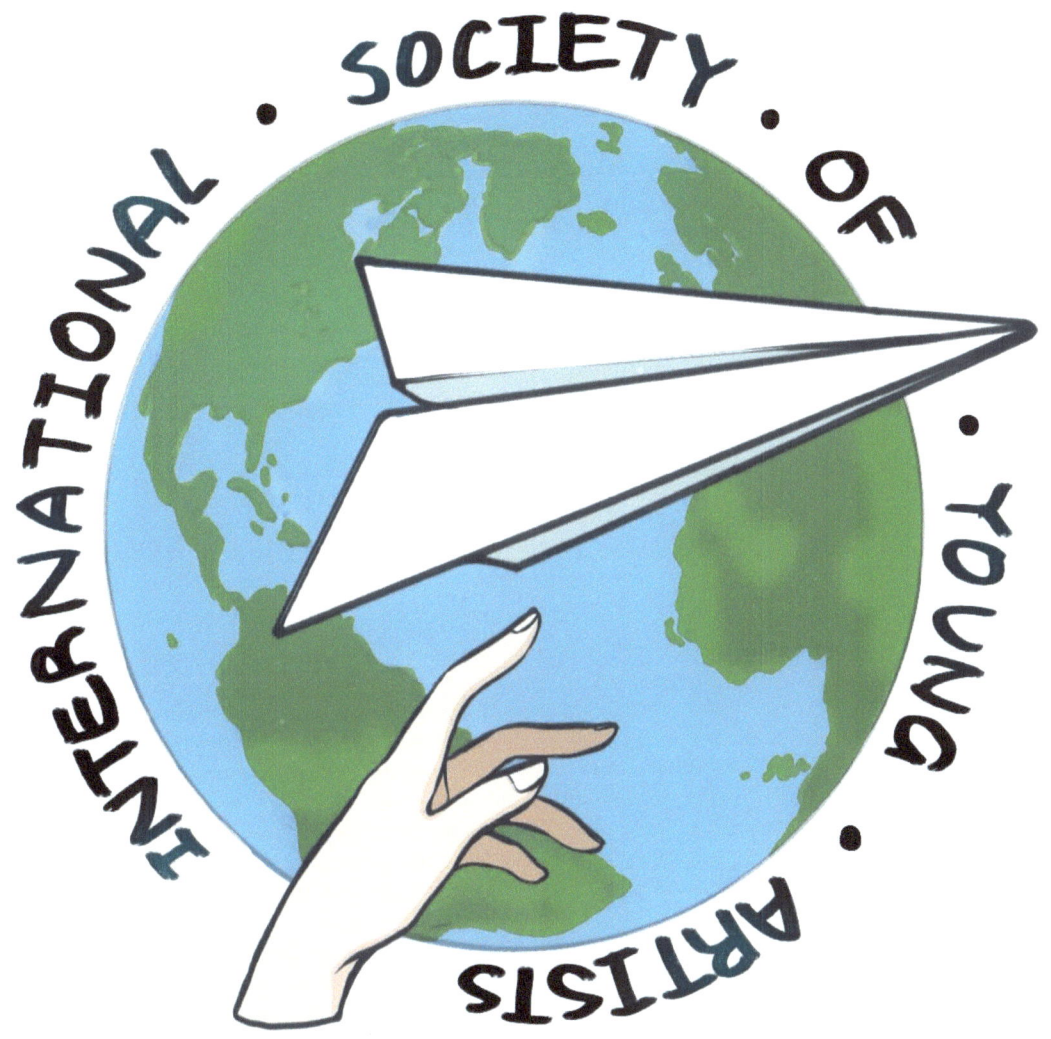

The Logo of International Society of Young Artist, digital, 2021

The publication of this book is part of a benevolent program - "The Vibrant Future" International Education Project for Young Artists, sponsored by the International Society of Young Artists. All of the earnings from the publication of this book will be donated to improve education for young artists.

Copyright © 2021 by International Society of Young Artists

All rights reserved.

Published in the United States by Losget Press, Los Angeles

Originally published in Paperback in the United States by Losget Press, in 2021

Title: Beaming Youth: International Youth Artist Artwork Series-2

Description: First Edition. | Los Angeles: Losget Press, 2021.

Identifiers: LCCN: 2021900120 | ISBN-13: 978-1-951364-07-6 | ISBN-10: 1-951364-07-4

www.losget.com

E-mail: contact@losget.com

First Printing. 2021.

www.ingramcontent.com/pod-product-compliance
Lightning Source LLC
Chambersburg PA
CBHW051148220526
45473CB00003B/700